Experiments Against Reality

ROGER KIMBALL

Experiments Against Reality

THE FATE OF CULTURE
IN THE POSTMODERN AGE

Chicago

IVAN R. DEE

Library of Congress Cataloging-in-Publication Data:
Kimball, Roger, 1953–
    Experiments against reality : the fate of culture in the postmodern
age / Roger Kimball.
        p. cm.
    Includes bibliographical references and index.
    ISBN 1-56663-430-X (alk. paper)
        1. Philosophy, Modern. 2. Civilization, Modern. 3. Philosophy
and civilization. I. Title.
B791.K53 2000
190—dc21   00-059637

Contents

Acknowledgments

When I mentioned to a friend that I was thinking of calling this book *Experiments Against Reality* he said, "Don't you mean 'experiments *on* reality?'" With respect to normal English idiom, my friend was of course correct. But I had in mind Hannah Arendt's description of totalitarianism as a sort of "experiment against reality"— one that, among other things, encouraged people to believe that "everything was possible and that nothing was true." How much of modern culture that belief—relying as it does upon what Arendt called a "mixture of gullibility and cynicism"—seems to characterize! In the chapters that follow, I attempt to trace some of the common procedures that have been used to carry out those experiments. Accordingly, this book is largely a chronicle of spiritual disillusionment—by turns artfully resisted or eagerly embraced. I hasten to add, however, that readers will also find numerous affirmative moments; *Experiments Against Reality* bears witness not only to the diminishments of modernity but also to the often unexpected gestures of acknowledgment those diminishments have elicited. "Human kind," T. S. Eliot observed, "cannot bear very much reality." But how much reality must one have borne in order to come to terms with the truth of that observation?

Earlier versions of most of these essays appeared in *The New Criterion*. The essay on Wallace Stevens, here much expanded, began life as a review in *The Times Literary Supplement*. Parts of "The Trivialization of Outrage" appeared in *The Public Interest* and *The American Outlook*; I delivered an earlier version of this essay as The Vice-Chancellor's Lecture at "The American Century From Afar," a conference sponsored by the Boston, Oxford, Melbourne Conversazione Society in Melbourne, Australia, in 1999.

On a more personal note, I wish to record my deep gratitude to Hilton Kramer, whose editorial intercessions over the course of nearly twenty years now have both inspired me and saved me from untold errors. I would also like to acknowledge the friendship and expert editorial ministrations of my colleagues, past and present, at *The New Criterion*: Christopher Carduff, Erich Eichman, Sara Lussier, Robert Messenger, Robert Richman, Maxwell Watman, and David Yezzi. I am grateful to them all. Finally, it gives me great pleasure to acknowledge the definitive support and steadfast intellectual companionship of Alexandra Kimball, *coniunx sine qua non*.

RK *July 2000*

Experiments
Against Reality

*I do not have much use for notions like "objective value" and
"objective truth."*
—Richard Rorty

*The man who cannot believe his senses, and the man who cannot
believe anything else, are both insane, but their insanity is proved
not by any error in their argument, but by the manifest mistake
of their whole lives.*
—G. K. Chesterton

IN THE FOREWORD to his magnum opus, *European Literature and the Latin Middle Ages* (1948), the great
German scholar Ernst Robert Curtius noted that his book,
for all its daunting scholarship, was "not the product of
purely scholarly interests." Rather, it

> grew out of a concern for the preservation of Western cul-
> ture. It seeks to serve an understanding of the Western
> cultural tradition in so far as it is manifested in literature. It
> attempts to illuminate the unity of that tradition . . . by the
> application of new methods. . . . In the intellectual chaos of
> the present it has become necessary . . . to demonstrate that
> unity. But the demonstration can only be made from a

universal standpoint. Such a standpoint is afforded by
Latinity.

It would not be easy to find a passage more at odds, in
tone or substance, with the sensibilities that dominate the
cultural landscape today. Curtius's talk of "new methods"
might at first elicit some enthusiasm from advocates of
trendy literary theory: after all, the word "method" can be
counted on to affect them the way a ringing bell affected
Pavlov's dog. In fact, though, they would find Curtius's
patient investigation of literary *topoi*—for that was what
he meant by "new methods"—hopelessly *retardataire*. And
Curtius's method is the least of what sets him apart from
the reigning sensibilities. Much more important is his quiet
but determined concern for the "preservation of Western
culture," his effort to exhibit the "unity of that tradition,"
his faith in a "universal standpoint" from which the "intellectual chaos" of his time could be effectively addressed.
Even his turn to Latin, "the language of the educated
during the thirteen centuries which lie between Virgil and
Dante," marks him as an oddity in the present intellectual
climate.

Today, the very idea that there might be something distinctive about the Western cultural tradition—something,
moreover, eminently worth preserving—is under attack on
several fronts. Multiculturalists in the academy and other
cultural institutions—museums, foundations, the entertainment industry—busy themselves denouncing the West
as racist, sexist, imperialistic, and ethnocentric. The cultural unity that Curtius celebrated is challenged by intellectual segregationists eager to champion relativism and to
attack what they see as the "hegemony" of Eurocentrism
in art, literature, philosophy, politics, and even in science.
The ideal of a "universal standpoint" from which the

achievements of the West may be understood and disseminated is derided by partisans of postcolonial studies, cultural studies, and neo-pragmatism as parochial and, even worse, dangerously, arrogantly, "foundationalist."

Writing in the immediate aftermath of World War II, Curtius naturally had the assaults of totalitarianism chiefly in mind when he spoke of the "intellectual chaos" of his time. Today's cultural commissars do not—not yet, anyway—control any governments or police forces. But the intellectual and spiritual chaos they endorse is potentially as disruptive and paralyzing as any brand of nihilism. The political philosopher Hannah Arendt once described totalitarianism as an "experiment against reality." She had in mind, among other things, the peculiar mixture of gullibility and cynicism that totalitarian movements inspire: an amalgam that fosters an intellectual twilight in which people believe "everything and nothing, think that everything was possible and nothing was true." It is in this sense that the cultural relativists of today display a totalitarian cast of mind. Their efforts to disestablish the intellectual tradition of the West are so many experiments against reality: the reality of our cultural and spiritual legacy.

It is a simple matter to give examples and describe the effects of such experiments against reality. But uncovering their precise nature—what motivates them, what they portend—is more difficult. They are as amorphous as they are widespread and virulent. It is consequently easy to get lost in the maze of competing barbarisms: deconstruction, structuralism, postcolonialism, and queer theory for breakfast, postdeconstructive cultural studies and Lacanian feminism for lunch. Who can say what will be served up for dinner? The menu is endless, and endlessly hermetic. And yet there are recurrent themes, arguments, and attitudes. Above all there are unifying suppositions, often only half-articulated, about the stability of human nature, the meaning of tradition, the scope and criteria of knowledge. In an appendix to his *Essays on European Literature*, Curtius again provided a striking counterexample to today's received wisdom when he speaks of the "essential connection between love and knowledge" and emphasized the critic's *receptivity*, his subservience to the reality he seeks to understand. "Reception is the essential condition for perception," Curtius wrote, "and this then leads to conception." At a time when the hubris of the critic is matched only by the fatuousness of his theories, Curtius's insistence that knowledge owes a perpetual debt to reality —that scholarship, as he puts it, "must always remain objective"—sounds a refreshingly discordant note.

In some ways, Curtius's reflections on the responsibilities of scholarship are—or would once have been—commonplace. The problem today is that such commonplaces have become exceptionally uncommon. The scholarly ideal of patient attentiveness is as démodé as a commitment to the ideal of objectivity. So it is that in these passing remarks Curtius touched on a matter of critical importance for anyone concerned with the future of the European past. Behind his insistence on the essentially receptive attitude of the critic is an acknowledgment that reality ultimately transcends our efforts to master it. It is reality that speaks to us, not we who lecture it. At the same time, Curtius's entire commitment to scholarship and "the preservation of Western culture" rests on a faith that the search for truth is not futile. If we must wait upon truth, we do not wait in vain. This twofold attitude—an acceptance of human limitation together with an affirmation of human capability— underlies his scholarly endeavor and links it to the great humanistic tradition of which he was a late, eloquent spokesman. It is also, finally, what sets him at odds with the enemies of that tradition. There are two large questions at issue in this conflict: the relation between truth and cultural value, and the authority of tradition as the custodian of mankind's spiritual aspirations.

Of the many things that have characterized the main current of European culture, perhaps none has been more central than faith in the liberating power of truth. At least since Plato described truth as the "food of the soul" and linked it to the idea of the good, truth has had, in the West, a normative as well as an intellectual component. In this sense, knowing the truth has been held to be a matter not only of comprehension but also of enlightenment, its attainment a moral as well as a cognitive achievement. The habit of judging "according to right reason," in Aristotle's famous formula, was seen to be as much an expression of character as intelligence. Saying yes to the truth involved ascent as much as assent. Philosophy, the "love of wisdom," proposed freedom not simply from ignorance but also, centrally, from illusion. "You shall know the truth," the Gospel of St. John tells us, "and the truth shall set you free." The optimism inherent in this imperative underlies not only the mainsprings of Western religion but also the development of its science and political institutions from the time of the Greeks through the Enlightenment and beyond.

Of course, this edifying picture has had plenty of competition. "What is truth?" asked Pontius Pilate as he washed his hands, thus providing a role model for countless generations of cynics. At the end of *The Republic*, Socrates says that the philosopher's "main concern" should be "to make a reasoned choice between the better and the worse life, with reference to the nature of the soul." But earlier in that dialogue he admits that many who devote themselves single-mindedly to philosophy become cranks if not, indeed, *pamponērous* ("thoroughly depraved"). The character of Thrasymachus, taunting Socrates with the declaration that "justice is nothing but the advantage of the stronger," provides an enduring image of the kind—or one of the kinds—of moral nihilist whose influence Plato feared.

In the modern age, no one has carried forward Thrasymachus's challenge more subtly or more radically than Friedrich Nietzsche. In a celebrated epigram, Nietzsche wrote that "we have art lest we perish from the truth." His disturbing thought was that art, with its fondness for illusion and make-believe, did not so much grace life as provide grateful distraction from life's horrors. But Nietzsche's real radicalism, as I try to show below in "The Legacy of Friedrich Nietzsche," came in the way that he attempted to read life *against* truth. Inverting the Platonic-Christian doctrine that linked truth with the good and the beautiful, he declared truth to be "ugly." Suspecting that "the will to truth might be a concealed will to death," Nietzsche boldly demanded that "the value of truth must for once be experimentally *called into question.*" This is as it were the moral source of all those famous Nietzschean formulae about truth and knowledge—that "there are no facts, only interpretations," that "to tell the truth is simply to lie according to a fixed convention," etc. As Nietzsche recognized, his effort to provide a genealogy of truth led directly "back to the moral problem: *Why have morality at all* when life, nature, and history are 'not moral'?"

Nietzsche's influence on contemporary intellectual life can hardly be overstated. "I am dynamite," he declared shortly before sinking into irretrievable madness. He was right. In one way or another, his example is an indispensable background to almost every destructive intellectual movement this century has witnessed. The philosopher

Richard Rorty summed up Nietzsche's importance when he enthusiastically observed that "it was Nietzsche who first explicitly suggested that we drop the whole idea of 'knowing the truth.' "

It can be argued that part of Nietzsche's influence has been due to misunderstanding. It was not entirely Nietzsche's fault, for example, that he became in effect the house philosopher of the Nazis. But it is not possible to exonerate Nietzsche entirely on that score, either. He would have been repelled by National Socialism, had he lived to see it, especially its anti-Semitism and *lumpen* elements. But his consistent glorification of violence, his doctrine of "the will to power," his distinction between "master" and "slave" morality, his image of the *Ubermensch* who is "beyond good and evil": they all played so neatly into the Nazis' hands because the brutality of those ideas answered to the brutality of the Nazis' requirements. Even if Nietzsche meant something different from what the Nazis meant, there was an element of like appealing to like when it came to their use of his ideas and rhetoric.

Nietzsche's intellectual and moral influence on our contemporaries betrays similar complexities. One imagines that Nietzsche would have loathed such poseurs as Jacques Derrida and Michel Foucault (to name only two). Such bad taste! Such bad writing! But their philosophies are inconceivable without Nietzsche's example. And, once again, there is a great deal in Nietzsche's thought that answers to the requirements of deconstruction, poststructuralism, and their many offshoots and permutations. Nietzsche's obsession with power once again is central, in particular his subjugation of truth to scenarios of power. (Foucault's insistence that truth is always a coefficient of "regimes of power" is simply Nietzsche done over in black leather.) And where would our deconstructionists and poststructuralists be without Nietzsche's endlessly quoted declaration that truth is "a moveable host of metaphors, metonymies, and anthropomorphisms"? A deconstructionist without the word "metonymy" is a pitiful thing, like a dog missing its favorite bone.

Conceptually, such signature Nietzschean observations as "everything praised as moral is identical in essence with everything immoral" add little to the message that Thrasymachus had for us twenty-five-hundred years ago. They are the predictable product of nominalism and the desire to say something shocking, a perennial combination among the intellectually impatient. Nietzsche's real radicalism arises from the grandiosity of his hubris. His militant "God is dead" atheism had its corollary: the dream of absolute self-creation, of a new sort of human being strong enough to dispense with inherited morality and create, in Nietzsche's phrase, its "own new tables of what is good." This ambition is at the root of Nietzsche's goal of effecting a "transvaluation of all values." It is also what makes his philosophy such an efficient solvent of traditional moral thought.

At least, that is the *substance* of what makes Nietzsche philosophical "dynamite." The detonator is supplied by Nietzsche's remarkable style. As a stylist Nietzsche had many faults. His rhetoric can be as grandiose as his megalomania. But almost everyone agrees that Nietzsche was an extraordinarily seductive, if sometimes hectoring, writer. And it must be said, too, that Nietzsche's rhetorical excesses were generally at the service of an abiding seriousness about deep issues. He may have been wrong about a great many things—about the most important things— but he was never frivolous. Unfortunately, many of Nietzsche's imitators and disciples have copied the extravagance of his manner while neglecting his ultimately

serious purpose. Indeed, his example has done a great deal
to enfranchise frivolity—what the philosopher David Stove
aptly called *enfant terriblisme*—as an acceptable academic
tic. When combined with the polysyllabic portentousness
of Nietzsche's disciple Martin Heidegger—another major
influence on the style of deconstruction—the effect is
deadly: portentous frivolity, the worst of both worlds.
Nietzsche once wrote that "one does not only wish to be
understood when one writes, one wishes just as surely *not*
to be understood." How he would have rued that sentence
had he foreseen the rebarbative quality of the academic
prose his writings helped to inspire!

One could easily fill a book with examples of the way
that philosophy and the humanities generally have abandoned not only any commitment to clarity of expression
but also the search for truth and, ultimately, faith in their
own power as instruments of moral illumination. Such is
the stuff of which glittering academic reputations are made
today: humanists whose message is the end of humanism,
philosophers bent on demonstrating the utter nullity of
philosophy. Let us confine ourselves here to a couple of
characteristic examples from one of Nietzsche's most influential heirs, the French deconstructionist Jacques Derrida. Inspired by Nietzsche, Derrida is always talking
about philosophy as a "game" or a form of "play." So he
begins his book *Dissemination* with this sentence: "This
(therefore) will not have been a book." "Therefore," indeed. This is followed by a . . . no, it is not an explanation,
but a sort of exfoliation, a luxuriance of verbal curlicues
designed not to clear things up but to festoon the initial
obscurity with cleverness. Such "games" pall quickly, of
course, and so Derrida, like so many of his epigoni, tries to
spice things up by injecting sex-talk wherever possible. He
can't mention Rousseau without dilating on masturbation,

EXPERIMENTS AGAINST REALITY

reflect on writing without bringing in incest, and so on. It's what D. H. Lawrence called sex in the head: an academic's frenetically anemic effort to demonstrate that, despite appearances to the contrary, there really is blood in his (or her) veins.

It can all be pretty distasteful, as anyone familiar with current scholarship in the humanities well knows. But the real obscenity is practiced upon language. Here is a relatively mild passage from the beginning of "Plato's Pharmacy," Derrida's famous essay on the *Phaedrus*:

> A text is not a text unless it hides from the first comer, from the first glance, the law of its composition and the rules of its game. A text remains, moreover, forever imperceptible. Its law and its rules are not, however, harbored in the inaccessibility of a secret; it is simply that they can never be booked, in the *present*, into anything that could rigorously be called a perception. . . . If reading and writing are one, as is easily thought these days, if reading *is* writing, this oneness designates neither undifferentiated (con)fusion nor identity at perfect rest; the *is* that couples reading with writing must rip apart.
>
> One must then, in a single gesture, but doubled, read and write. And that person would have understood nothing of the game who, at this, would feel himself authorized merely to add on; that is, to add any old thing. . . . The reading or writing supplement must be rigorously prescribed, but by the necessities of a *game*, by the logic of *play*, signs to which the system of all textual powers must be accorded and attuned.

Perhaps this is the appropriate place to recall Chesterton's definition of madness as "using mental activity so as to reach mental helplessness." If one penetrates behind the skeins of Derrida's rhetoric, a moment's thought will show that the "rigorously prescribed" logic of his play is completely short-circuited by a simple fact: that reading is not, as it happens, the same thing as writing. Never was, never will be.

Such deliberate stupefaction—Derrida's proposition that writing is prior to speech provides another example—is at the heart of deconstruction. Derrida's most famous sentence is undoubtedly *il n'y a pas de hors-texte*, "there is nothing outside the text." This is short hand for denying that words can refer to a reality beyond words, for denying that truth has its measure in something beyond the web of our language games. It is, of course, a simple matter to *say* "There is nothing outside the text." It has a clever, radical sound to it. But is it true? If so, then there is at least one thing "outside" the text, namely the truth of the statement "There is nothing outside the text."

It is the same with all such pronouncements: "There is no such thing as literal meaning" (Stanley Fish), "All readings are misreadings" (Jonathan Culler), "Truth . . . cannot exist independently of the human mind" (Richard Rorty). Or, in slightly less staccato form, here is Fredric Jameson:

> The very problem of a relationship between thoughts and words betrays a metaphysics of "presence," and implies an illusion that universal substances exist, in which we come face to face once and for all with objects; that meanings exist, such that it ought to be possible to "decide" whether they are initially verbal or not; that there is such a thing as knowledge which one can acquire in some tangible and permanent way.

Not only are all these statements essentially self-refuting— does Stanley Fish literally mean "There is no such thing as literal meaning"?—but they also have the handicap of being continually refuted by experience. When Derrida leaves Plato's pharmacy and goes into a Parisian one, he depends mightily on the fact that there *is* an outside to language, that when he asks for *aspirine* he will not be given *arsenic* instead.

A great deal of Derrida's philosophy depends on the linguistic accident that the French verb *différer* means both "to differ" and "to defer." Out of this pedestrian fact he has spun a dizzying argument, the upshot of which is that the meaning of any text is perpetually put off, *deferred*. But, of course, if some unscrupulous pharmacist were to substitute arsenic for aspirin, Derrida would learn to reconnect the signifier with the signified right speedily, and he would lament, in the time that remained to him, his apostasy from the logocentric "nostalgia" for the "metaphysics of presence."

It is often pointed out today that deconstruction and structuralism have become old hat, that the parade of academic fashion has passed on to other entertainments: to cultural studies and various neo-Marxist hybrids of "theory" and the politics of grievance (so-called "Subaltern" and postcolonial studies, queer theory, gender studies, etc.). This is partly true. It is certainly the case that the terms "deconstruction" and "structuralism" no longer have the cachet they possessed in the 1980s and early 1990s. Nor does the name "Derrida" automatically produce the reverence and wonder among graduate students that it once did. ("Foucault," however, seems to have retained its talismanic charm.) There are basically two reasons for this. The first has to do with the late Paul de Man, the Belgian-born Yale professor of comparative literature, who in addition to being one of the most prominent practitioners of deconstruction, was—it was revealed in the late 1980s—an enthusiastic contributor to Nazi newspapers during World War II. That discovery, and above all the flood of obscurantist mendacity disgorged by the deconstructionist-structuralist brotherhood—not least by Derrida himself—to exonerate de Man, has cast a permanent shadow over deconstruction's status as a widely accepted instrument of intellectual liberation. Derrida began his response as follows:

> Unable to respond to the questions, to all the questions, I will ask myself instead *whether responding is possible* and what that would mean in such a situation. And I will risk in turn several questions *prior to* the definition of a *responsibility*. But is it not an act to assume in theory the concept of responsibility? One's own as well as the responsibility to which one believes one ought to summon others?

Derrida concluded by turning the tables on de Man's critics, arguing that to criticize de Man was "to reproduce the exterminating gesture against which one accuses de Man of not having armed himself sooner with the necessary vigilance." In other words, to criticize de Man is somehow to implicate oneself in Nazi brutally.

The second reason that deconstruction has faded is simply that, like any academic fashion, deconstruction's methods and vocabulary, once so novel and forbidding, have gradually become part of the common coin of academic discourse. It is important to recognize, though, that this very process of assimilation has assured the continuing influence of deconstruction and structuralism. The *terms* "deconstruction" and "structuralism" are not invoked as regularly today as they once were; but the fundamental ideas about language, truth, and morality that they express are more widespread than ever. Once at home mostly in philosophy and literature departments, their nihilistic tenets are cropping up further and further afield: in departments of history, sociology, political science, and architecture; in law schools and—God help us—business schools. Outside the academy, the rhetoric of deconstruction has penetrated into museums and other cultural institutions. Indeed, deconstructive themes and presuppositions have increasingly become part of the general intellectual atmosphere: absorbed to such an extent that, like the ideas of psychoanalysis, they float almost unnoticed, part of the ambient spiritual pollution of our time. Who can forget the politician who, accused of wrongdoing, said in his defense that "it all depends on what the meaning of the word 'is' is"?

Although the language of deconstruction and structuralism is forbidding, the appeal of the doctrines is not hard to understand. It is basically a Nietzschean appeal. As the late English philosopher and novelist Iris Murdoch observed in *Metaphysics as a Guide to Morals* (1992), "the new anti-metaphysical metaphysic promises to unburden the intellectuals and set them free to play. Man has now 'come of age' and is strong enough to get rid of his past."

That, at least, is the idea—the promise issued but, like meaning in a deconstructionist's fantasy, always deferred. As Murdoch noted, part of what is objectionable in the deconstructivist-structuralist ethos "is the damage done to other modes of thinking and to literature." Dissolving everything in a sea of unanchored signifiers, deconstruction encourages us to blur fundamental distinctions: distinctions between intellectual disciplines, between fact and fiction, between right and wrong. Because there is "no such thing" as intrinsic value, there is at bottom no reason to respect the integrity of literature, philosophy, science, or any other intellectual pursuit. All become fodder for the deconstructionist's "play"—or perhaps "folly" would be a more appropriate term. The crucial thing lost is truth: the ideal, in Murdoch's words, of "language as truthful, where 'truthful' means faithful to, engaging intelligently and responsibly with, a reality which is beyond us."

With its doctrine of *il n'y a pas de hors-texte*, deconstruction is an evasion of reality. In this sense it may be described as a reactionary force: it hides from rather than engages with reality. But because deconstruction operates by subversion, its evasions are at the same time an attack: an attack on the cogency of language and the moral and intellectual claims that language has codified in tradition. The subversive element inherent in the deconstructive enterprise is another reason that it has exercised such a mesmerizing spell on intellectuals eager to demonstrate their radical *bona fides*. Because it attacks the intellectual foundations of the established order, deconstruction promises its adherents not only an emancipation from the responsibilities of truth but also the prospect of engaging in a species of radical activism. A blow against the legitimacy of language, they imagine, is at the same time a blow against the legitimacy of the tradition in which language lives and has meaning. They are not mistaken about this. For it is by undercutting the idea of truth that the decontructionist also undercuts the idea of value, including established social, moral, and political values. And it is here, as Murdoch points out, that "the deep affinity, the holding hands under the table, between structuralism and Marxism becomes intelligible." Most deconstructionists would seem to be unlikely revolutionaries; they are academics, after all, not rabble-rousers; but their attack on the inherited values of our culture is as radical and potentially destabilizing as anything devised for Mr. Molotov.

The deconstructionist impulse comes in a variety of flavors, from bitter to cloyingly sweet, and it can be made to serve a wide range of philosophical outlooks. That is part of what makes it so dangerous. One of the most beguiling and influential American deconstructionists is Richard Rorty. Once upon a time, Rorty was a serious analytic philosopher. Since the late 1970s, however, he has increasingly busied himself explaining why philosophy must jettison its concern with outmoded things like truth and human nature. According to him, philosophy should turn itself into a form of literature or—as he sometimes puts it—"fantasizing." He is set on "blurring the literature-philosophy distinction and promoting the idea of a seamless, undifferentiated 'general text,'" in which, say, Aristotle's *Metaphysics*, a television program, and a French novel might coalesce into a fit object of hermeneutical scrutiny. Thus it is that Rorty believes that "the novel, the movie, and the TV program have, gradually but steadily, replaced the sermon and the treatise as the principal vehicles of moral change and progress." (One does not, incidentally, have to believe that sermons or treatises were ever "the principal vehicles of moral change and progress" to be convinced that novels, movies, and TV programs are nothing of the sort now.)

As almost goes without saying, Rorty's attack on philosophy and his celebration of culture as an "undifferentiated 'general text'" have earned him many honors. In the early 1980s, he left his professorship at Princeton for an even grander one at the University of Virginia; upon retiring, in 1998, he accepted a five-year appointment at Stanford. He is the recipient of a MacArthur Foundation "genius" award; and he has lately emerged as one of those "all-purpose intellectuals . . . ready to offer a view on pretty much anything" that he extols in his book *Conse-*

quences of Pragmatism (1982). Indeed, Richard Rorty is widely regarded today as he regards himself: as a sort of secular sage, dispensing exhortations on all manner of subjects, as readily on the op-ed page of major newspapers as between the covers of an academic book of philosophical essays. The tone is always soothing, the rhetoric impish, the message nihilistic but cheerful. It has turned out to be an unbeatable recipe for success, patronizing the reader with the thought that there is nothing that cannot be patronized.

In "Ironist Theory to Private Allusions," his essay about Derrida in *Contingency, Irony, Solidarity* (1989), Rorty writes about the French philosopher in glowing terms as someone who "simply drops theory" for the sake of amoral "fantasizing" about his philosophical predecessors, "playing with them, giving free rein to the trains of association they produce." He himself strives to follow this procedure. He does not, however, call himself a deconstructionist. That might be too off-putting. Instead, he calls himself a "pragmatist" or, more recently, a "liberal ironist." What he wants, as he explained in *Philosophy and the Mirror of Nature* (1979), his first foray into postphilosophical waters, is "philosophy without epistemology," that is, philosophy without truth, and especially without Truth with a capital *T*.

In brief, Rorty wants a philosophy (if we can still call it that) which "aims at continuing the conversation rather than at discovering truth." He can manage to abide "truths" with a small *t* and in the plural: truths that we don't take too seriously and wouldn't dream of foisting upon others: truths, in other words, that are true merely by linguistic convention: truths, that is to say, that are not true. What he cannot bear—and cannot bear to have us bear—is the idea of Truth that is somehow more than that.

Rorty generally tries to maintain a chummy, easygoing persona. This is consistent with his role as a "liberal ironist," i.e., someone who thinks that "cruelty is the worst thing we can do" (the liberal part) but who, believing that moral values are utterly contingent, also believes that what counts as "cruelty" is a sociological or linguistic construct. (This is where the irony comes in: "I do not think," Rorty writes, "there are any plain moral facts out there . . . nor any neutral ground on which to stand and argue that either torture or kindness are [sic] preferable to the other.") Accordingly, one thing that is certain to earn Rorty's contempt is the spectacle of philosophers without sufficient contempt for the truth. "You can still find philosophy professors," he tells us witheringly, "who will solemnly tell you that they are seeking *the truth*, not just a story or a consensus but an honest-to-God, down-home, accurate representation of the way the world is." That's the problem with liberal ironists: they are ironical about everything except their own irony, and are serious about tolerating everything except seriousness.

As Rorty is quick to point out, the "bedrock metaphysical issue" here is whether we have any non-linguistic access to reality. Does language "go all the way down"? (Like Derrida, Rorty subscribes to the doctrine of *il n'y a pas de hors-texte*.) Or does language point to a reality beyond itself, a reality that exercises a legitimate claim on our attention and provides a measure and limit for our descriptions of the world? In other words, is truth something that we invent? Or something that we discover?

The main current of Western culture has overwhelmingly endorsed the latter view. For example, the "receptivity" that Curtius insisted upon for the critic is unintelligible without some such presupposition. But Rorty firmly endorses the idea that truth is merely a human invention. He wants us to drop "the notion of truth as correspondence with reality altogether" and realize that there is "no difference that makes a difference" between the statement "it works because it's true" and "it's true because it works." He tells us that "Sentences like . . . 'Truth is independent of the human mind' are simply platitudes used to inculcate . . . the common sense of the West." Of course, Rorty is right that such sentences "inculcate . . . the common sense of the West." He is even right that they are "platitudes." The statement "The sun rises in the east" is another such platitude. It is worth pointing out, however, that "the common sense of the West" has a lot to be said for it and that even platitudes can be true.

Rorty cavalierly tells us that he does "not have much use for notions like 'objective value' and 'objective truth.'" But then the list of things that Rorty does not have much use for is very long. For example, he wants us to get rid of the idea that "the self or the world has an intrinsic nature" because it is "a remnant of the idea that the world is a divine creation." Since for Rorty "socialization" (like language) "goes all the way down," he believes that there is no such thing as a self apart from the social roles it inhabits: "the word 'I' is as hollow as the word 'death.'" ("Death," he assures us, is an "empty" term.)

Rorty looks forward to a culture—he calls it a "liberal utopia"—in which the "Nietzschean metaphors" of self-creation are finally "literalized," i.e., made real. For philosophers, or people who used to be philosophers, this would mean a culture that "took for granted that philosophical problems are as temporary as poetic problems, that there are no problems which bind the generations together in a single natural kind called 'humanity.'" ("Humanity" is another one of those notions that Rorty cannot think about without scare quotes.)

Rorty recognizes that most people ("most nonintellectuals") are not yet liberal ironists. Many people still believe that there is such a thing as truth independent of their thoughts. Some even continue to entertain the idea that their identity is more than a distillate of biological and sociological accidents. Rorty knows this. Whether he also knows that his own position as a liberal ironist crucially depends on most people being *non*-ironists is another question. One suspects not. In any event, he is clearly impatient with what he refers to as "a particular historically conditioned and possibly transient" view of the world, that is, the pre-ironical view for which things like truth and morality still matter. Rorty, in short, is a connoisseur of contempt. He could hardly be more explicit about this. He tells us in the friendliest possible way that he wants us to "get to the point where we no longer worship *anything*, where we treat *nothing* as a quasi divinity, where we treat *everything*—our language, our conscience, our community —as a product of time and chance." What Rorty wants is philosophy without philosophy. The "liberal utopia" he envisions is a utopia in which philosophy as traditionally conceived has conveniently emasculated itself, abandoned the search for truth, and lives on as a repository of more or less bracing exercises in fantasy.

In his book *Overcoming Law* (1995), the jurist and legal philosopher Richard Posner criticizes Rorty for his "deficient sense of fact" and "his belief in the plasticity of human nature," noting that both are "typical of modern philosophy." They are typical, anyway, of certain influential strains of modern philosophy. And it is in the union of these two things—a deficient sense of fact and a belief in the unbounded plasticity of human nature—that the legacy of Nietzsche bears its most poisonous fruit. As the philosopher Susan Haack, one of Rorty's most penetrating

critics, has pointed out, "if one really believed that criteria
of justification are purely conventional, wholly without
objective grounding, then, though one might conform to
the justificatory practices of one's own epistemic community, one would be obliged to adopt an attitude of
cynicism towards them, to think of justification always in
covert scare quotes." Richard Rorty is fond of describing
himself as an "ironist," but really, Haack argues, he is "a
cynic hiding behind a euphemism." In bidding farewell to
truth, he at the same time bids farewell to serious inquiry
of any kind. As Haack observes, "unless there is such a
thing as better and worse evidence for accepting this or
that proposition as true—objectively better or worse evidence, that is—there can be no real inquiry of any kind:
epistemological, . . . or scientific, forensic, historical,
mathematical."

The cognitive pessimism espoused by figures such as
Derrida and Rorty has moral as well as intellectual implications. When Rorty, expatiating on the delights of his
liberal utopia, says that "a postmetaphysical culture seems
to me no more impossible than a postreligious one, and
equally desirable," he perhaps speaks truer than he pur-
posed. For despite the tenacity of non-irony in many sections of society, there is much in our culture—the culture
of Europe writ large—that shows the disastrous effects of
Nietzsche's dream of a postmetaphysical, ironized society
of putative self-creators. And of course to say that such a
society would be as desirable as a postreligious society
amounts to saying also that it would be just as *un*desirable.

Like his fellow liberal ironists, Rorty takes radical secularism as an unarguable good. For him, religion, like
truth—like anything that transcends our contingent self-
creations—belongs to the childhood of mankind. Ironists
are beyond all that, and liberal ironists are beyond it with

a smile and a little joke. But of course whether our culture really is "postreligious" remains very much an open question. That liberal ironists such as Richard Rorty make do without religion does not tell us very much about the matter. In an essay called "The Self-Poisoning of the Open Society," the Polish philosopher Leszek Kolakowski observes that the idea that there are no fundamental disputes about moral and spiritual values is "an intellectualist self-delusion, a half-conscious inclination by Western academics to treat the values they acquired from their liberal education as something natural, innate, corresponding to the normal disposition of human nature." Since liberal ironists like Richard Rorty do not believe that anything is natural or innate, Kolakowski's observation has to be slightly modified to fit him. But his general point remains, namely that "the net result of education freed of authority, tradition, and dogma is moral nihilism." Kolakowski readily admits that the belief in a unique core of personality "is not a scientifically provable truth." But he argues that, "without this belief, the notion of personal dignity and of human rights is an arbitrary concoction, suspended in the void, indefensible, easy to be dismissed," and hence prey to totalitarian doctrines and other intellectual and spiritual deformations.

The Promethean dreams of writers such as Derrida and Rorty depend critically on their denying the reality of anything that transcends the prerogatives of their efforts at self-creation. Traditionally, the recognition of such realities has been linked with a recognition of the sacred. It is a mistake typical of intellectuals to believe that this link can be severed with impunity. This, too, is something that Kolakowski sees clearly. As he argues in another essay, "The Revenge of the Sacred in Secular Culture," "culture, when it loses its sacred sense, loses all sense."

With the disappearance of the sacred, which imposed limits to the perfection that could be attained by the profane, arises one of the most dangerous illusions of our civilization—the illusion that there are no limits to the changes that human life can undergo, that society is "in principle" an endlessly flexible thing, and that to deny this flexibility and this perfectibility is to deny man's total autonomy and thus to deny man himself.

It is a curious irony that self-creators from Nietzsche through Derrida and Richard Rorty are reluctant children of the Enlightenment. In his essay "What is Enlightenment?," Immanuel Kant famously observed that the motto of the Enlightenment was *sapere aude*, "Dare to know!" For the deconstructionist, the liberal ironist, and other paragons of disillusionment, that motto has been revised to read "Dare to believe that there is nothing to know." The Enlightenment sought to emancipate man by liberating reason and battling against superstition. It has turned out, however, that when reason is liberated entirely from tradition—which means also when it is liberated entirely from any acknowledgment of what transcends it—reason grows rancorous and hubristic: it becomes, in short, something irrational.

It is in this sense that anyone concerned with the future of the European past must approach the Enlightenment and its legacy with conflicted feelings: in a spirit that is as ready to criticize as to endorse. To be sure, few of us would wish to do without the benefits of the Enlightenment. As the sociologist Edward Shils pointed out in his 1981 book *Tradition*, the Enlightenment's "tradition of emancipation from traditions is . . . among the precious achievements of our civilization. It has made citizens out of slaves and serfs. It has opened the imagination and the reason of human beings." Nevertheless—as Shils also understood—to the extent that Enlightenment rationalism turns against the tradition that gave rise to it, it degenerates into a force destructive of culture and the manifold directives that culture has bequeathed us. Like so many other promises of emancipation, it has contained the seeds of new forms of bondage. Philosophy has been an important casualty of this development. It is no accident that so much modern philosophy has been committed to bringing us the gospel of the end of philosophy. Once it abandons its vocation as the love of wisdom, philosophy inevitably becomes the gravedigger of its highest ambitions, interring itself with tools originally forged to perpetuate its service to truth.

Reflecting on the ambiguous legacy of the Enlightenment, especially the accelerating campaign against traditional sources of moral and intellectual direction, Shils went on to warn that "the destruction or discrediting of these cognitive, moral, metaphysical, and technical charts is a step into chaos. Destructive criticism which is an extension of reasoned criticism, aggravated by hatred, annuls the benefits of reason and restrained emancipation." Today, the effects of that annulment are evident everywhere. At stake is not simply the future of an academic discipline but the deepest sources of our moral and intellectual self-understanding. In *Philosophical Investigations*, Wittgenstein remarked that "all philosophical problems have the form 'I have lost my way.'" At a moment when so much of intellectual life has degenerated into an experiment against reality, perhaps our primary task is facing up to the fact that many of the liberations we crave have served chiefly to compound the depth of our loss.

Part One

Art v. Aestheticism:
The Case of Walter Pater

In an age when the lives of artists were full of adventure, his life is almost colourless.
—Walter Pater, "Sandro Botticelli"

If we had not welcomed the arts and invented this kind of cult of the untrue, then the realization of general untruth and mendaciousness that now comes to us through science—the realization that delusion and error are conditions of human knowledge and sensation—would be utterly unbearable. Honesty *would lead us to nausea and suicide. But now there is a counterforce against our honesty that helps us avoid such consequences: art as the* good *will to appearance.*
—Friedrich Nietzsche, *The Gay Science*

F OR MOST OF US, the Victorian essayist Walter Pater survives chiefly as a kind of literary aroma punctuated by a handful of famous phrases. Having grown up with the astringent qualms of modernism—which ostentatiously defined itself in opposition to the earnest aestheticism of writers such as Pater—we are likely to find that aroma a bit cloying. Few serious modern writers indulged themselves in prose so effulgently purple as did Pater. His meticulous adumbrations of mortal things quickened into beauty by death will strike most contemporary readers as quaint, neurasthenic, or both. Perhaps the notion that *"All art constantly aspires towards the condition of music,"* as Pater wrote in "The School of Giorgione," is sufficiently abstract and elusive still to occasion productive meditation. But the idea—another of Pater's nuggets—that Leonardo's *Mona Lisa* "is older than the rocks among which she sits; like the vampire, she has been dead many times, and learned the secrets of the grave" seems little more than a set-piece of timid *fin-de-siècle* morbidity. Even the celebrated apothegm from the conclusion of *The Renaissance*, Pater's first and most famous book, is troublesome: "To burn always with this hard, gem-like flame, to maintain this ecstasy, is success in life." Is it? For most of us, the scintillations will long ago have been quenched by too-frequent repetition.

It is a matter of some curiosity, then, that the well-known literary critic Denis Donoghue should have undertaken a critical biography of Walter Pater. Although he has written on a wide range of topics and figures, including Swift, Emily Dickinson, and the critic R. P. Blackmur, Donoghue is familiar to most of his readers as a champion of high modernism and its decidedly un-Pateresque ambitions.

At least, we might have thought them un-Pateresque. It is part of Donoghue's purpose in *Walter Pater: Lover of Strange Souls* (Knopf, 1995) to restore Pater to his place as an important, though largely unacknowledged, precursor of modernism. "Pater," he writes, "gave modern literature its first act. The major writers achieved their second and third acts by dissenting from him and from their first selves." It is not, Donoghue thinks, so much a question of "influence" as of "presence." He sets out to show that Pater is "a shade or trace in virtually every writer of significance from Hopkins and Wilde to Ashbery."

In addition to those just named, his roster of Pater's literary heirs includes Henry James, Yeats, Pound, Ford, Woolf, Joyce, Eliot, Aiken, Hart Crane, Fitzgerald, Forster, Borges, Stevens, and A. R. Ammons. The first "poem" in Yeats's eccentric edition of the *Oxford Book of Modern Verse* (1936) is a versified snippet from Pater's expostulation on the *Mona Lisa*. The mature T. S. Eliot would take sharp exception to Pater and everything he stood for; indeed, his essay "Arnold and Pater," from 1930, is a *locus classicus* in modernism's attack on Victorian aestheticism; but early works such as "Preludes," "Portrait of a Lady," and "The Love Song of J. Alfred Prufrock" are instinct with a Pateresque languor, brimming as they are with personages measuring out lives with coffee spoons while they come and go, talking of Michelangelo.

Similarly, the early Stevens is full of Pateresque themes and aspirations. Pater certainly does not hold the copyright on the idea (as Stevens put it in "Sunday Morning") that "death is the mother of beauty." But taken in conjunction with complacent peignoirs, late coffee and oranges, and "the holy hush of ancient sacrifice," the identification of mortality as the condition of beauty assumes a distinctly Pateresque coloring. Again, Pater was hardly the first to favor evocation over declaration; but his *style* of embracing intimation echoes plainly in "Thirteen Ways of Looking at a Blackbird":

> I do not know which to prefer,
> The beauty of inflections
> Or the beauty of innuendoes,
> The blackbird whistling
> Or just after.

If Donoghue is right, Pater's presence is more than a collection of echoes and insinuations. "Whatever we mean by modernity," he insists, Pater "is an irrefutable part of it." His first published essay, on Coleridge, in 1866 sounds the distinctive, disabused note: "Modern thought is distinguished from ancient by its cultivation of the 'relative' spirit in place of the 'absolute.' . . . To the modern spirit nothing is, or can be rightly known, except relatively and under certain conditions." Then, too, Pater's interest in French literature and German aesthetics helped to make English literature more cosmopolitan, more worldly. And the French element, especially, opened up exotic new avenues of feeling.

In brief, Pater instigated for English letters something like what such writers as Baudelaire, Rimbaud, Verlaine, Huysmans, and Mallarmé did for the French. He made the forbidden, the outlandish, the silent a central literary preoccupation—though he did so quietly, with the greatest possible tact. If he was a "lover of strange souls" (Donoghue's subtitle comes from Pater's essay on Leonardo in The Renaissance), if "strangeness and beauty" was his "favorite conjunction," it was for him a matter of discriminating delectation not abandonment. In this respect, he betrays a kinship with Mallarmé, who advocated painting "not the thing itself, but the effect that it produces," and who once defined poetry as "a brief tearing of silence." Pater's route to exquisiteness was not through absinthe, hashish, sexual extravagance, or conscious blasphemy, but via a diffident voraciousness of appreciation.

Nevertheless, despite Pater's enormous reserve, there is a direct line of descent from The Renaissance (which was first published in 1873) to Oscar Wilde's The Picture of Dorian Gray (1890) and other such turn-of-the-century manifestations of arty decadence. Mario Praz was right (in The Romantic Agony, his classic study of the literature of decadence) to identify Pater as "the forerunner of the Decadent Movement in England." Not for nothing did Pater expatiate on the "fascination of corruption" and the poetic aspects of a countenance tinged with a deathly pallor. Algernon Swinburne was not only a friend but also a spiritual brother. Especially in his early years, Pater liked to think of himself as a champion of pagan virtues. But an underside of pagan vices clings firmly to Pater's prose. G. K. Chesterton perceptively noted the duality that accompanies the championship of paganism:

> A man loves Nature in the morning for her innocence and amiability, and at nightfall, if he is loving her still, it is for her darkness and her cruelty. He washes at dawn in clear water as did the Wise Men of the Stoics, yet, somehow at the dark end of the day, he is bathing in hot bull's blood, as did Julian the Apostate.

Donoghue duly registers this aspect of Pater's legacy, but he shifts the emphasis: "It was Pater, more than Arnold, Tennyson, or Ruskin, who set modern literature upon its antithetical—he would have said its antinomian—course." That is to say, Donoghue highlights those elements of Pater's achievement that anticipate the critical, Romantic side of modernism: the side that exalted art as spiritual armor suited to a secular age and that found expression (for example) in Nietzsche's dictum that "we have art lest we perish from the truth." (Or—Nietzsche again—"Only as an aesthetic phenomenon is life and the world eternally justified.") As it happens, Pater claims us less through his ideas than through his sensibility, his style. He was not, Donoghue notes, really "learned in the history of art or in any of the subjects he took up—Greek myths, English poetry, Greek philosophy." Indeed, he was not an original thinker: virtually every idea he expressed can be traced to a source in English, French, or German writers. He is a force in the criticism of these subjects because he devised a distinctive style of writing about them: the Pateresque, a new color in the palette.

Donoghue's book is an effort to define and nurture that "new color," to recommend it anew as a compensation for the diminishments and losses of modernity. It is a measure of his eloquence that he succeeds in rendering the Pateresque at least momentarily plausible; it is a measure of the limitations of his chosen subject that that plausibility remains momentary, episodic.

Donoghue has segregated the biographical portion of his story in a "brief life" of some seventy pages at the beginning of the book. In some ways, it is remarkable that he was able to draw it out as long as he did. Pater extended his discretion even into the minutiae of his biography: his was a life notable above all for its lack of notable incident. We do, however, have the usual official signposts. We know that he was born Walter Horatio Pater near Stepney in 1839, the second son and third child of Richard and Maria Pater. A fourth child, Clara Ann, was born in 1841. Pater's father, a surgeon who catered to the poor, died shortly after Clara's birth at the age of forty-five. The family then moved to Enfield and, later, to Canterbury. In 1854, Pater's mother died, leaving the children in the care of their aunt Elizabeth. Pater was educated at the King's School, Canterbury, and then at Queen's College, Oxford, where he read widely but took an indifferent degree in 1862. While at Oxford he studied with the great Platonist Benjamin Jowett and came under the influence of Matthew Arnold and John Ruskin. He also, like so many university students then and later, used his college years as an opportunity to shed his religious faith. By 1859, Donoghue reports, Pater's attitude toward Christianity was "frivolous." He was, for example, overheard to say that it would be great fun to take Holy Orders without believing a word of Christian doctrine. His effort to put this scheme into effect was prevented by a friend who wrote to the Bishop of London, acquainting him with the state of Pater's beliefs.

In 1862, Pater's aunt Elizabeth died, and he set up house in London with Clara and his elder sister, Hester. In 1864, he won a provisional fellowship to Brasenose College, Oxford. The fellowship was confirmed the following year, and Pater settled into the pattern he would maintain for the rest of his life. Cared for by his maiden sisters, he shuttled quietly between Oxford and London, made occasional trips to the continent, and devoted himself to reading, writing, teaching, and aesthetic refinement. His circle of friends included Edmund Gosse, Mr. and Mrs. Humphry Ward, the classicist Ingram Bywater, as well as the influential Oxford don Mark Pattison and his young wife, twenty-seven years his junior, who are generally thought to have provided George Eliot with her models for Mr. Casaubon and Dorothea in *Middlemarch*. Pater's first visit to Italy, in the summer of 1865, was a revelation. He found in the Renaissance paintings he saw in Ravenna, Pisa, and Florence "the imagery of a richer, more daring sense of life than any to be seen in Oxford." It was then that he began "to associate the Italian Renaissance with freedom" and abundant sensuous life. In effect, "the Renaissance" for Pater named not a historical period but a state of mind, a promise of fulfillment.

It is here, just as Pater's career is about to begin, that things get difficult for the biographer. Like his image of Botticelli, Pater's life was "almost colourless." Donoghue notes that most people who write about Pater assume that "he must have had more life than appears, since otherwise he would have to be deemed a freak of nature." But the record shows that "by comparison with his grand contemporaries, he seems hardly to have lived." Thomas Hardy, meeting Pater in London in 1886, noted that his manner was "that of one carrying weighty ideas without spilling them." Deliquescence was as much a theme in his life as in his work. "There are," Donoghue notes, "weeks or even months in which he seems to have taken his favorite theme of evanescence and drifted away. We assume that he is still alive, but the evidence for his breathing is meagre."

Although he was clearly homosexual by disposition, Pater's fastidious nature—what Christopher Ricks called his "greed for fineness"—forbade anything so obvious as a love affair or a sex life. He was, as Edmund Wilson put it, "one of those semi-monastic types . . . that the English universities breed: vowed to an academic discipline but cherishing an intense originality, painfully repressed and incomplete but in the narrow field of their art somehow both sound and bold." In the event, Pater contented himself with a few passionate friendships and an ardent contemplation of youthful male beauty wherever it chanced to present itself. It was a great sorrow to him, a lover of elegance, that he was himself physically unprepossessing: bald, bulky, and bushy in his formidable mustachios. Nonetheless, beginning in 1869 Pater dressed the part of a dandy. Donoghue equips him with top hat, black tailcoat, silk tie of apple green, dark-striped trousers, yellow gloves, and patent leather shoes. Pater appears as Mr. Rose in W. H. Mallock's satire *The New Republic* (1877): a "pale creature, with large moustache, looking out of the window at the sunset. . . . [H]e always speaks in an undertone, and his two topics are self-indulgence and art." In 1894, the last year of his life, Pater was invited to meet Mallarmé, who was then lecturing at Oxford. Mallarmé taught English in a *lycée*; Pater's French was excellent; but the two connoisseurs of intimation apparently thought it too vulgar actually to speak. According to one account, they "regarded each other in silence, and were satisfied."

Pater was not entirely without gumption; only he tended to hoard it for his imagination. The infamous Frank Harris—editor of the *Saturday Review*, sexual braggart, and author of the pornographic fantasy *My Life and Loves* (four volumes)—is notoriously an unreliable witness. But his anecdote about Pater has the ring of authenticity:

> He seemed at times half to realize his own deficiency. "Had I So-and-so's courage and hardihood," he cried once, "I'd have—." Suddenly the mood changed, the light in the eyes died out, the head drooped forward again, and with a half smile he added. "I might have been a criminal—he, he," and he moved with little careful steps across the room to his chair, and sat down.

The problem with Harris's anecdote is that it traps Pater in his caricature. It may be true; but it is not the whole truth. Such stories make it difficult to understand the genuine boldness of Pater's work: to appreciate, for example, the enormous scandal that *The Renaissance* caused when it was first published in 1873. Originally titled *Studies in the History of the Renaissance*, the slim volume consists of nine essays, some of which had been already published in one form or another, plus a brief preface and (in most editions) a conclusion. As Pater's friend Mrs. Mark Pattison noted in an otherwise friendly review of the book, the title is "misleading" because "the historical element is precisely that which is wanting. . . . [T]he work is in no wise a contribution to the history of the Renaissance." Pater took the point. In subsequent editions it was called by the title we know today, *The Renaissance; Studies in Art and Poetry.*

Not that the change of title really addressed Mrs. Pattison's criticism. "The book," another contemporary reviewer warned, "is not for any beginner to turn to in search of 'information.'" "Facts" and historical accuracy are not the coin in which Pater traded. For him, history was a mine to be worked for the *frisson* of insight; a certain amount of poetic license only aided the process.

Perhaps the chief instance of poetic license concerned the term "Renaissance." That Pater's conception of the Renaissance was idiosyncratic is clear first of all from the topics that he aggregated under the rubric. The book includes essays on such bona fide Renaissance figures as Pico della Mirandola, Leonardo, and Michelangelo; his essay on Botticelli did much to introduce the relatively unknown painter to the public. But the book also deals with figures like the medieval philosopher and ill-fated lover Abelard and the eighteenth-century art historian and impresario for "the glory that was Greece" Johann Winckelmann.

Pater noted that although interest in the Renaissance "mainly lies" in fifteenth-century Italy, he understands the term in "a much wider scope than was intended by those who originally used it to denote that revival of classical antiquity in the fifteenth century." For him, the Renaissance was a distinctive "outbreak of the human spirit" whose defining characteristics include "the care for physical beauty, the worship of the body, the breaking down of those limits which the religious system of the middle ages imposed on the heart and the imagination." Thus it is that although Winckelmann (who had long been one of Pater's culture heroes) was born in 1717, Pater concluded that he "really belongs in spirit to an earlier age" by virtue of "his enthusiasm for the things of the intellect and the imagination for their own sake, by his Hellenism, his life-long struggle to attain to the Greek spirit." For Pater, "Renaissance" was shorthand for a certain species of aesthetic vibrancy.

It was not necessarily a wholesome vibrancy. Part of what made Pater's debut scandalous was the hothouse atmosphere that he reveled in: the ripe, over-ripe sensorium that was so distant from the brisk admonitions of such pragmatic partisans of culture as Matthew Arnold. Pater's fascination with violence and death, with the interpenetration of death and beauty, was part of that ripeness. In his essay on Michelangelo, for example, Pater tells us that that great artist, like "all the nobler souls of Italy," "is much occupied with thoughts of the grave, and his true mistress is death—death at first as the worst of all sorrows and disgraces; . . . afterwards, death in its high distinction, its detachment from vulgar needs, the angry stains of life and action escaping fast." For Pater every genuine love was a kind of *Liebestod*. How Pater must have resonated to the end of Shelley's *Adonais*:

> Life, like a dome of many-coloured glass,
> Stains the white radiance of Eternity,
> Until Death tramples it to fragments.—Die,
> If thou wouldst be with that which thou dost seek!

But it was not only the atmosphere of Pater's book that shocked readers. Even more important was the blithe, aesthetic paganism that was implicit throughout *The Renaissance* and that Pater explicitly set forth in his conclusion. Dilating on "the splendour of our experience and its awful brevity," he recommended seizing the moment, regardless of the consequences: "Not the fruit of experience, but experience itself, is the end." Since "a counted number of pulses only is given to us of a variegated, dramatic life," "our one chance" lies in "expanding that interval, in getting as many pulsations as possible into the given time." Neither morality nor religion figured in Pater's equation. What mattered was the intensity, the ecstasy of experience. Consequently, we must grasp "at any exquisite passion, or any contribution to knowledge that seems by a lifted horizon to set the spirit free for a moment, or any stirring of the senses, strange dyes, strange colours, and curious odours, or work of the artist's hands, or the face of one's friend." For Pater, the measure of life was not its adherence to an ideal but the perfection of self-satisfaction. "To burn always with this hard, gem-like flame, to maintain this ecstasy, is success in life." Pleasure, not duty, was the cardinal imperative. Life was not a continuously unfolding whole but a series of lyric moments: "In a sense it might even be said that our failure is to form habits."

Aesthetes embraced Pater's expostulation. The young Oscar Wilde declared that *The Renaissance* was "the golden book of spirit and sense, the holy writ of beauty." Others were not so enthusiastic. The Rev. John Wordsworth, a colleague of Pater's at Brasenose, acknowledged the book's "beauty of style" and "felicity of thought." But he objected that the fundamental message of the book was immoral: "I cannot disguise from myself," he wrote in a letter to Pater,

> that the concluding pages adequately sum up the philosophy of the whole; and that that philosophy is an assertion that no fixed principles either of religion or morality can be regarded as certain, that the only thing worth living for is momentary enjoyment and that probably or certainly the

soul dissolves at death into elements which are destined never to reunite.

Nor were Christian clergymen the only critics of Pater's hedonism. The book was widely regarded as an invitation to moral frivolity. George Eliot spoke for many when she wrote that it was "quite poisonous in its false principles of criticism and false conceptions of life." No one was more shocked by the scandal that *The Renaissance* precipitated than Pater himself. He did not abandon his aestheticism. But he did attempt to modulate it. In the second edition of *The Renaissance* he dropped the conclusion altogether. Later, he restored it, but with cosmetic modifications and a note informing readers that he had worried that "it might possibly mislead some of those young men into whose hands it might fall." When *The Picture of Dorian Gray* was published, Pater took the opportunity to distinguish his version of Epicureanism from Wilde's:

A true Epicureanism aims at a complete though harmonious development of man's entire organism. To lose the moral sense therefore, for instance, the sense of sin and righteousness, as [does] Mr. Wilde's hero—his heroes are bent on doing as speedily, as completely as they can—is to lose, or lower, organisation, to become less complex, to pass from a higher to a lower degree of development. . . . Lord Henry, and even more the, from the first, suicidal hero, loses too much in life to be a true Epicurean.

Pater attempted to provide a portrait of the "true Epicurean" in *Marius the Epicurean* (1885), an overwrought, somewhat ponderous autobiographical novel that describes the spiritual journey of its hero from paganism to the threshold of Christianity. (Pater much preferred hovering on the threshold of commitment to actually embracing any definite faith.) According to Donoghue, "the main reason [for writing the book] was to refute the charge, levelled against *Studies in the History of the Renaissance*, that he was a hedonist, an epicurean and—the implication was clear—that he instructed his undergraduates at Brasenose to live for pleasure alone." In fact, Pater did believe in living for pleasure alone. But he thought that careful discrimination among pleasures redeemed his aestheticism from vulgar hedonism or immorality.

Did it? In part. Pater would certainly have recoiled in horror from the crude narcissism and decadence that his work helped to inspire. But it is not at all clear that George Eliot was mistaken in castigating his "false principles of criticism and false conceptions of life." Donoghue wishes to resuscitate Pater partly because he thinks that a Pateresque aestheticism encourages readers to deal with art on its own terms, as affording an experience valuable in itself. "There are," he writes, "some experiences which are best approached on the assumption that their value is intrinsic." This is certainly true. And it may be that Pater's view of art, as Donoghue claims, can help to immunize art from ideology. Because he held that art "has no moral design upon us," Pater would have had no patience with efforts to subject aesthetic experience to politics—or any other "external" value. "In its primary aspect," he wrote in *The Renaissance*, "a great picture has no more definite message for us than an accidental play of sunlight and shadow for a few moments on the wall or floor."

Yet this is not the whole story. Donoghue writes that "the purpose of art is to offer the distressed soul release, however temporary." This is not a new theme for him. In his book *The Arts Without Mystery* (1984), for example, Donoghue worried that our commitment to scientific rationality had drained the arts of their power to enchant and to kindle the imagination. He sought to "reinstate mystery" into the arts while at the same time distinguishing mystery "from mere bewilderment or mystification." For Donoghue, the artist is most truly himself when he stands in an antagonistic or (one of his favorite words) "antinomian" attitude toward society. Yet this Romanticism is sharply qualified by prudence, the most un-Romantic of virtues. Donoghue understands that the main business of society cannot countenance the extravagances that the artistic imagination furnishes.

> The arts are on the margin, and it doesn't bother me to say they are marginal. What bothers me are the absurd claims we make for them. I want to say the margin is the place for those feelings and intuitions which daily life doesn't have a place for, and mostly seems to suppress. . . . With the arts, people can make a space for themselves, and fill it with intimations of freedom and presence.

Pater would have agreed. In his essay on Winckelmann, he wrote that

> What modern art has to do in the service of culture is so to rearrange the details of modern life, so to reflect it, that it may satisfy the spirit. And what does the spirit need in the face of modern life? The sense of freedom. . . . The chief factor in the thoughts of the modern mind concerning itself is the intricacy, the universality of natural law, even in the moral order. For us, necessity is . . . a magic web woven through and through us, like that magnetic system of which modern science speaks, penetrating us with a network,

subtler than our subtlest nerves, yet bearing in it the central forces of the world. Can art represent men and women in these bewildering toils so as to give the spirit at least the equivalent for the sense of freedom?

The real question, for Donoghue as well as for Pater, is whether that "equivalent for the sense of freedom" is anything more than illusion. Does Pater's philosophy—does any thoroughgoing aestheticism—really leave room for "intrinsic value" as Donoghue claims?

In his preface to *The Renaissance*, Pater begins by *seeming* to agree with Matthew Arnold's famous definition of criticism, but he then slyly inverts Arnold's meaning:

> "To see the object as in itself it really is," has been justly said to be the aim of all true criticism whatever; and in aesthetic criticism the first step towards seeing one's object as it really is, is to know one's own impression as it really is, to discriminate it, to realise it distinctly. . . . What is this song or picture, this engaging personality presented in life or in a book, to *me*? . . . [T]he picture, the landscape, the engaging personality in life or in a book . . . are valuable for their virtues, as we say, in speaking of an herb, a wine, a gem; for the property each has of affecting one with a special, a unique, impression of pleasure.

For Pater, "one's own impression" trumps meaning. And it is a curious irony, as the critic Adam Phillips has observed, that although Pater insists on the value of discrimination and accurate identification of the critic's "impressions," his vocabulary is "notably vague." Thus it is that he "exploited the invitation of inexact words: 'sweet,' 'peculiar,' 'delicate,' and above all 'strange.'"

Donoghue rightly notes that Pater "looked at an object

under the sign of pleasure, not of truth." He approvingly quotes another critic who spoke of "the disjunction of sensation from judgment" in Pater's work. The "Paterian imagination," he writes, seeks "relations" instead of "duties." "It follows that Pater practised consciousness not as a mode of knowledge but as an alternative to knowledge. . . . One of the ways in which Pater was antinomian was in his being ready to think that understanding wasn't everything." Indeed, his chief concern was "his pleasure in feeling alive." "Aesthetic criticism" in Pater's sense deals "not with objects, works of art, but with the types of feeling they embodied. . . . Ontology is displaced by psychology."

"Ontology is displaced by psychology": in other words, what matters for Pater are states of feeling, not truth. At the end of his book, Donoghue acknowledges the "risks" of aestheticism: "triviality, exquisiteness, solipsism." An additional risk is losing the weight or reality of one's experience. T. S. Eliot criticized Pater for propounding "a theory of ethics" in the guise of a theory of art. What he meant was that Pater's conception of "aesthetic criticism" offered not a principle of criticism but a way of life. At the center of that way of life is the imperative to regard all experience as an occasion for aesthetic delectation: a seemingly attractive proposition, perhaps, until one realizes that it depends upon a narcissistic self-absorption that renders every moral demand negotiable. "The sense of freedom" is indeed the essence of aestheticism; but it is the cold and lonely freedom of the isolated individual. This was something that Kierkegaard exposed with great clarity in his anatomy of "the aesthetic mode of life" in *Either/Or*. Donoghue tells us that "the part of Aestheticism which should now be recovered . . . is its concern for the particularity of form in every work of art." The problem is that although aestheticism begins by emphasizing form, it ends by dissolving form into the "pleasurable sensations" and "pulsations" that Pater so valued. In this sense, aestheticism is the enemy of the intrinsic. Donoghue criticized Eliot's essay on Pater as "extravagant" and "cruel." But Eliot was right: the theory of "art for art's sake" is "valid in so far as it can be taken as an exhortation to the artist to stick to his job; it never was and never can be valid for the spectator, reader or auditor."

The Importance
of T. E. Hulme

*The fundamental principle of all morality is that man is a being
naturally loving justice. In* Emile *I have endeavored to show how
vice and error, foreign to the natural constitution of man, have
been introduced from outside, and have insensibly altered him.*
—Jean-Jacques Rousseau

*The "classical" point of view I take to be this. Man is by his
very nature essentially limited and incapable of anything
extraordinary. He is incapable of attaining any kind of
perfection, because, either by nature, as the result of original
sin, or the result of evolution, he encloses within him certain
antinomies. There is a war of instincts inside him, and it is part
of his permanent characteristics that this must always be so.*
—T. E. Hulme

"THE HISTORY of philosophers we know, but who will
write the history of the philosophic amateurs and
readers?" Thus did the Imagist poet and essayist T. E.
Hulme begin "Cinders," a posthumously published collection of notes and aphorisms about art, life, and language
that he scribbled in his early twenties while traveling across
Canada working on railways, farms, and in timber mills.
Hulme (the name is pronounced "Hume") was himself a

conspicuously philosophical amateur. Or perhaps one should say "amateur philosopher" (I use "amateur," as he did, in its most flattering sense to indicate passionate, almost amatory, involvement with ideas).

Among much else, Hulme was a translator and—for a few years, anyway—a champion of the work of the French philosopher Henri Bergson, a thinker who, though all-but forgotten today, was immensely influential in the opening decades of the twentieth century. Hulme was an early and voluble reader of Edmund Husserl, G. E. Moore, Alexius Meinong, Georges Sorel (whose *Réflexions sur la Violence* he also translated), Max Scheler, and other difficult, path-breaking thinkers; he was the first to disseminate in England Wilhelm Worringer's ideas about the origins of the "urge to abstraction" in art; he was an enthusiastic proponent of certain strains of avant-garde art, an implacable critic of others. Above all, Hulme was a committed if idiosyncratic Tory, an ardent propagandist for "classicism" and "the religious attitude," an adamant scourge of pacificism and anything that he could construe as "romanticism" or "humanism."

Today, Hulme merits an extended footnote in the history of English modernism—the high modernism of T. S. Eliot, Ezra Pound, and Wyndham Lewis. In her edition of Hulme's writings for Oxford's Clarendon Press, Karen Csengeri calls Hulme "one of the most misunderstood figures in twentieth-century letters." He is at any rate one of the most fugitive. Hulme is one of those curious figures whose influence outruns his achievement—or at least whose achievement is difficult to reckon by the usual standards. The aesthetic movement with which he is most closely associated—Imagism—is, as René Wellek observed, based on ideas that are "extremely simple and even trite." Poetry, Hulme wrote in one typical exhortation, should be "a visual concrete" language that "always endeavors to arrest you, and to make you continuously see a physical thing, to prevent you gliding through an abstract process."

Well, OK. But even in the Teens that was not exactly press-stopping material. And Hulme's own poetry? In bulk, anyway, his contribution was comically modest. "The Complete Poetical Works of T. E. Hulme" consists of five short poems first published together in the magazine *New Age* in 1912 and then, later that year, as an appendix to Ezra Pound's *Ripostes*. Of course, the title was partly a joke. But it was hardly an exaggeration. Hulme's total poetic *oeuvre* runs to eight poems, the longest of which is fourteen lines. They belong to the same genre as Pound's famous "In a Station of the Metro." Here is "Autumn":

A touch of cold in the Autumn night—
I walked abroad,
And saw the ruddy moon lean over a hedge
Like a red-faced farmer.
I did not stop to speak, but nodded,
And round about were the wistful stars
With white faces like town children.

Charming, yes; memorable, perhaps; but surely rather . . . *small*.

The diminution is deliberate. "The old poetry," Hulme wrote in "A Lecture on Modern Poetry" (1908), "dealt essentially with big things. . . . But the modern is the exact opposite of this, it no longer deals with heroic action, it has become definitely and finally introspective and deals with expression and communication of momentary phases in the poet's mind." It is not surprising that Hulme went on to quote with approval G. K. Chesterton on the difference between old and new poetry: "the old dealt with

the Siege of Troy, the new attempts to express the emotions
of a boy fishing."

Hulme's philosophical musings are more ambitious, but he
not did make any notable theoretical advances. He was an
amusingly original *character* but—as his friend and biographer Michael Roberts acknowledged—he was "not an
original thinker, he solved no problems."

Sometimes, however, simply articulating problems can
be as fruitful as solving them. In his book *Romantic Image*,
Frank Kermode devotes an entire chapter to Hulme. Kermode winds up being highly critical, almost dismissive, but
he does admit that Hulme was "in some respects, the most
influential" member of his literary coterie. Many critics
come away from Hulme feeling this way. He was somehow
more than the sum of his parts. Hulme was a human
tuning fork, vibrating powerfully to certain intellectual and
spiritual currents. And—what turned out to be more important—he managed to set off vibrations in others. As
Jewel Spears Brooker pointed out in " 'Ole T. E. H.': Pio-
neer of Modernism," Hulme "was more than one of the
founding fathers of modern poetry; in all the arts, he was a
prophet of and an advocate for modernism."

Perhaps the greatest eminence who responded to
Hulme's battle cry was T. S. Eliot. In 1924, seven years
after Hulme's death, his friend Herbert Read, the art critic,
assembled a chrestomathy of Hulme's writing and published it under the title *Speculations: Essays on Humanism
and the Philosophy of Art*. Reviewing *Speculations* in *The
Criterion*, Eliot lavished praise on both the book and its
author. Hulme, Eliot wrote, was

> the forerunner of a new attitude of mind, which should be
> the twentieth-century mind, if the twentieth century is to

have a mind of its own. Hulme is classical, reactionary, and revolutionary; he is the antipodes of the eclectic, tolerant, and democratic mind of the end of the last century.

"Classical," "reactionary," suspicious of the "democratic mind": Eliot's lexicon had no higher encomia. In his Clark Lectures of 1926, Eliot referred to Hulme as "the most *fertile* mind of my generation." Elsewhere, he described him variously as "the most remarkable theologian of my generation" and even a "great poet." "The poems of T. E. Hulme," Eliot wrote in "The Function of Criticism," "only needed to be read aloud to have an immediate effect."

Of course, not everyone was as susceptible to Hulme's spell as Eliot. Ezra Pound, for example, was an early enthusiast but soon became disenchanted with the cult growing up posthumously around Hulme. Pound did everything he could to minimize Hulme's role in defining the Imagist aesthetic. "Mr. Hulme is on his way to mythological glory," Pound complained in the 1930s, dismissing one appreciative study of Hulme with a summary, Poundian "bullshit."

If Hulme has remained a somewhat shadowy figure, one reason is that he has, until now, been poorly served by his editors. In 1955, Samuel Hynes published a second Hulme miscellany, *Further Speculations*, and other writings by Hulme have appeared in appreciations (now out of print) by Michael Roberts and Alun Jones. But Herbert Read's *Speculations* is the volume most people interested in Hulme know. As Karen Csengeri points out in her introduction to the Oxford edition of Hulme's writings, *Speculations* provides a highly misleading view of Hulme's thought. The essays are arranged more or less in reverse chronological order, and Read provides no clues to their dates of composition. Thus the volume opens with "Humanism and the Religious Attitude," a version of Hulme's very last piece of philosophical writing that Read abridged and adorned with his own title. (Csengeri prints the original version under Hulme's title, "A Notebook.") Read also left out several important essays, slighting Hulme's political writing, his writing about art, and his writing about the war. Even more problematic was Read's inclusion of so much of Hulme's writing about Bergson. As Csengeri notes, *Speculations* makes Bergson "seem to be the centre-piece of Hulme's intellectual life, instead of simply an important step to the extremely individual views of his later work." Hulme was not a systematic thinker, but his thought did develop out of a consistent worldview; *Speculations* obscures both the development of Hulme's thought and its underlying emotional consistency.

Although it is occasionally marred by typos—"Hulme" printed as "Hume," mangled Greek (and this in a Clarendon Press book!), etc.—Csengeri's edition of Hulme's writings supersedes the other collections of his work and deserves praise. Not only has she done a professional job of editing and annotating Hulme's text, but also she has supplied a balanced and insightful introduction that goes a long way toward situating Hulme's achievement. She recognizes Hulme's virtues as a thinker—above all his "intellectual honesty"—but does not overstate his importance. In short, she has made newly accessible to us the work of a neglected conservative thinker of great if fragmentary suggestiveness, formidable rhetorical skill, and keen passion.

Thomas Ernest Hulme was born in September 1883, in North Staffordshire to a family in comfortable circumstances; his father was a gentleman farmer and businessman. In 1902, Hulme won a mathematics exhibition to St. John's College, Cambridge. A teetotaler himself, Hulme apparently consorted with some who were unburdened by an aversion to alcohol. He was at any rate sent down in 1904 for what Herbert Read delicately called "indulging in a brawl." A college document that might have slipped out of Bertie Wooster's dossier mentions "over-stepping the limits of the traditional license allowed by the authorities on Boat Race night." On another occasion, a policeman reprehended Hulme as he relieved himself in broad daylight in Soho Square: "You can't do that here." Buttoning himself up, Hulme replied "Do you know you are addressing a member of the middle classes?" The policeman said, "I beg pardon, sir," and went on.

Herbert Read correctly noted that Hulme's temperament was "not one that could submit readily to an academic mould." After being sent down, he knocked about London and studied briefly at the University of London before embarking on his trek across Canada. Succeeding years found him in Brussels, back in London lecturing to the Poets' Club, in Bologna for a meeting of the Philosophical Congress, absorbing ideas from Pierre Lasserre and *L'Action française* in Paris, and from Worringer in Berlin. His writings appeared regularly—sometimes under the pseudonym "Thomas Gratton"—in A. R. Orage's magazine *New Age* and other journals. In 1912, he applied to be readmitted to St. John's. Henri Bergson, his reputation then at its height, supplied a rousing letter of recommendation describing his disciple as "un esprit d'une grande valeur . . . rares qualités de finesse, de vigueur, et de pénétration." Hulme was duly readmitted.

Instead of continuing his studies, however, Hulme had to flee the country when an enraged father threatened to prosecute him for trying to seduce his sixteen-year-old daughter. When the war came, Hulme was quick to enlist; in April 1915, he was wounded and sent home to recuperate.

The following year he was granted a commission in the Royal Marines Artillery and returned to the front.

"Always seek the hard, definite, personal word," Hulme admonished in "Cinders." In the course of his short life —he was just thirty-four when killed in action near Nieuport, Flanders, in September 1917—Hulme ostentatiously sought the hard, the definite, the impersonally personal in every aspect of his life. The sculptor Jacob Epstein—a close friend—proudly noted that Hulme "was capable of kicking a theory as well as a man downstairs when the occasion demanded." Epstein's bust of Hulme is reproduced on the cover and frontispiece of *Speculations*. It reveals an English officer right out of central casting: chiseled features, neatly trimmed moustache, reserved and coolly assessing gaze. A monocle and riding crop would not have been out of place.

Force of personality was one reason that Hulme—a young provincial, after all—was able to make such an impression on his generation. Force of style was another. Hulme commanded a brisk, tonic prose; just as he favored the concrete image over abstraction in poetry, so he managed to endow even the most abstruse philosophical issues with palpable immediacy. Hulme's essays and lectures tend to be episodic and epigrammatic. In places, they seem inconsecutive; they are never rote. To read Hulme is to participate in a vigorous intellectual quest, cheerful, serious, impatient. Typical is the way he begins the important essay "A Tory Philosophy" (1912): "It is my aim to explain in this article why I believe in original sin, why I can't stand romanticism, and why I am a certain kind of Tory."

Hulme's pugnacious style made him particularly effective on the attack. "A Tory Philosophy" is in part a brief for what he calls the "classic" world view, a view that, suspicious of claims to moral progress, emphasizes order, discipline, and tradition. "As man is essentially bad,"

Hulme wrote in one typical passage, "he can only accomplish anything of value by discipline—ethical and political. Order is thus not merely negative, but creative and liberating. Institutions are necessary."

Hulme realized that such prescriptions were not new, but he was careful to distinguish his own brand of "classicism" from others he regarded as spurious. Here, for example, is what he has to say about Nietzsche in "A Tory Philosophy":

> Most people have been in the habit of associating these kinds of views with Nietzsche. It is true that they do occur in him, but he made them so frightfully vulgar that no classic would acknowledge them. In him you have the spectacle of a romantic seizing on the classic point of view because it attracted him purely as a theory, and who, being a romantic, in taking up this theory, passed his slimy fingers over every detail of it. Everything loses its value. The same idea of the necessary hierarchy of classes, with their varying capacities and duties, gets turned into the romantic nonsense of the two kinds of morality, the slave and the master morality, and every other element of the classic position gets transmuted in a similar way into something ridiculous.

Philosophically, Hulme was not at all in Nietzsche's league; but his observations are to the point and, as far as they go, quite devastating. One feels that Hulme could have done for Nietzsche what Nietzsche did for Wagner.

Hulme could be especially brutal about his contemporaries. An avid admirer of Jacob Epstein's sculpture, he did not take kindly to obtuse criticism of Epstein's work. In "Mr. Epstein and the Critics" (1913), he reviews some of what he considers the most egregious writing about Epstein's art. He devotes hilarious attention to one Anthony Ludovici, who, as it happens, was an early (and notoriously muddled) commentator on Nietzsche. "What," Hulme asks, "is the particular type of charlatan revealed in this book on Nietzsche?"

Mr. Ludovici, writing on Nietzsche, might be compared to a child of four in a theatre watching a tragedy based on adultery. . . . You picture then a spruce little mind that has crept into the complicated rafters of philosophy—you imagine him perplexed, confused—you would be quite wrong. . . . [On the contrary, he] blots out all the complexity which forms the reality of the subject, so that he is simply unaware of its existence. He sees only what is akin to his mind's manner of working, as dogs out for a walk only scent other dogs, and as a Red Indian in a great town for the first time sees only the horses. . . . That a man should write stupid and childish things about Nietzsche does not perhaps matter very much. . . . But when a little bantam of this kind has the impertinence to refer to Mr. Epstein as a "minor personality" . . . then the matter becomes so disgusting that it has to be dealt with. The most appropriate means of dealing with him would be a little personal violence. By that method one removes a nuisance without drawing more attention to it than its insignificance deserves.

Hulme was more subtle, and perhaps more effective, in his attacks on the pacifism of Bertrand Russell and the Bloomsbury art critic Clive Bell in "War Notes," the miscellaneous commentaries he wrote while convalescing in 1915–16. In his foreword to *Speculations*, Herbert Read described Hulme as "a militarist by faith." This is misleading. Hulme was hardly insensitive to the horrors of the war.

Nor was he a thoughtless hawk. In "Diary from the Trenches," which originated as letters to his family, he wrote that life in the trenches was "a kind of nightmare, in which you are in the middle of an enormous saucer of mud with explosions and shots going off all round the edge." "As soon as you had seen someone hurt," he noted, "you began to look at shelling in a very different way": "there is nothing picturesque about it. It's the most miserable existence you can conceive of."

Hulme understood and indeed sympathized with the pacifist revulsion at war. But he also understood that, in the war with Germany, what was at stake made that revulsion a form of moral cowardice. "Bad as the consequences for Europe from our Balance of Power may be," Hulme observed, "the consequences from the German hegemony would be far worse. No politics is ideal; but in a world of real politics, the German is hateful to all but Germans. . . . What is being settled in the present war is the political, intellectual, and ethical configuration of Europe for the coming century."

The "enlightened" pacifism of Russell and Bell arose from an ideology that "finds no place whatever for the heroic," that deeply discounted the importance of honor, and that was prepared to sacrifice virtually any principle for the sake of peace. Hulme had nothing but contempt for it. "It comes to this," he wrote, "that for the emancipated man death is too great a price to pay for anything. Life and comfort are the ultimate goods." Noting the socialist rhetoric with which the well-to-do Bell was wont to festoon his pacifist protestations, Hulme made an observation that is as pertinent and withering today as it was in 1916: "It is a widespread but entirely mistaken idea to suppose that you amend for the advantages of wealth by asserting verbally that you are a Socialist."

Emphasizing the idea of original sin; proclaiming a classicist aesthetic; disparaging the romantic ideology of progress; insisting on the importance of honor and physical courage: in these and other ways Hulme was about as politically incorrect, *avant la lettre*, as it was possible to be. That, in fact, is one reason he remains fresh and engaging. But there are deeper reasons for the importance of T. E. Hulme. His opinions were the product not of superficial attitudinizing but of a passionate engagement with fundamental spiritual questions. Hulme lived at a moment when cataclysmic social change and naïve optimism about the power and beneficence of rationality combined to threaten the survival of any values not subject to a utilitarian calculus. As Csengeri notes, a major source of Hulme's passion was "fear that the modern world, carrying with it a scientific and philosophical baggage from the Victorian past, was trying to merge the sphere of values with that of science. To allow the two to be merged could only lead to the destruction of the ethical." In this, as she points out, Hulme looks forward to many later thinkers, including Wittgenstein.

At bottom, no matter what the subject at hand, Hulme spoke as a moralist. In "Cinders," he proclaimed the irreducible plurality of the world and issued nominalistic warnings about the seductions of language: "Symbols . . . picked out and believed to be realities." His long flirtation with Bergson developed because he hoped that Bergson's notion of "intuition" could provide a convincing response to the dehumanizing, mechanistic world view that, gaining ground everywhere around him, threatened to obliterate the very idea of moral freedom and transform the world into a place where "the word 'value' has clearly no meaning." Bergson, as the philosopher Leszek Kolakowski observed, promised to liberate French intellectual life from "scientism,"

> from the belief that natural science . . . had provided us with an unsurpassed model of genuine knowledge, that all criteria of validity and truth had been established in the procedures of empirical and mathematical science and that all cognitive results worthy of this name derive their legitimacy from the correct application of these criteria. From mechanism, that is, from the . . . [ambition] to reduce all branches of knowledge to physics. From the determinists' contention that the future has always been settled in all its details, in particular that our use of terms such as "free choice" or "creativity" results from our ignorance of causes. . . . From the positivist dismissal of all the questions dealing with the meaning of life, the calling of humanity, the divine origin of the universe, the qualitative distinctions between various forms of being.

Bergson's philosophy, in short, was like catnip to Hulme. If he eventually repudiated Bergson, it was primarily because, under the influence of Pierre Lasserre, he came to believe that Bergson's solution to the problem of scientism, especially his confusion of theology and biology, rested on a species of sentimentality—that it was, in fact, "nothing but the last disguise of romanticism."

Hulme was always looking for spiritual escape hatches; temperamentally, he could endorse only those exits which he could present to himself as conquests. His attack on Romanticism—on sentimentality, on "humanism"—was at bottom an attack on the demeaning capitulations exacted by modernity. Hence his attraction to Wilhelm Worringer's theory about the psychological origins of abstract art. Hulme embraced abstract art not for its aesthetic but for what he took to be its existential potential. He hoped that the rise of abstraction might presage the renewal of a fundamental spiritual resource that had been obscured by long addiction to superficial humanism. "Our difficulty now," he wrote in 1915, "is that we are really incapable of understanding how any other view but the humanistic, could be seriously held by intelligent and emancipated men." Abstract art, he thought, might be a handmaiden in the task of articulating a convincing alternative to desiccated humanism. In his 1908 book *Abstraktion und Einfühlung* ("Abstraction and Empathy") Worringer argued that throughout the ages representational art tended to flourish when mankind felt at home in the world, felt "empathy" with his natural surroundings. By contrast, Worringer identified a feeling of "inner unrest inspired . . . by the phenomena of the outside world" as the primary "urge to abstraction" in the arts:

> The simple line and its development in purely geometrical regularity was bound to offer the greatest possibility of happiness to the man disquieted by the obscurity and entanglement of phenomena. For here the last trace of connection with, and dependence on, life has been effaced, here the highest absolute form, the purest abstraction has been achieved; here is law, here is necessity, while everywhere else the caprice of the organic prevails.

Hulme eagerly seized upon Worringer's ideas. "The re-emergence of geometrical art," he wrote in a 1914 lecture called "Modern Art and Its Philosophy,"

> may be the precursor of the corresponding attitude towards the world, and so, of the break up of the Renaissance humanistic attitude. The fact that this change comes first in

art, before it comes in thought, is easily understandable for this reason. So thoroughly are we soaked in the spirit of the period we live in, so strong is its influence over us, that we can only escape from it in an unexpected way, as it were, a side direction like art.

Many of Hulme's critics have been quick to point out that his use of terms like "humanism" and "Renaissance" —to say nothing of "romanticism" and "original sin"—is Pickwickian at best. They are of course correct. But there is an important sense in which such criticisms are beside the point. Hulme did not pretend to be a scholar: he was after not accurate verbal taxonomy but an accurate description of man's spiritual condition. Thus, for example, he freely acknowledged that he is "not . . . concerned so much with religion, as with the attitude, the 'way of thinking,' . . . from which a religion springs." Any threat to this way of thinking, he believed, was also a threat to the spiritual integrity of man. What he called "romanticism" was naturally hostile to the religious attitude because it encouraged sentiments of delusive self-infatuation. The "root of all romanticism," for Hulme, was the belief that "man, the individual, is an infinite reservoir of possibilities; and if you can so rearrange society by the destruction of oppressive order then these possibilities will have a chance and you will get Progress." Again, there are plenty of Romantics (including, some would say, Hulme himself) to whom this description does not apply. But Hulme's characterization located a spiritual temptation that is as alive today as it was when he wrote.

In a famous passage from his essay "Romanticism and Classicism" (c. 1911), Hulme remarked that "part of the fixed nature of man is the belief in the Deity." "This should," Hulme wrote, be as fixed and true for every man as belief in the existence of matter and in the objective world. . . . Now at certain times, by the use of either force or rhetoric, these instincts have been suppressed. . . . The inevitable result of such a process is that the repressed instinct bursts out in some abnormal direction. So with religion. By the perverted rhetoric of Rationalism, your natural instincts are suppressed and you are converted into an agnostic. Just as in the case of the other instincts, Nature has her revenge. The instincts that find their right and proper outlet in religion must come out in some other way. You don't believe in God, so you begin to believe that man is a god. You don't believe in Heaven, so you begin to believe in a heaven on earth. In other words, you get romanticism. The concepts that are right and proper in their own sphere are spread over, and so mess up, falsify and blur the clear outlines of human experience. It is like pouring a pot of treacle over the dinner table. Romanticism then, and this is the best definition I can give of it, is spilt religion.

The exact nature of Hulme's own religious beliefs is a matter of some dispute; but one need not, I think, subscribe to any particular credo to see the power of his objection: "That man is in no sense perfect," as Hulme put it elsewhere, "but a wretched creature, who can yet apprehend perfection." It is not perhaps a cheerful philosophy, but it has the advantage of being true. Which was why Hulme concluded that he did not "put up with the dogma for the sake of the sentiment, but . . . may possibly swallow the sentiment for the sake of the dogma."

A Craving for Reality:
T. S. Eliot Today

It is not to ring the bell backward
Nor is it an incantation
To summon the spectre of a Rose.
We cannot revive old policies
Or follow an antique drum.
—T. S. Eliot, "Little Gidding," 1942

For the immediate future, and perhaps for a long way ahead, the
continuity of our culture may have to be maintained by a very
small number of people.
—T. S. Eliot, in *The Criterion*, 1939

It is now our unsparing obligation to disclaim the reactionary
Eliot.
—Cynthia Ozick, "T. S. Eliot at 101," 1989

MISTAH ELIOT—he dead. This is the message that the natives are sending back about T. S. Eliot. From our vantage point at the start of a new millennium (maybe it should be called our "disadvantage" point), the extraordinary literary and critical authority that Eliot once commanded is almost incomprehensible. This is not simply because Eliot no longer occupies the exalted place he once did. It is also because that exalted place is itself largely unavailable. The culture that Eliot's authority both presupposed and helped to sustain—the culture of high modernism—seems to be everywhere out of stock, back-ordered: no longer carried because no longer called for. Today, Eliot subsists mostly as a toppled icon: the source of a handful of indelible phrases, a venerable addition to academic bibliographies, reliable sustenance for the literary jackals who practice the indelicate art of diminution-through-biography. It is the same with the culture that Eliot sought to salvage through his poetry and critical writings. One gets the impression that, especially for younger observers, the entire world that Eliot's sometime authority animated is irrecoverably strange and distant. For many, Eliot's vaunted power is little more than an occult blend of mystification and tyranny—a bit like the iron charisma exercised by Conrad's character Kurtz, whom Eliot famously memorialized in the epigraph to "The Hollow Men" (1925): "Mistah Kurtz—he dead." It is difficult to say what is more remarkable: the potency of Eliot's influence at its peak or the suddenness of its eclipse.

It was not that long ago, after all, that Eliot was an inescapable presence. William Empson spoke for many when he confessed, in 1958, that "I do not know for certain how much of my own mind [Eliot] invented, let alone how much of it is a reaction against him or indeed a consequence of misreading him. He is a very penetrating influence, perhaps not unlike the east wind." It is worth noting, too, that Eliot's influence was many-sided as well as penetrating. It did not rest only on his achievement as a poet—though it was the poetry, I believe, that provided the ultimate imprimatur, the final sanction, for his authority. Edmund Wilson, a keen but far from uncritical admirer of Eliot's work, noted that "his verses have an emotional vibration, a curious life of their own, that seems almost to detach them from the author." The syllables of "The Love Song of J. Alfred Prufrock" (1915), "Gerontion" (1920), *The Waste Land* (1922), "The Hollow Men," parts of the *Four Quartets* (1935–1942), and other poems were for many people irreplaceable mental furnishings. The realities they evoke was—is?—*our* reality.

Consider the following medley from several poems:

"Let us go then, you and I,
When the evening is spread out against the sky
Like a patient etherised upon a table;
Let us go, through certain half-deserted streets,
The muttering retreats
Of restless nights in one-night cheap hotels
And sawdust restaurants with oyster shells."

"In the room the women come and go
Talking of Michelangelo."

"After such knowledge, what forgiveness? Think now
History has many cunning passages, contrived corridors
And issues, deceives with whispering ambitions,
Guides us by vanities. Think now
She gives when our attention is distracted
And what she gives, gives with such supple confusions
That the giving famishes the craving. Gives too soon
Into weak hands, what's thought can be dispensed with
Till the refusal propagates a fear. Think
Neither fear nor courage saves us. Unnatural vices
Are fathered by our heroism. Virtues
Are forced upon us by our impudent crimes."

"April is the cruellest month, breeding
Lilacs out of the dead land, mixing

63

Memory and desire, stirring
Dull roots with spring rain."

"Unreal City,
Under the brown fog of a winter dawn,
A crowd flowed over London bridge, so many,
I had not thought death had undone so many."

"These fragments I have shored against my ruins."

*"This is the way the world ends
Not with a bang but a whimper."*

"At the still point of the turning world."

These and other passages from Eliot's slender body of published verse (think of Sweeney, of Madame Sosostris, of "the young man carbuncular") reverberated pregnantly throughout the literary imagination of the twentieth century. They were not merely "memorable speech" (Auden's shorthand definition of poetry): they were existential signposts, landmarks in modernity's spiritual battle for a survivable culture.

A roster of equally memorable phrases, or nearly so, could be made from Eliot's critical prose: "Objective correlative"; "dissociation of sensibility"; the monuments of literature forming "an ideal order among themselves, which is modified by the introduction of the new (the really new) work," the progress of the artist as "a continual self-sacrifice, a continual extinction of personality"; "genuine poetry can communicate before it is understood." These and other famous ideas helped to inaugurate the New Criticism, an approach to literature and culture that once seemed—and perhaps still is—the most supple, serious, and responsive of any formulated in the twentieth century.

Indeed, if Eliot's poetic stature loomed large, his stature as a critic—as a critic of literature, first of all, but also, more parochially, as a social, moral, and religious critic—loomed even larger. The effect of his essays on literary, religious, and educational subjects is little short of mesmerizing. Then, too, there was his work as an editor. From 1925, his position at Faber and Faber allowed him to help shape contemporary taste by publishing such figures as W. H. Auden, Stephen Spender, Cecil Day-Lewis, Ezra Pound, Edwin Muir, Robert Lowell, Marianne Moore, Ted Hughes, and Sylvia Plath. And as editor of *The Criterion*, the magazine he founded in 1922 and edited until its demise in 1939, Eliot helped to change the critical temper of his age. "No modern critic," R. P. Blackmur wrote, "has had anything like the effect of Eliot on . . . literary people." He was, Hugh Kenner affirmed, "the most gifted and most influential critic in English in the twentieth century—very likely the best since Coleridge." Clement Greenberg—like Wilson, an enthusiastic but distinctly qualified admirer of Eliot's work—went even further in his praise of Eliot's critical power. After mentioning "Aristotle, Johnson, Coleridge, Lessing, Goethe," and other figures from the critical pantheon, Greenberg concluded that "T. S. Eliot may be the best of all literary critics."

The mid-1970s, when I was in college, was probably the last moment when Eliot's greatness could be taken for granted, could be *felt* as an ineluctable challenge. Everyone even remotely interested in literature knew his poems and essays. They were also likely to know the essentials of his biography: that he was born in St. Louis, the last of seven children, in 1888; that he studied at Harvard with such figures as George Santayana and Irving Babbit; that he nearly took a doctorate in philosophy with a thesis on the British idealist F. H. Bradley; but that he decided instead to transplant himself to England where for several years (until 1925) he worked at Lloyds Bank. In the mid-1970s, Eliot's stature was still acknowledged, but grudgingly: it had degenerated into a matter of "Yes, but . . ." "Yes, he was an important poet, but what about his reactionary politics?" "Yes, he was a powerful critic, but what about his reactionary, hierarchical view of culture?" "Yes, he was an important cultural spokesman, but what about his reactionary allegiance to orthodox Christianity?" By 1975, the age was well advanced against T. S. Eliot and everything he stood for. Eliot had once declared himself "classical in literature, royalist in politics, and Anglo-Catholic in religion." Could his worst enemy have drawn up a more damning indictment? (Actually, yes, as several enemies subsequently showed.) Since the mid-1960s, what the age demanded was formless subjectivity in literature, egalitarianism in politics, and low-church or no-church romanticism in religion.

Eliot won the Nobel Prize in 1948 and by the time he died, at the beginning of 1965, his reputation seemed unassailable. In fact, the seeds of its defeat were already sprouting. It is true that death is a reliable (though often temporary) depressant of reputations, especially of reputations that have enjoyed a long triumph. Among much else, death is an invitation for revisions, reconsiderations, reevaluations. The inevitable direction of those operations, it seems, is downward. Celebrations and fond recollections and Festschriften may abound: the dominant note is nevertheless usually deflationary.

Still, the fate of Eliot's reputation cannot be explained by appealing to this process of posthumous readjustment.

Other elements were and are at work. Perhaps the most important element has been the evaporation of seriousness about literature and culture. The loss of seriousness, with all its corollary diminutions, marks the divide between the strenuous modernism of figures like Eliot and Joyce and the flaccid postmodernism that has flourished in its wake. It has often been said that Eliot provided a kind of literary conscience for his age. More to the point, his example discouraged people from neglecting their *own* literary consciences. If Eliot was a "literary dictator," as was sometimes maintained, this had more to do with what, inspired by Eliot's practice, educated people habitually required of themselves in the way of taste, judgments, and standards than with anything Eliot might have wished to require of them. It is possible—just—to imagine a lugubriously comic figure like the Yale literary critic Harold Bloom pontificating about the "anxiety of influence" and deprecating Eliot's achievement when Eliot's influence was still intact. But in Eliot's heyday no one would have regarded Bloom's blimpish Freudian melodramas with anything other than neglect or condign ridicule.

Eliot's poetry always attracted numerous critics. At the beginning, criticism focused largely on Eliot's tone. With poems like "Prufrock," "Preludes," "Portrait of a Lady," and "Morning at the Window" ("I am aware of the damp souls of housemaids / Sprouting despondently at area gates"), Eliot introduced a new emotional register to English poetry. Modelling his work closely on the poetry of the ill-fated French Symbolist Jules Laforgue (1860–1887), which Eliot discovered in 1908 through Arthur Symons's book *The Symbolist Movement in Literature* (1899), Eliot achieved a poetry that was urban, urbane, ironic, and full of sophisticated wearinesses. (It was, as Symons said of Laforgue, "alert, troubled, swaying, deliberately uncertain.") Predictably, Eliot's suave, emotionally attenuated manner—he spoke of his *aboulie*—outraged conventional Georgian taste, which distrusted irony almost as much as it disliked urbanism. ("His 'poems,'" sniffed an anonymous reviewer of *Prufrock* in *The Times Literary Supplement*, "will hardly be read by many with enjoyment.")

But the critical reaction to Eliot's early poems was nothing compared to the paroxysms of rage that greeted *The Waste Land* with its polyglot dyspepsia and trembling mosaic-like structure (or anti-structure, according to those who disliked it). *The Waste Land* was hated by all the right people. ("Virtuosity for its own sake," "so much waste paper," "deliberate mystification.") The response to *The Waste Land* catapulted Eliot to canonical notoriety. He was, one critic notes, "hailed as the sceptic of the hour, the spokesman for a 'lost' generation, venting the bitterness of its disillusion with the elders who had led them into a needless war."

Ironically, by the time the poem was published, in October of 1922 (first in the inaugural issue of *The Criterion*, then in New York in *The Dial*), Eliot had distanced himself considerably from the poem's powerful vision of cultural and spiritual despair. "My present ideas," he noted in November 1922, "are very different." Indeed, there is a sense in which his ideas had *always* been very different. As is well known, we owe *The Waste Land*—which Eliot had originally intended to call "He do the Police in Different Voices" (a line from Dickens's *Our Mutual Friend*)—partly to the massive editorial interventions of Ezra Pound. Not for nothing did Eliot dedicate the poem to Pound with a tag from Dante: *il miglior fabbro*—"the better craftsman." Pound cut the poem from about a thousand lines to its present 433. He supplied several important emendations of diction—e.g., he made Mr. Eugenides speak "demotic" rather than "abominable" French, and where Eliot had Lil's husband "coming out of the Transport Corps," Pound saw that he was "demobbed," a great improvement. More significantly, Pound's excisions subtly downplayed the element of religious yearning in the poem. The result, he wrote to Eliot's New York patron John Quinn in 1922, was a "damn good poem. . . . About enough, Eliot's poem, to make the rest of us shut up shop."

Pound's editorial contributions to Eliot's poetry ended with "The Hollow Men." The religious dimension of Eliot's verse, and life, became more and more prominent, which is to say both became distinctly un-Poundian. By 1928, the year after Eliot converted to high-Church Anglicanism (and also became a British subject), an anonymous reviewer for *The Times Literary Supplement* was complaining that Eliot had rejected "modernism for medievalism." This complaint was reinforced with the publication of religious poems like *Ash Wednesday* (1930) and the *Four Quartets*. In a letter to Paul Elmer More in 1929, Eliot responded that it was "rather trying to be supposed to have settled oneself in an easy chair, when one has just begun a long journey afoot."

Still, there is a sense in which he would have agreed with the *TLS* reviewer. Modernist though his later poetry is in structure, in attitude it marks a radical flight from certain modernist presuppositions. Indeed, in 1928 Eliot wrote in *The Criterion* that "modernism" (which in the context he took to be synonymous with "humanism") "is a mental blight." The *Four Quartets* are full of remarkable poetry. But Donald Davie was undoubtedly right when he observed, in 1956, that the response to *Four Quartets* was "flagrantly ideological": "the religiously inclined applaud the Quartets, the more or less militantly secular and 'humanist' decry them. As simple as that."

In some ways, Eliot presented an easy target for detractors. His panoply of learned allusions—he later claimed that the footnotes to *The Waste Land* were a sort of joke, but were they?—opened him to the charge of pedantry. "Eliot's work," as Edmund Wilson noted in an important essay from 1958 called "'Miss Buttle' and 'Mr. Eliot,'" "is fatally suited to the needs of American teachers of courses in English." Then, too, Eliot's phrasing and poetic voice were consistently so distinctive, even mannered, that parody—unintentional as well as intentional—was irresistible. Wilson quotes generously from *The Sweeniad* by Myra Buttle ("My Rebuttal"), a pseudonym for the English don Victor Purcell.

> Between the mystification
> And the deception
> Between the multiplication
> And the division
> Falls the Tower of London
>
> Many Nouns in *is* we find
> To the Masculine assigned
> Amnis, axis, caulis, collis,
> Clunis, crinis, fascis, follis. . . .
> Take away the number you first thought of . . .
> Stop breeding . . .
> Stop breathing . . .
>   *Pop!*

All very amusing, that (though not as amusing as Mr. Purcell's "serious" verse, snatches of which Wilson quotes). Such parodies are in the end a kind of unintended homage, betraying the strength and ubiquity of the original. What makes "Miss Buttle's" effort funny is that we instantly recognize the strains of "The Hollow Men" behind it. The philistine attack on Eliot was one thing. Far more damaging is the absorption of philistinism by the literary elite. That, too, is a feature of our postmodern condition. When Harold Bloom tells us that John Ashbery is a "stronger" poet than Eliot, our first reaction is to feel sorry for the generations of Yale students Bloom has inflicted himself on. But when a gifted and sensitive writer like Cynthia Ozick attacks Eliot as the epitome of a reactionary high culture whose time has passed, the result is far more shocking. In "T. S. Eliot at 101," a long and bitter article published in *The New Yorker* in 1989, Miss Ozick combined *ad hominem* venom and fashionable cultural populism to assault both Eliot and the demanding vision of high art that he articulated. Eliot himself she castigated as an "autocratic," "inhibited," "narrow-minded," and "considerably bigoted fake English-man," while at the same time rejecting the culture of high modernism he represented as otiose. "High art," Miss Ozick concluded, "is dead." One of the things that made Cynthia Ozick's performance so dispiriting was the fact that she had previously arrayed herself, if not on the side of Eliot, exactly, then at least on the side of the kind of seriousness about art and culture for which Eliot stood. She presented her essay as an exercise in "nostalgia." In fact, it was a form of valedictory defection. Lyndall Gordon's *T. S. Eliot: An Imperfect Life* (Norton, 1998) leaves one with a similar feeling.

Gordon's book is a compilation and expansion of her two earlier biographical volumes about Eliot, *Eliot's Early Years* (1977) and *Eliot's New Life* (1988). In her foreword to *T. S. Eliot: An Imperfect Life*, she says that the rewriting and changes she made "go beyond revision." Indeed they do. The earlier volumes provided a somewhat pedestrian but workmanlike biography of Eliot. With Peter Ackroyd's *T. S. Eliot: A Life* (1984), they were among the first. But Gordon's new book is less an account of than an all-out attack on Eliot's life. Gordon was never burdened with a gift for narrative, but in her original volumes she presented the paraphernalia of Eliot's life and career clearly and succinctly. The new book introduces a thick patina of animus. Gordon tells us that her aim was not to demystify Eliot but "to follow the trials of a searcher whose flaws and doubts speak to all of us whose lives are imperfect." In fact, she never misses an opportunity to highlight—often, to exaggerate—Eliot's failings. It is almost comical to compare *T. S. Eliot: An Imperfect Life* with its predecessors: everywhere she has turned up the volume of criticism.

The difference between the earlier volumes and the revised offering is epitomized by a rubric in Gordon's index. In the original volumes, under "Eliot, Thomas Stearns," one finds the category "Opinions." In *Imperfect Life*, that heading is recast as "Opinions and Prejudices." In the original biography, Gordon dilated at times on Eliot's "misogyny." There is a lot more of that in *Imperfect Life*. She describes the mildly obscene poetical sports that the young Eliot sent to friends in letters as "loathsome things": "There's sick fury here," Gordon writes in one typical addition, "an obsessional hatred of women and sex, punitive in its virulence."[1]

In the new book, Gordon also predictably expatiates on Eliot's anti-Semitism—a growth industry these days—going

---

[1] Eliot never published these (mostly very minor) poems. They, and other early poems—drafts for "Prufrock" and so on—have been collected and embroidered with extensive scholarly apparatus in *Inventions of the March Hare, Poems 1909–1917*, edited by Christopher Ricks (Harcourt Brace, 1996).

so far as to say that "he did not hold back from the mass-prejudice that played a part in the largest atrocity of the century." Meaning what? That Eliot was some sort of covert Nazi? Eliot was undoubtedly anti-Semitic. Critics long ago pointed out the handful of anti-Semitic lines in Eliot's poetry: "And the jew squats on the window sill," "Rachel née Rabinowitz," etc. And the comment he made in a 1933 series of lectures—published as *After Strange Gods*, a book he never reprinted—that "reasons of race and religion combine to make any large number of free-thinking Jews undesirable" quickly became notorious.

But to insinuate, as Gordon does, a connection between Eliot's all-too-common brand of social anti-Semitism and the Holocaust is both preposterous and anachronistic. For example, it is worth noting that the real focus of his comment in *After Strange Gods* was on "free-thinking," not "Jews." It is consonant with his disapproving observation, later in that same book, that "the Anglo-Saxons display a capacity for *diluting* their religion, probably in excess of that of any other race." This is not to deny Eliot's anti-Semitism, only to qualify it. Eliot's anti-Semitism was of a piece with his anti-secularism. The young Eliot may have been a modernist, but there were aspects of modernity that terrified him. His criticism was directed primarily against those aspects of modern, industrial society that encouraged social uprootedness and undermined continuity with the past. The problem, as Eliot put it in *The Idea of a Christian Society* (1940), was the "tendency of unlimited industrialism . . . to create bodies of men and women . . . detached from tradition, alienated from religion, and susceptible to mass suggestion: in other words a mob. And a mob will be no less a mob if it is well fed, well clothed, well housed, and well disciplined."

Eliot's chief claims on our attention are as a poet and a

critic, not as a social or political theorist. Nevertheless, there is some irony, as Hilton Kramer observed in connection with the question of Eliot's anti-Semitism,

> that Eliot was himself an outstanding example of the deracinated cosmopolitanism he so much feared and despised. As a polyglot expatriate American who had severed his native roots in order to make his way in an alien society that was deeply opposed to the modernism he practiced as a poet, Eliot found himself as much at odds with the culture and politics of his adopted country as he believed himself to be with those of his homeland.

None of these deeper issues is appropriately dealt with in Gordon's biography. She is too busy looking for "strains of virulence" and "racial hatred." This search even spills over into her comments on some figures who influenced Eliot. Thus Jules Laforgue is accused of writing "women-riddled poetry"—unlike the other kind, I suppose.

Gordon has assembled a lot of information in her decades of work on Eliot. And she makes some memorable observations along the way. About Eliot's first trip to Paris in 1910, for example, she notes that where Laforgue before him was a participant, Eliot was "an inspector of vice. . . . While Laforgue tended to reproach women for his sense of banality, Eliot understands the banality of vice itself."

Notwithstanding such insightful aperçus, however, it is clear that whatever drew Gordon to Eliot to begin with was supplanted somewhere along the line with a swarm of fashionable grievances. There is even a dollop of academic social-constructivism about sex: "Who can now determine," she asks in a section about Eliot's relation with his friend Jean Verdenal (to whom *Prufrock and Other Observations* is dedicated), "the exact ways people of the past bent their inclinations in order to construct gender according to the absurd models of masculinity and femininity?" Right: "I Tiresias, though blind, throbbing between two lives. . . ."

In both *Eliot's Early Years* and *T. S. Eliot: An Imperfect Life*, Gordon says that her aim is "to trace the continuity of Eliot's career and to see the poetry and the life as complementary parts of one design, a consuming search for salvation." Whether or not she succeeded, that aim was patent in *Eliot's Early Years*. In the new book, the original ambition is buried underneath recurrent litanies about Eliot's "trajectory" "leaving broken lives in its wake" and his "intolerance for the masses, for women and Jews." Gordon emits declarations of high-mindedness at regular intervals ("biography . . . can't reduce a man to the adversarial categories—guilty or not guilty—of the courtroom"), but she then proceeds immediately with some damning aside: "undoubtedly, an infection is there in Eliot—hate."

Gordon's animus even extends to Eliot's forebears. In her original biography, she tells us that Andrew Eliot "was believed to have officiated at the Salem witch trials." In her new redaction we read instead that "he was drawn into the frenzy of the Salem witch trials, where he condemned innocents to death." The implication, presumably, is that we shouldn't be surprised that Eliot turned out to be a fanatic: after all, the man had witch-burners in his background.

I earlier quoted Edmund Wilson's observation that Eliot's "verses have an emotional vibration, a curious life of their own, that seems almost to detach them from the author." Wilson continues: "Of no other poet, perhaps, does a bon mot of Cocteau's seem so true: The artist is a kind of prison from which the works of art escape."

Wilson was right. And it is something that requires uncommon tact and delicacy from any biographer who wishes to present us with Eliot the artist and not a pathetic caricature. (Eliot explicitly stated that he did not want a biography: now we know why.) Eliot is worthy of attention not because he had certain attitudes about women or Jews or education or religion of which we disapprove today. He is worthy of attention first of all because he wrote poetry possessed of those "vibrations," that "curious life," which Wilson noted. Of course there is a biographical correlative to much of Eliot's poetry. And when we read this oft-quoted passage from *The Waste Land*—

> "My nerves are bad to-night. Yes, bad. Stay with me.
> "Speak to me. Why do you never speak? Speak.
> "What are you thinking of? What thinking? What?
> "I never know what you are thinking. Think."

—it is perhaps illuminating to know that Eliot wrote most of the poem while recuperating from a nervous breakdown in 1921 and that his first wife, Vivienne Haigh-Wood, was a drug-sodden hysterical invalid who eventually went mad. Bertrand Russell, who had an affair with Vivienne not long after she married Eliot, wrote about it to a friend: "At last I spent a night with her. *It was utter hell*. There was a quality of loathsomeness about it which I can't describe." "She gave the impression of absolute terror," another acquaintance recalled,

> of a person who's seen a hideous goblin. . . . Her face all drawn and white, with wild, frightened, angry eyes. An over-intensity over nothing, you see. Supposing you were to say to her, "Oh, will you have some more cake," she'd say "What's that? What do you mean? What do you say that for?" She was terrifying. At the end of an hour I was ab-

solutely exhausted, sucked dry. And I said to myself: Poor Tom, this is enough! But she was his muse all the same.

Well, maybe. Vivienne undoubtedly made her contributions to Eliot's work. It was she, for example, who came up with the title for *The Criterion*: Eliot had intended to call it *The London Review*. But lots of people have hysterical, half-mad spouses. Few are great poets. Eliot himself once remarked that "various critics have done me the honour to interpret [*The Waste Land*] in terms of criticism of the contemporary world, have considered it, indeed, as an important bit of social criticism. To me it was only the relief of a personal and wholly insignificant grouse against life; it was just a piece of rhythmical grumbling." But that was disingenuous. The grouse may have been personal and insignificant; the poem—*qua* poem, not biographical artifact—is neither merely personal nor insignificant. As Eliot famously noted in "Tradition and the Individual Talent" (1919),

> It is not in his personal emotions, the emotions provoked by particular events in his life, that the poet is in any way remarkable or interesting. His particular emotions may be simple, or crude, or flat. The emotion in his poetry will be a very complex thing, but not with the complexity of the emotions of people who have very complex or unusual emotions in life. . . . Poetry is not a turning loose of emotion, but an escape from emotion; it is not the expression of personality, but an escape from personality. But, of course, only those who have personality and emotions know what it means to want to escape from these things.

For Eliot, writing *The Waste Land* may have been in part a personal catharsis. For us, it is the *impersonality* of the emotion that makes the poem significant. It speaks to us not of Eliot's trauma but of a trauma inseparable from our culture.

The chaos of Eliot's emotional life in the 1910s and early 1920s did not prevent him from carefully stage-managing his literary career. As soon as he gave up on an academic career, in 1914, he threw himself into London literary life. Writing to his mother in 1919, he spoke proudly of the "privileged position" he occupied: "There is a small and select public which regards me as the best living critic, as well as the best living poet, in England. . . . I really think that I have far more *influence* on English letters than any other American has ever had, unless it be Henry James." His pride was all the more justified because, as he noted in another letter, for an American, "getting recognized in English letters is like breaking open a safe." Eliot displayed great deliberation and canniness in his pursuit of literary fame. There are, he wrote to a former teacher from Harvard in 1919, "only two ways in which a writer can become important":

> to write a great deal, and have his writings appear everywhere, or to write very little. It is a question of temperament. I write very little, and I should not become more powerful by increasing my output. My reputation in London is built upon one small volume of verse, and is kept up by printing two or three more poems in a year. The only thing that matters is that these should be perfect in their kind, so that each should be an event.

And so it was. Eliot's collected poems, excluding the children's verse, runs to one-hundred-and-forty-odd pages; thirty or more of those pages are given over to "minor" or "unfinished" poems. But Eliot made up in concentration what he lacked in quantity. From *Prufrock* and *The Waste Land* through the *Four Quartets* and the late plays, publication of Eliot's work always was a galvanizing literary event, riveting attention even when it did not elicit unqualified assent.

The chief reason that Eliot commanded the attention he did was doubtless the originality, power, and quality of his work. The work was the indispensable presupposition. But beyond that, Eliot animated everything he touched with a rare passion and urgency of conviction. This is evident in his uncompromising partisanship on behalf of high culture. "Culture," Eliot wrote in *Notes Towards the Definition of Culture* (1948), "may even be defined as that which makes life worth living." And although after his conversion he always viewed culture as inseparable from religion ("if Christianity goes," he said, "the whole of our culture goes"), he nonetheless communicated through his poetry and criticism a sense that matters of great, of absolute, moment were being broached.

At the same time it is important to note that Eliot did not fetishize culture. "Boil down Horace, the Elgin Marbles, St. Francis and Goethe," he wrote in "Second Thoughts About Humanism," "and the result will be pretty thin soup." "Culture," he concluded, "is not enough, even though nothing is enough without culture." The distinction is crucial. If reading Eliot is partly an apprenticeship in seriousness, it is also an introduction to the limits or decorum of seriousness.

Eliot was not always somber. Far from it. There is an element of impish playfulness in much of his work, from the "Shakespeherian Rag" of *The Waste Land* to his 1923 essay on the music hall singer Marie Lloyd. W. H. Auden was right that in the household that was T. S. Eliot, a stately archdeacon lived together with a querulous old peasant woman who had experienced famines, pogroms, the lot, as well as a mischievous boy prone to practical jokes. It is not surprising that the author of *The Waste Land* was also the author of *Old Possum's Book of Practical Cats* or that he was an avid admirer of vaudeville and the Marx Brothers.[2] The great critic E. R. Curtius, who translated *The Waste Land* into German, recalled that when he first read the poem "it captivated me with sudden and dazzling flashes of mystery and music, with a resonant happiness."

At first, "resonant happiness" may seem odd. After all, as Curtius went on to note, "with Eliot the depressive element predominates": *The Waste Land*, "The Hollow Men," *Ash Wednesday*: the very titles communicate gravity. In the early poems there is often a permeating nimbus of impotence, exhaustion, dryness. (Think of Prufrock, the narrator of "Gerontion," the "velleities and carefully caught regrets" in "Portrait of a Lady.") Later, that texture

---

2 Gordon recounts the visit that Groucho Marx and his wife made to meet the Eliots in 1964. Groucho fortified himself by reading *Murder in the Cathedral* twice, *The Waste Land* three times, and brushing up on *King Lear* for good measure. "Well, sir," Groucho wrote in a letter,

> as the cocktails were served, there was a momentary lull. . . . So, apropos of practically nothing . . . I tossed in a quotation from *The Waste Land*. That, I thought, will show him I've read a thing or two besides my press notices from Vaudeville.
>
> Eliot smiled faintly—as though to say he was thoroughly familiar with his poems and didn't need me to recite them. So I took a whack at *King Lear*. . . .
>
> That, too, failed to bowl over the poet. He seemed more interested in discussing *Animal Crackers* and *A Night at the Opera*. He quoted a joke—one of mine—that I had long since forgotten. Now it was my turn to smile faintly.

of feeling is absorbed into an atmosphere of religious angst. And yet Curtius is right. Reading Eliot imparts a peculiar sense of buoyancy, of tensed vitality—in Edmund Wilson's phrases, "vibrations" and "curious life." One reason for this, I believe, is that Eliot was everywhere embarked on a voyage of discovery. Many critics have noted a progression in Eliot's development from the aestheticism of Arnold and Pater through ironic despondency to resignation and, finally, to Christian affirmation.

I have no doubt that there is some such itinerary in Eliot's thought. But the defining leitmotif of Eliot's journey is a craving for reality. That craving—the fulfillment of that craving—is the source of the "resonant happiness" Curtius discerned. It is the source of Eliot's religious convictions— "Man is man," he wrote in an essay on humanism, "because he can recognize supernatural realities, not because he can invent them." Eliot's craving for reality also stands behind his repeated admonitions about the perils of accepting aesthetic substitutes—of attempting "to preserve emotions without the beliefs with which their history has been involved." (How unlike a poet such as Wallace Stevens, who—as we shall see—for much of his career seems to have entertained the hope that poetic invention could supersede belief.) Eliot, like T. E. Hulme before him, was suspicious, by temperament and conviction, of all such ambitions. Both men castigated "Romanticism" in part because they feared the seductive power of simulacra.

The comments that Eliot made about passion in *After Strange Gods* illustrate this fear. "It is a cardinal point of faith in a romantic age," he wrote, "to believe that there is something admirable in violent emotion for its own sake, whatever the emotion or whatever the object." Eliot disagreed, branding such "extreme emotionalism" as "a symptom of decadence":

It is by no means self-evident that human beings are most real when they are most violently excited; violent physical passions do not in themselves differentiate men from each other, but rather tend to reduce them to the same state; and the passion has significance only in relation to the character and behavior of the man at other moments of his life and in other contexts. Furthermore, strong passion is only interesting or significant in strong men, those who abandon themselves without resistance to excitements which tend to deprive them of reason, become merely instruments of feeling and lose their humanity; and unless there is moral resistance and conflict there is no meaning.

Anyone who delves into Eliot's work knows that the word "emotion" plays a complicated role in his thought; whatever else can be said, it seems clear that he tended to regard the value, the reality, of an emotion as directly proportional to the resistance it encounters. Belief— genuine moral commitment—is a trophy of obstacles overcome.

"We know too much and are convinced of too little," Eliot warned in "A Dialogue on Dramatic Poetry" (1928). "Our literature is a substitute for religion, and so is our religion." In *The Use of Poetry and the Use of Criticism* (1933), in a discussion of Matthew Arnold, he reflects more fully on this point:

Nothing in this world or the next is a substitute for anything else; and if you find you must do without something, such as religious faith or philosophic belief, then you must just do without it. I can persuade myself . . . that some of the things that I can hope to get are better worth having than some of the things I cannot get; or I may hope to alter myself so as to want different things; but I cannot persuade

myself that it is the same desires that are satisfied, or that I
have in effect the same thing under a different name.

Eliot was obsessed with reality. That is the ultimate source
of his power as a poet and his authority as a critic. He was
everywhere engaged in a battle against ersatz: ersatz culture, ersatz religion, ersatz humanity. That, finally, is what
makes even the late, religious Eliot congenial to modernism: his impatience with imposture. In "Burnt Norton,"
the first of his *Four Quartets*, Eliot wrote that "human
kind / Cannot bear very much reality." It was his lonely
task to remind us of this even as he set about coaxing us
toward greater and greater feats of endurance.

Wallace Stevens:
Metaphysical Claims Adjuster

From this the poem springs: that we live in a place
That is not our own and, much more, not ourselves
And hard it is in spite of blazoned days.
—Wallace Stevens, *Notes Toward a Supreme Fiction*

"POETRY," Wallace Stevens wrote in a well-known aphorism, "must resist the intelligence almost successfully."
Stevens must have liked this formulation, for he used
it again, with only slight variation, in "Man Carrying
Thing," a poem from the late 1940s. Stevens's detractors,
never in short supply, would doubtless be tempted to quip
that he must have regarded his own poems as especially
successful, since so many seem to resist the intelligence not
almost but with total success.

Such objections miss the point of Stevens's poetic
achievement, which was always more a matter of evocation—"half colors of quarter-things," as he put it in "The
Motive for Metaphor"—than demonstration. But charges
of obscurity and of precious obfuscation have followed
Stevens since before the publication of *Harmonium*, his
first book, in 1923. Part of the problem lies in Stevens's
linguistic extravagance, an inheritance from Pateresque
decadence and the French Symbolists. Like Mallarmé,

Stevens often sought to capture "not the thing itself, but the effect that it produces," a policy guaranteed to favor exquisiteness.

In an appreciative review of the second, expanded edition of *Harmonium* (1931), R. P. Blackmur remarked that "the most striking if not the most important thing" about Stevens's verse was its vocabulary, a heady confect including such rarities as "fubbed," "girandoles," "diaphanes," "pannicles," "carked," "ructive," "cantilene," "fiscs," and "princox." Contrasting him with e.e. cummings, Blackmur praised Stevens as a master of an ambiguity that was "dense with being."

Others were less admiring. In 1915, when he was thirty-six and still virtually unknown, Stevens went with his wife, Elsie, to read from his recent work at the New York studio of the rich dilettante and art collector Walter Arensberg. Stevens had lately written some of *Harmonium*'s best-known poems, including "Sunday Morning," "Disillusionment at Ten O'Clock," and "Peter Quince at the Clavier":

Beauty is momentary in the mind—
The fitful tracing of a portal;
But in the flesh it is immortal.

One guest recalled that, as they gathered to listen, Stevens "remarked that his wife, who had hinted disapproval before he began, did not like his poems. 'I like Mr. Stevens's things,' she said, 'when they are not affected; but he writes so much that is affected.'" ("Mrs. Stevens," her husband wrote in a letter of 1922, is "a fascinating creature whom one cannot exactly get away from.")

Stevens's marriage, like the rest of his interior life, seems to have been heavily mortgaged to his imagination. He met

Elsie on a visit home to Reading, Pennsylvania, in 1904. He was twenty-six, fresh from Harvard, New York, and law school. She was eighteen, shy, poorly educated, painfully insecure. Although time would rob Elsie of her looks with cruel rapidity, she was possessed of an extraordinary chiseled beauty when young. (Her features were later immortalized on the Liberty Head dime by Adolph Alexander Weinman.) From the beginning, she seems to have been more muse than companion. Ever prudent, Stevens insisted that they delay getting married until he was well enough established in his career. With Stevens in New York and Elsie in Reading, their five-year courtship unfolded mostly on paper. In retrospect, it seems that Stevens preferred it that way: it made the interior soliloquies so much easier. (Consider "Final Soliloquy of the Interior Paramour": the title alone registers an inviolable inwardness.) His biographers paint a chilly picture of Mr. and Mrs. Stevens occupying separate suites in their fine house in Hartford: she remonstrative, censorious; he lost in the intricate fabrications of his mind. No doubt Elsie was, or became, intolerable; the detail that she prohibited their daughter, Holly, from calling her "mommy" seems to capture some essential emotional hardness. But equally how intolerable to be the occasion rather than the object of a husband's imaginings.

Elsie Stevens, whose literary taste ran to Longfellow and *Good Housekeeping*, was perhaps not the best judge of her husband's work. But she was hardly alone in her judgment. Ezra Pound, not exactly the plain man's poet, memorably groused that Stevens was "a schoolgirl straining for originality." And in the early 1940s, in a volume tellingly called *The Anatomy of Nonsense*, Yvor Winters complained of (among other things) Stevens's logic-flouting "hedonism." Of course, it is possible to celebrate Stevens for precisely the things that Winters deprecated. Hedonism? Poetry "must give pleasure," Stevens declared in *Notes Toward a Supreme Fiction*. But the question remains, what pleasures does this "hedonist" really provide?

Stevens is often described as a "philosophical" poet. Much effort has been expended tracing influences and showing similarities between Stevens and Nietzsche, Wittgenstein, William James, Santayana, Emerson, Zen Buddhism, Hans Vaihinger (author of a Kant-inspired book called *The Philosophy of "As If"*), Bergson, and many others. Such expeditions are always successful, and I have no doubt that Stevens read and absorbed something from many if not all of the above-listed sources. But the danger in calling someone a philosophical poet is the temptation of replacing the poetry with the ideas the poetry is supposed to express or "symbolize." Stevens was always reluctant to "explain" his poems, rightly fearing that the explanation would then take the place of the poem, diminishing it in the process. The peculiarity of Stevens's poetry is that it inhabits, *as poetry*, mental regions generally occupied by philosophers and theologians. But it does so not with propositions or arguments but with tones, feelings, moods, music. Consequently, it does not draw conclusions, it entertains possibilities. Stevens was undoubtedly moved by some of the same concerns that move philosophers: think only of the place that the word "being" occupies in his poetry. But Stevens's response to those concerns is primarily linguistic, not conceptual, exactitude. He strives less for intellectual affirmation—the product of argument—than its emotional coefficient—the product of poetry. What Stevens is after is

Not an attainment of the will
But something illogically received,

A divination, a letting down
From loftiness, misgivings dazzlingly
Resolved in dazzling discovery.

This makes for a curious situation. In an earlier chapter,
I quoted T. S. Eliot's reflection on Matthew Arnold's efforts
to find in culture a substitute for religion: "nothing in this
world or the next is a substitute for anything else; and if
you find you must do without something, such as religious
faith or philosophic belief, then you must just do without
it." It would be difficult to find a passage more at odds
with Wallace Stevens's sensibility. Indeed, his poetic career
may be described as a long series of attempts to conjure
just such substitutions. Writing to the critic Hi Simons in
1940, Stevens noted that "it is a habit of mind with me to
be thinking of some substitute for religion. . . . My trouble,
and the trouble of a great many people, is the loss of belief
in the sort of God in Whom we were all brought up to
believe." Stevens's hope—rather than his answer, exactly—
was that art, that poetry would provide the necessary
substitute. "After one has abandoned a belief in god," he
wrote, "poetry is that essence which take its place as life's
redemption."

There was a polemical side to this hope, an aggressive
secularism that recast "life's redemption" in a steady ver-
nacular. "The great poems of heaven and hell have been
written," Stevens wrote in *The Necessary Angel*, a collection of essays, "and the great poem of the earth remains
to be written." Whether or not that judgment is accurate
(what, for example, was Wordsworth writing if not poems
"of the earth"?), it stands as a declaration of purpose that
Stevens fulfilled chiefly by recognizing its limitations. In
"The Poems of Our Climate," published in *Parts of a
World* (1942), Stevens begins with an image of cool aes-

thetic perfection: "Clear water in a brilliant bowl, / Pink
and white carnations." The beguiling promise of that
"world of clear water, brilliant-edged" was a "complete
simplicity" that "stripped one of all one's torments." In the
end, Stevens acknowledges, the very simplicity of this min-
imalist dream makes it dehumanizing: "one would want
more, one would need more, / More than a world of white
and snowy scents." What "more" is there for a Stevensian
aesthete? The "more" of partial redemptions, incomplete
unities, fragmentary wholenesses:

> The imperfect is our paradise.
> Note that, in this bitterness, delight,
> Since the imperfect is so hot in us,
> Lies in flawed words and stubborn sounds.

Building disappointment into delight insured against the
deeper disappointment of unbudgeted failure.

Stevens is famous partly as the ultimate aesthete who was
also a hard-nosed legal advisor for the Hartford Accident
and Indemnity Company. Like Anthony Trollope before
him, Stevens took his professional obligations with the ut-
most seriousness. And just as Trollope prospered in his
career at the Post Office, so Stevens rose to become, as one
of his colleagues in the insurance business put it, "the dean
of surety-claims men in the whole country." It seems pe-
culiarly appropriate that Stevens's professional life, too,
should have been centrally involved with substitutions. For
insurance works only to the extent that losses can be made
good; ultimately, it depends upon the idea of fungibility:
that one thing can validly substitute for another. Stevens
devoted his professional life to adjudicating claims for tan-
gible losses; in his poetic life, he endeavored to be a kind of

metaphysical claims adjuster, proferring remedies supplied by his imagination for spiritual losses incurred elsewhere.

"Money," Stevens wrote in *Adagia*, a collection of aphorisms, "is a kind of poetry." Perhaps he meant that money is the currency with which insurance redeems its losses. Similarly, belief is the currency of the spirit. It is often said that Stevens's poetry is about the relation between imagination and reality. This is true enough, but the central drama in that relationship concerns the nature and vitality of belief. William James, who taught at Harvard when Stevens was a student there at the turn of the century, devoted a short book to *The Will to Believe*. Stevens devoted his entire life to the subject. In "Flyer's Fall" he imagined death as "a dimension in which / We believe without belief, beyond belief." Does this make sense? I am not sure. But there can be no doubt that at the center of Stevens's poetry is a dialectic of hypothesis and affirmation, a modernist's grammar of plausible assent. "The final belief," he wrote in one typical reflection, "is to believe in a fiction, which you know to be a fiction, there being nothing else. The exquisite truth is to know that it is a fiction and you believe in it willingly."

The extreme aestheticism inherent in such a pronouncement is often taken to be at the core of Stevens's thought. I believe it is only the starting point. The 1997 Library of America collection of Stevens's work reinforces this belief. Selected by Frank Kermode and Stevens's chief biographer, Joan Richardson, it is the most comprehensive single volume of his work yet published. It gathers together virtually all of Stevens's poetry—including some previously unpublished juvenilia—most of his prose, his three plays, and a handful of letters and journal entries. There are no surprises here. The newly published juvenilia is indifferent, apprentice stuff: Stevens before he became Stevens. Nevertheless, reading through the Library of America volume, a new image of the poet emerges—though not, perhaps, the one the editors intended. It is the image of the poet as spiritual pilgrim as well as aesthetic conjuror.

In a letter about *Notes Toward a Supreme Fiction*, his longest and probably most ambitious poem, Stevens spoke about his hope that, "in the various predicaments of belief, it might be possible to yield, or to try to yield, ourselves to a declared fiction." In this scenario of acquiescence, the emphasis is at least as much on the "predicaments of belief" as on the "declared fiction." As he put it in *Adagia*,

> The relation of art to life is of the first importance especially in a skeptical age since, in the absence of a belief in God, the mind turns to its own creations and examines them, not alone from the aesthetic point of view, but for what they reveal, for what they validate and invalidate, for the support that they give.

The key contrast is between "the aesthetic point of view" by itself and what is revealed, validated, invalidated. It is clear that by "fiction" Stevens did not mean arbitrary, unanchored imaginings. His severe attitude toward surrealism shows that he was not a prophet of relativism or irrationalism: "The essential fault of surrealism," he noted, "is that it invents without discovering." For Stevens, invention without discovery was sterile. It is true that in the late 1930s, in response to Marxist criticism of his work, he announced that "I am, in the long run, interested in pure poetry." Especially in his work before 1940, Stevens indulged in a great deal of humor, verbal play, and incantatory word magic, which sometimes amounted to little more than a species of nonsense verse. Think, for example, of "The Emperor of Ice-Cream," which Stevens once claimed was his favorite of his own poems, or these lines from "Bantams in Pine-Woods":

Chieftain Iffucan of Azcan in caftan
Of tan with henna hackles, halt!

Damned universal cock, as if the sun
Was blackamoor to bear your blazing tail.

Fat! Fat! Fat! Fat! I am the personal.
Your world is you. I am my world.

Et cetera. It is from this unpromising poetic tributary that one finally arrives at the weary nonsensical knowingness of John Ashbery.

But such verbal ejaculations, though in one sense typically Stevensian, represent Stevens doodling. They show him playing with the elements, but not the driving spirit, of his poetry. What matters in Stevens are not his submissions but his resistances. If Stevens was "in the long run" interested in "pure poetry," it turns out that the purest poetry is that which is tempered by and responsive to reality. Again, it is true that Stevens, like William Blake, could at times assert that "God and the imagination are one." But he also maintained that in the relation between imagination and reality, reality does not easily or always capitulate. In a note from his college years, Stevens observed that "Art for art's sake is both indiscreet and worthless. . . . Beauty is strength. But art—art all alone, detached, sensuous for the sake of sensuousness, not to perpetuate inspiration or thought, art that is mere art—seems to me to be the most arrant as it is the most inexcusable rubbish." This uncharacteristically strong language reverberates again in a letter from 1945, in which Stevens insists that "If poetry is limited to the vaticination of the imagination, it soon becomes worthless. The cognitive element involves the consciousness of reality."

The truth is that as Stevens matured, he increasingly acknowledged the recalcitrance of reality in the face of the blandishments of the imagination. This is matched by a gradual loss of exuberance—or, to put the same thing more positively, it is matched by a growing tautness in his verse. For the young Stevens, Florida was not only a preferred holiday spot, it also served as an emblem of imaginative consummation. Despite early poems such as "The Snow Man" with its "mind of winter" and "listener" who, "nothing himself, beholds / Nothing that is not there and the nothing that is," the dominant mode of Stevens's early poetry is lush, gorgeous, tropical: "Coffee and oranges in a sunny chair, / And the green freedom of a cockatoo," as in "Sunday Morning." An animal melancholy—the down side of paganism—suffuses many of the poems in *Harmonium*, but there is no resignation, no sense of ultimacy.

The growing dryness of his later verse is fed by an increasing clarity, which oscillates between serenity and despondency. "To an Old Philosopher in Rome," Stevens's homage to his old Harvard teacher George Santayana, is one of the gentlest late poems, its vision of "the celestial possible" vibrating with hope and gratitude. But many of the final notes are melancholy indeed. In "As You Leave the Room," the last poem in the Library of America volume, we hear the speaker ask: "I wonder, have I lived a skeleton's life, / As a disbeliever in reality, . . ." From about 1950 on, there is a recurrent feeling, as Stevens put in "The Plain Sense of Things," that "A fantastic effort has failed."

It is in this sense the whole of Stevens's poetry appears as a kind of prolegomenon—necessary, delectable, but essentially incomplete. As Janet McCann noted in *Wallace Stevens Reconsidered* (1995), her excellent study of the poet's spiritual development, Stevens's "late poems show his gradual approach to the religious commitment that took place at the margin of his creative life, beyond the last written poem."

The nature of that commitment is no secret. As has been established by Milton Bates and others, in the spring and summer of 1955 during his last illness, Stevens was instructed in the Roman Catholic faith, was baptized in the Church, and received Communion. Of course, the movement from aesthete to convert has been a familiar "last act" among decadents from Oscar Wilde on down: a final gesture scandalizing, for once, the wits who had devoted their lives to scandal. Stevens's biographer spoke for many when she suggested that his turn to Rome amounted to little more than a "final prank." I am not so sure. Given the central place that the problem of belief had in Stevens's work, his conversion has a special poignancy. Pranks there are aplenty in Stevens's work. Yet behind the pranks there is generally a pulsing seriousness. In 1954, John Crowe Ransom praised Stevens for "arguing on behalf of a secular culture based on Nobility." Long before that, however, Stevens had come to distrust the nobility that Ransom extolled. "Humanism would be the natural substitute," he wrote in a letter from 1940, "but the more I see of humanism the less I like it." In the end, Stevens is a poet of departures, thresholds, beckonings: full of delectations, but full, too, of warinesses. The "gusty emotions / on wet roads on autumn nights" ("Sunday Morning") that he celebrates in his early poetry turn out to be tokens of insufficiency: spiritual pointers, not ends in themselves. "The Sail of Ulysses," written in 1954, went about as far as Stevens the poet was prepared to go: "We come to knowledge when we come to life. / Yet always there is another life, / A life beyond this present knowing, . . ."

The Permanent Auden

"It's such a pity Wystan never grows up."
—W. H. Auden, *Letter to Lord Byron*

"I shall only ask you to apply to the work of the deceased a very simple test. How many of his lines can you remember?"
—W. H. Auden, "The Public v. the Late Mr. W. B. Yeats"

IN JUNE 1994, shortly before Princeton University Press brought out its edition of W. H. Auden's juvenilia, *The New Criterion* published a handful of those apprentice poems from the mid-to-late 1920s. While working on a brief introduction to accompany the selection, I happened to have a conversation with a visiting English critic whose work I admire. I told him I was writing something about Auden's juvenilia. Without missing a beat he said, "It's all juvenilia, isn't it?"

I joined him in a laugh. But his comment did take me aback. W. H. Auden, perhaps the most accomplished poetic craftsman since Yeats—the man who once claimed to have written poems exemplifying every form discussed in George Saintsbury's *History of English Prosody* (three volumes)—a lifelong purveyor of juvenilia? Surely not. Auden was one of the most urbane and insightful essayists of the twentieth century. That much is indisputable. But his poetic stature?

There seem to be two main schools of thought. No one denies the prodigious skill, the cleverness, the wide if quirky erudition on display in Auden's poetry. And very few would deny the strength of many—well, anyway several—poems published between 1930, when his first volume appeared, and around 1940, the year after he emigrated (his enemies said "fled") to the United States. These were the years of most of Auden's anthology pieces: "The Secret Agent," "Lullaby," "As I Walked Out One Evening," "Musée des Beaux Arts," "In Memory of W. B. Yeats," "September 1, 1939," "In Memory of Sigmund Freud," and one or two others. Opinion has long been divided about Auden's later work, especially his work after 1945. And since 1973, when Auden died at the age of sixty-six, opinion has also been increasingly divided about the larger question of what his poetic achievement really adds up to. Does it rival or even surpass that of Yeats or Eliot, say? Or has the discipline of posterity made it seem less capacious, less vital, less necessary?

Auden's champions include many distinguished and articulate figures: poets like Joseph Brodsky, Richard Wilbur, and John Fuller, whose 1998 reference work, *W. H. Auden: A Commentary*, is a meticulous labor of love and scholarship. A much-expanded and revised version of his 1970 *Reader's Guide* to Auden's poems, Fuller's *Commentary* attempts "to say something useful about every original poem, play or libretto of his written in English that has so far reached print (with the exception of most of the juvenilia . . .)."

Among Auden's other commentators, the palm must go to Edward Mendelson, the poet's literary executor, chief editor, bibliographer, and most devoted critic. In *Early*

Auden (Viking, 1981), Mendelson distinguished between the traditions of "civil poetry" and "vatic poetry," locating Auden firmly in the former. "He had no wish to achieve an imaginative triumph over common reality," Mendelson wrote in his introduction. "His poems were not visionary autonomous objects, exempt from the practical and ethical standards appropriate to all other human works. They were made to be judged both for their art and their truth." What Auden wanted, Mendelson wrote later in the book, is "poetry that reflected the formal and linguistic lessons of modernism yet could still serve the public good. The art he wished to create was intent less on autonomy and stasis than on enlightenment and action."

Early Auden followed its subject's career through the eve of his emigration to the United States, in January 1939, with his friend, sometime lover, and occasional collaborator Christopher Isherwood. *Later Auden* (Farrar, Straus, 1999) picks up the story from there, providing a history and interpretation of Auden's work from 1939 through his death in 1973.

Later Auden is a scrupulous and inviting piece of literary-critical scholarship, crisply written and full of the quiet authority that comes with intimate mastery of a subject. Indeed, I doubt whether anyone can claim greater mastery of the Auden corpus than Mendelson. He began with a doctoral dissertation on Auden. In 1970, when the poet was thinking about putting together a collection of his book reviews and review essays, he found he was unable to remember exactly what he'd written or where. But Mendelson, who had met Auden while working on his doctoral thesis, had amassed photocopies of virtually everything. Auden—who was spectacularly disorganized himself—was duly impressed by this display of order (and doubtless by the homage it implied) and entrusted the selection of the volume that became *Forewords and Afterwords* (1973) to him. In 1972, Mendelson was appointed Auden's literary executor (joining Monroe K. Spears and William Meredith), and he has devoted himself to Audeniana ever since. In addition to his critical studies, he is a founding member of the Auden Society. He has also edited almost all of Auden's posthumous works:[1] the last collection of poems, entitled *Thank You, Fog* (1974), *Collected Poems* (1976), *The English Auden: Poems, Essays, and Dramatic Writings 1927–1939* (1977), and the ongoing *Complete Works of W. H. Auden* of which three volumes (plays, libretti, and prose to 1938) have thus far appeared from Princeton University Press. All of which is to say that there is precious little about Auden's work that Mendelson doesn't know.

Although it is half again as long as its predecessor, *Later Auden* does not come with the same kind of interpretative scaffolding. In *Early Auden*, by arguing for the merits of what he called the "civil tradition" of poetry, Mendelson challenged the prevailing critical climate that gave precedence to the Romantic-Modernist tradition with its emphasis on the isolated individual and the autonomy of the work of art. His detailed discussion of Auden's early development was at the same time a brief for the view of poetry—and by implication, the view of society and man's place in it—that Auden came to represent. At bottom, it is an eighteenth-century view, according to which the purpose of art is to delight and instruct.

In *Later Auden*, such larger arguments are more implicit than explicit. In his introduction, Mendelson lays out various oppositions—between myth and parable, between

---

1 An exception is the aforementioned *Juvenilia: Poems, 1922–1928,* which was edited by Katherine Bucknell (Princeton, 1994).

"the Ariel-dominated poet and the Prospero-dominated poet," between the poem as "verbal contraption" (Auden's phrase) and moral artifact—with which Auden's poetry contended. But the text proper is a tightly focused, sometimes almost abrupt, tour of Auden's work from the elegy for Yeats, which was written a few weeks after he arrived in New York, to the "concluding carnival" of his last, chatty poems. As in his earlier volume, Mendelson quietly punctuates his critical narrative with aptly chosen biographical details. While no substitute for a full-fledged biography, this procedure does provide readers with a kind of precis of Auden's movements, activities, and infatuations. Those interested in a fuller account of Auden's life may consult the excellent biography by Humphrey Carpenter (Houghton Mifflin, 1981) and the briefer, more thematic life by Richard Davenport-Hines (Pantheon, 1995).

Early Auden argued for Auden's surpassing greatness ("the most inclusive poet of the twentieth century, its most technically skilled, and its most truthful"), *Later Auden* assumes it. It is revisionist in that it places Auden's later work on a par with, or even ahead of, his early work. Mendelson is far from uncritical; about some poems from the early Forties, for example, he writes that "the contemplative saints briefly but disastrously took over much of his work, and they ruined every poem they touched." But such local criticisms occur in the context of presumed greatness. They tend to underscore the boldness of Mendelson's arresting claim that "much of [Auden's] most profound and personal work was written in the last fifteen years of his life," that is from 1958 on. "Personal" of course it may be; any doodle might be personal. And in fact Auden, who famously declared that he did not want a biography written about him, often noted that his poems were full of coded autobiographical references. "For a poet like myself," he wrote, "an autobiography would be redundant since anything of importance that happens to one is immediately incorporated, however obscurely, in a poem." The task of identifying such references has kept scholars busy for years and is one of the things that makes John Fuller's *Commentary* so valuable. Among other things, Fuller is almost always able to provide the relevant biographical correlative: "Auden wrote this poem while staying at the new Pennsylvania home of Caroline Newman, his patron," "Auden spent the night of 19 January in Paris, *en route* with Isherwood for Marseilles," "The circumstances of this early poem to [his lover, Chester] Kallman are," etc.

But by "profound" Mendelson means artistically significant: not only technically accomplished but also (given Auden's understanding of art) morally wise and aesthetically compelling. Mendelson argues this case passionately and intelligently; whether he argues it convincingly is another matter. There are many ways in which one can trace Auden's poetic development. The road from existential bafflement to religious affirmation charts one course (in 1940, at the age of thirty-three, Auden began "in a tentative and experimental way" to return to the Anglo-Catholic faith of his youth). The movement from lyric isolation to deliberate didacticism marks another trajectory. A third path has to do with what we might call diminishing poetic tautness. I do not mean a loss of prosodic virtuosity. Auden's astonishing technical mastery never left him; if anything he became more facile with age. His stupendous example helped make us more aware of the ways in which technical facility can be the precondition of poetic achievement. It may also have encouraged us to neglect the fact that technique, uncatalyzed by sensibility and subject matter, can be the enemy of poetic achievement. In any event, for Auden technical fluency sometimes resulted in poetry that seemed to proceed on verbal autopilot. Auden often remarked on his fondness for the *Oxford English Dictionary*. In later life, it provided some of his favorite reading matter and indeed was the source of many of the lexical curiosities that—increasingly—bedizened his poetry. Humphrey Carpenter notes that the most prominent object in the workroom of Auden's house in Kirchstetten, Austria (where he summered from 1958 to the end of his life), was the OED. The set, Carpenter writes, would always be "missing one volume, which was downstairs, Auden invariably using it as a cushion to sit on when at table—as if (a friend observed) he were a child not quite big enough for the nursery furniture." Auden's raids on the lexicon resulted in some bewildering rarities. In a review of *Epistle to a Godson* (1972), one critic lists "blouts, pirries, stolchy, glunch, sloomy, snudge, snoachy, scaddle, cagmag, hoasting, drumbles," among others. How many do you know? How many were chosen because the poet felt he had stumbled upon the one absolutely right word for the thought or feeling he was trying to express? How many did he adopt because he happened to pick them up from yesterday's trip through the dictionary and they filled a metrical hole? Auden regularly described poetry as a verbal puzzle, akin to a crossword. Well, it is and it isn't. Not all poems are verbal puzzles—not even all good ones—and it should go without saying that not all verbal puzzles are poems. These are distinctions that some of Auden's later poetry elides.

In 1936, Auden said that "the first, second and third thing in . . . art is subject. Technique follows from and is governed by subject." Possibly he later changed his mind;

he certainly changed his practice. Auden's love of complicated verse forms and unusual words was doubtless partly
an expression of a poet's delight in the resources of language and his ability to manipulate them skillfully. It may
also have been an attempt to compensate for the diminishing tautness I mentioned: an effort to inject arbitrary verbal complexity to distract readers—and even, perhaps,
himself—from the lack of genuine poetic density that
characterizes so many of his later poems. In this regard, it
seems significant that the word "cosy" came to loom large
in Auden's vocabulary in later years.

These features of Auden's poetry have not gone unremarked. Already in 1940, when reviewing *Another Time*,
Randall Jarrell complained that, unlike Auden's early
"oracular" verse, the present poems seemed "moral, rational, manufactured, written by the top of the head for
the top of the head." Although he was full of generalized
compliments about Auden's talent, Jarrell also wrote that
"the poems say often now, 'Be good.' They ascend through
moral abstractions, gnomic chestnuts, to a vaguish humanitarian mysticism." And this was only 1940. By 1955,
when he reviewed *The Shield of Achilles*, Jarrell was
resorting to sarcasm: "non-Euclidean needlepoint, a man
sitting on a chaise longue juggling four cups, four saucers,
four sugar lumps, and the round-square: this is what great
and good poets do when they don't bother even to try to
write great and good poems."

One of the most devastating reflections on Auden's
development—or decline, rather—was Philip Larkin's review of *Homage to Clio* in 1960. Entitled "What's Become
of Wystan?" (a play on Browning's line "What's become of
Waring"), Larkin begins by praising Auden's pre-1940
poetry and proceeds to describe his later verse as "too ver-
bose to be memorable and too intellectual to be moving."

Larkin readily acknowledges Auden's large ambition and poetic virtues—"the wide-angled rhetoric, the seamless lyricism, the sudden gripping dramatisations"—but he insists that "almost all we value is still confined to the first ten years" of his career. Auden, he wrote, had "become a reader rather than a writer" with the result that his poetry suffered a "loss of vividness" and "a certain abstract windiness." The "rambling intellectual stew of 'New Year Letter,'" Larkin wrote, "was hardly more than a vamp-till-ready." The poems in *Homage to Clio* were "agreeable and ingenious" but their "poetic pressure is not high." Too often, he mused, readers find "a wilful jumble of Age-of-Plastic nursery rhyme, ballet folk-lore, and Hollywood Lemprière served up with a lisping archness that sets the teeth on edge." As an example, Larkin quotes this bit from "Plains" (1953), part of Auden's sequence *Bucolics*:

> Romance? Not in this weather. Ovid's charmer
> Who leads in quadrilles in Arcady, boy-lord
> Of hearts who can call their Yes and No their own,
> Would, madcap that he is, soon die of cold or sunstroke:
> Their lives are in firmer hands; that old grim She
> Who makes the blind dates for the hatless genera
> Creates their country matters.

Pretty bad, isn't it?

Tough as Larkin's review was, it exhibited disappointment as much as hostility. It was with sadness, not malice, that Larkin concluded that Auden, "never a pompous poet, has now become an unserious one" who "no longer touches our imaginations." It speaks extremely well of Auden that, a few months after this review appeared, he wrote about Larkin's first book *The Less Deceived* and, as Mendelson notes, "praised it without reservation."

The tweeness that Larkin discerned in Auden's verse was always a temptation for Auden; it was a temptation he gave into more and more as the years went by. Hence the increasing levity and campiness of Auden's poetry. This was something that Christopher Ricks registered with deadly precision in his review of *About the House* (1965). Ricks begins by describing the "disarming" quality that much of Auden's poetry displays; he then goes on to note that it is "harder to pinpoint the moment at which such a word has to be said accusingly rather than thankfully." Consider, for example, the prominence of the word "silly" in Auden's poetic vocabulary (e.g., from the elegy on Yeats: "You were silly like us.") As Ricks points out, Auden doubtless expected his readers to recall the etymology of "silly" ("blessed," "fortunate"), but the line depends mostly on the word's deflationary effect: a confidential, homey effect that can easily be overplayed. Increasingly, Auden did overplay it. Consider the lines that Ricks quotes from "Grub First, Then Ethics" (1958): "surely those in whose creed / God is edible may call a fine / omelette a Christian deed." At best, this is silly in the modern sense: "showing a lack of good sense," "frivolous." The fact that Auden wrote not to ridicule but out of professed commitment to Christian doctrine makes the poem in even more questionable taste.

Taste is the lodestar of art, the inner principle that accounts for the decorum of the appropriately said. Increasingly, Auden's faculty of taste functioned accurately only in a risible or mocking mode. Given the right subject and the right form, he could be very funny. He was, for example, a master of the clerihew:

No one could ever inveigle
Georg Wilhelm Friedrich Hegel

Into offering the slightest apology
for his *Phenomenology.*

Or:

Mallarmé
Had too much to say:
He could never quite
Leave the paper white.

But Auden had difficulty purging his poetry of such levity.
What works in a clerihew can be disastrous in a serious
poem. As Ricks points out, Auden's habit of supercili-
ousness shows itself with lamentable consequences in his
habit of irregular capitalization: "A Major Prophet taken
Short," "a Perfect social Number," etc. The effect is unsettling, and ultimately unserious. Exactly how, Ricks asks,
does it differ from A. A. Milne's procedure with Winnie the
Pooh: "A Good Hum, such as is Hummed Hopefully to
Others"?

This family of criticisms is broached even by some of
Auden's most stalwart admirers. In the 1940s and 1950s,
Edmund Wilson became a staunch booster of Auden. He
concluded his long tribute, "W. H. Auden in America"
(1956), by describing him as "a great English poet who is
also . . . one of the great English men of the world."
Nearly twenty years earlier, however, Wilson put his finger
on another dimension of Auden's sensibility: "W. H.
Auden has presented the curious spectacle of a poet with
an original language . . . whose development has seemed to
be arrested at the mentality of an adolescent schoolboy."
There is no doubt that Auden's poetry developed; the
question is whether it can really be said to have matured.
The quality that, in their different ways, Wilson, Jarrell,
Larkin, and Ricks dilate on has to do with a precocious-

ness that never ended. At the end, Auden presented the unsettling spectacle of a precocious sexagenarian. In later years, Auden took to referring to himself as "mother," especially in relation to the monumentally irresponsible Chester Kallman. (Although they were lovers only briefly, Auden supported Kallman for the rest of his life and the two periodically lived together.) More telling and finally more appropriate was the nickname Auden acquired at Oxford: "The Child." The coyness and prolixity that characterize Auden's later poetry are emblematic of what happens when the desire for perpetual adolescence fails to outgrow itself: it grows seedy instead. It is shocking, as one looks back over Auden's poetic oeuvre, to note how early the seediness set in.

Auden once memorably defined poetry as "memorable speech." How well does his own poetry do by this criterion? Auden certainly said and wrote some memorable things. His comment that Rilke was "the greatest lesbian poet since Sappho" may be described as unforgettable. Likewise his comment that his face, which in later years was ravaged by the thick furrows of Touraine-Solents-Gole syndrome, was "like a wedding cake left out in the rain." The widely memorable lines from his poetry are almost exclusively from poems written, as Larkin observed, from the first decade of his career. They also tend to be fragmentary: a line here, two or three lines there. "Lay your sleeping head my love / Human on my faithless arm" ("Lullaby," 1937); "About suffering they were never wrong, / The Old Masters" ("Musée des Beaux Arts," 1938); "In the prison of his days / Teach the free man how to praise" (the Yeats elegy, 1939: these lines also appear as the epitaph on Auden's memorial stone in Westminster Abbey); "sad is Eros, builder of cities, / And weeping anarchic Aphrodite" (the elegy for Freud, 1939).

It is ironical that what is probably Auden's single most famous poem, "September 1, 1939," was one that he disavowed and even, as he put in 1957, came to "loathe." Nevertheless, the poem contains some of Auden's most memorable poetry, from the ominous opening lines—

I sit in one of the dives
On Fifty-Second Street
Uncertain and afraid
As the clever hopes expire
Of a low dishonest decade
Waves of anger and fear
Circulate over the bright
And darkened lands of the earth,
Obsessing our private lives

—to the famous end of the eighth stanza: "We must love one another or die." As Mendelson points out, "this line was more widely quoted and admired than perhaps anything else" in Auden's work. E. M. Forster said that because Auden had written it, "he can command me to follow him." Which doubtless tells us a lot about Forster.

In any event, Auden soon had misgivings about the poem. In 1944, he abandoned the celebrated eighth stanza partly because he believed that in the context of the poem ("Hunger allows no choice / To the citizen or the police") the line about love reduced what should be a voluntary act to an instinctual drive like hunger. In 1964, Auden's dislike of the poem hardened into revulsion when an advertising consultant for Lyndon Johnson misappropriated the line in an infamous campaign commercial. As Richard Davenport-Hines reports in his biography, the commercial featured a little girl counting the petals of a flower; suddenly, she is interrupted by a stern male voice counting down from ten to zero, at which point the girl is replaced by the flash of an explosion and a mushroom cloud. Then Johnson's voice intoned: "These are the stakes: to make a world in which all of God's children can live, or go into the dark. We must love each other or we must die." Auden bitterly responded, "I pray to God that I shall never be memorable like that again." When he prepared his *Collected Shorter Poems* for publication the following year, he omitted the poem and refused to allow it to be reprinted in his lifetime.

Most readers will be able to cite a few other lines or poems—"At the Grave of Henry James" (1941), for example, with the beginning of its stern last stanza: "All will be judged." But after around 1940, most readers will find that the gems are fewer and farther between. It is sad that among Auden's later poems, one of the most memorable is the last verse he ever wrote, an often-reproduced haiku:

> He still loves life
> but O O O O how he wishes
> the Good Lord would take him.

(As Mendelson points out, the "O"s need to be elided to keep the haiku to the requisite seventeen syllables; but should they be read as three syllables, as he says, or two, as I suspect?) In the end, Auden's poetry has produced relatively faint echoes. He was a remarkable mimic; he did marvelous impersonations of seriousness; but his continual worries about the authenticity of his poems show that even in his own mind he did not transcend impersonation. In comparison, say, to the poetry of T. S. Eliot, Auden's poetry lacks density. His example has meant a great deal to several poets who came after him; his techniques are preserved in the practice of some of the best. But Auden's poetry has left indifferent traces on the sensibility of our time. It is accomplished, not ineluctable. Reverberations from "Prufrock," *The Waste Land*, "Gerontion," and the *Four Quartets* are everywhere: the meter and the matter of those poems are part of the poetic metabolism of the age. Auden wrote nothing that has entered our pulses so thoroughly.

The permanent Auden is found elsewhere, above all in the scintillating and companionable essays of *The Dyer's Hand* (1962), *Forewords and Afterwords*, and some of his lectures, especially *The Enchafèd Flood* (1949) and parts of *Secondary Worlds* (1968). He was always penetrating on literary subjects. His essay on Trollope in *Forewords and Afterwords* is a masterpiece. So is his essay on Shakespeare's sonnets. As in the scenario he described in "Musée des Beaux Arts," his essays hail the triumph and consolation of the ordinary in the face of the extraordinary. In the poem, "the expensive delicate ship" saw "something amazing, a boy falling out of the sky," but it had somewhere to go and "sailed calmly on." One of Auden's most salutary services was to remind us of the importance of sailing calmly on.

Auden wrote often and well about the contradictory desire to find in art both an escape from and a revelation of reality. In an essay on Robert Frost, he observed that

> we want a poem to be beautiful, that is to say, a verbal earthly paradise, a timeless world of pure play, which gives us delight precisely because of its contrast to our historical existence with all its insoluble problems and inescapable suffering; at the same time we want a poem to be true, that is to say, to provide us with some kind of revelation about our life which will show us what life is really like and free us from self-enchantment and deception, and a poet cannot

bring us any truth without introducing into his poetry the problematic, the painful, the disorderly, the ugly.

Auden was especially effective in his admonitory mode, warning about the hubris of art absolutized. In a prose passage of "The Sea and the Mirror" (1944), a character observes that "if the intrusion of the real has disconcerted and incommoded the poetic, that is a mere bagatelle compared to the damage which the poetic would inflict if it ever succeeded in intruding upon the real."

This admonition is a leitmotif in Auden's work. "Poetry," he wrote in *The Dyer's Hand*, "is not magic. In so far as poetry, or any other of the arts, can be said to have an ulterior purpose, it is, by telling the truth, to disenchant and disintoxicate." Later on in that volume, he expanded on this thought. The effect of formal beauty, he noted, is "evil to the degree that beauty is taken, not as analogous to, but identical with goodness, so that the artist regards himself or is regarded by others as God, the pleasure of beauty being taken for the joy of Paradise, and the conclusion drawn that, since all is well in the work of art, all is well in history." And again: "Orpheus who moved stones is the archetype, not of the poet, but of Goebbels." Poetry, Auden said in the elegy for Yeats, "makes nothing happen." Many of his essays expatiate on the mischief of trying to have it otherwise.

Auden's essays are rich and endlessly rewarding. Yet in them, too, there is a large element of impersonation. In "Reading," the opening essay of *The Dyer's Hand*, Auden remarks that "in literature, as in life, affectation, passionately adopted and loyally persevered in, is one of the chief forms of self-discipline by which mankind has raised itself by its own bootstraps." This is undoubtedly true, though not necessarily reassuring. It is also true, as Auden remarks a few pages later, that "some writers confuse authenticity, which they ought always to aim at, with originality, which they should never bother about." Authenticity and affectation are not opposites, exactly, but if they can co-exist, they must do so uneasily. Auden never really resolved such tensions; he exploited them. The beguiling urbanity of Auden's essays depends partly on his native brilliance and erudition, partly on what we might call his air of easygoing religious seriousness. He never simply reviewed a book, he made it part of an existential project. He managed to do this whether he was writing about Kierkegaard, migraines, or M. F. K. Fisher's *The Art of Eating*.

Auden was fond of quoting Yeats's line about being forced to choose between perfection of the life and perfection of the work. He early on chose the latter. "Charade" is too strong a word. But there is a startling disjunction in Auden between the avuncular moralist who has such remarkable things to say about art, pride, sin, self-deception, etc., and the disheveled, lickerish narcissist who habitually besotted himself with horrifying quantities of alcohol, benzedrine, and some fifteen-thousand cigarettes yearly, who talked about being "married" to the disreputable Chester Kallman and then diverted himself with a steady procession of call-boys. George Orwell retracted his description of Auden as "a sort of gutless Kipling," but not, I believe, his comment from 1940 (soon after Auden absented himself from the perils of war-threatened England by emigrating to the United States) that "Mr. Auden's brand of amoralism is only possible if you are the kind of person who is always somewhere else when the trigger is pulled." Auden later wrote to the British embassy offering to do "anything when and if the Government ask me," but he oughtn't have been surprised to find his offer rebuffed.

Auden mounted a campaign against an overly aestheticized view of the world, but he did so while remaining within the orbit of aestheticism. His anguish was no doubt genuine, but his solution always had something of a performance about it. This is not to say that it lacked pathos. In a sermon he delivered in Westminster Abbey in 1966, Auden poignantly observed that

> those of use who have the nerve to call ourselves Christians will do well to be extremely reticent on the subject. Indeed, it is almost the definition of a Christian that he is somebody who *knows* he isn't one, either in faith or morals. Where faith is concerned, very few of us have the right to say more than—to vary a saying of Simone Weil's—"I believe in a God who is like the True God in everything except that he does not exist, for I have not yet reached the point where God exists." As for loving and forgiving our enemies, the less we say about that the better. Our lack of faith and love are facts we have to acknowledge, but we shall not improve either by a morbid and essentially narcissistic moaning over our deficiencies. Let us rather ask, with caution and humour—given our time and place and talents, what, if our faith and love were perfect, would we be glad to find it obvious to do?

Referring to Christianity, G. K. Chesterton once said that anything worth doing is worth doing badly. It is a witty statement, partly true. But only partly. In both his art and his life, W. H. Auden leaned heavily on the resources of the subjunctive, even as he entertained his readers with dreams of indicative truth. When he was eight years old, his mother taught him the love duet from *Tristan*. Auden played Isolde. It is not clear that he ever ceased giving that performance.

The First Half
of Muriel Spark

*The poet should prefer probable impossibilities to improbable
impossibilities.*
—Aristotle, *Poetics*

*When I first started writing people used to say my novels were
exaggerated. They never were exaggerated, merely aspects of
realism.*
—Muriel Spark, *Loitering with Intent*

I N A REVIEW of the reissue of *London Labour and the
London Poor* in 1968, W. H. Auden remarked that
Henry Mayhew's sprawling portrait of Victorian London
street life—brimming with such vivid specimens as Jack
Black, Rat-Killer to Her Majesty—led him to revise his
understanding of Dickens. Far from being a "fantastic
creator of over-life-size characters," Auden concluded,
Dickens was in fact "much more of a 'realist' than he is
generally taken for."

One occasionally has a similar feeling when reading the
fiction of the Scottish-born novelist Muriel Spark. What
seems at first like caricature often turns out to pass, for the
moment anyway, as unvarnished reportage. Generally, the
reports are not encouraging. Perhaps, deep down, "the

facts" themselves express a species of caricature; and perhaps, on reflection, one realizes this. Spark's trick is to coax us into musing that, if one were to go deeper still, maybe . . . The presentiment often terminates in an ellipsis, a feeling of uneasiness, anxiety. Not for nothing is the imperative "Memento Mori"—*Remember that you shall die*—the title of one of her best-known and most accomplished books. In that sober tale, all the characters are aged and more than a few are senile. "Being over seventy," one of them observes, "is like being engaged in a war. All our friends are going or gone and we survive amongst the dead and dying as on a battlefield." By the end of the novel, the battlefield is wiped clear, and the reader is given a brief recap of the characters' particular fates: "Lettie Colston . . . comminuted fractures of the skull; Godfrey Colston, hypostatic pneumonia; Charmian Colston, uremia; Jean Taylor, myocardial degeneration; Tempest Sidebottome, carcinoma of the cervix;" etc., etc.

The grimly comic cultivation of such reminders is a Sparkian trademark. Doubtless, it has something to do with religion, specifically with Catholicism, the faith to which Spark converted in 1954. Our life on earth is a pilgrimage, a prolegomenon, and one mustn't forget it: This basic conviction figures prominently, though undogmatically, in all Spark's work, infusing it with the ambition of allegory. But the vertiginous effect of her fiction is not simply a coefficient of faith. It is also the product of a literary gift, a sensibility.

Many of the settings, events, and characters that populate Spark's fiction have antecedents, more or less distant, in her life: a charismatic school teacher, an ailing grandmother, a club for women in wartime London, a friend who was murdered by her husband who in turn killed himself. All appear transmuted—*transfigured*, to use a

Sparkian adjective—in her novels and stories. Spark is a
dab hand at presenting the wrong end of the telescope and
then exclaiming, "See, I told you it was like that!" Her imaginings are frequently extravagant. It is business as usual
in Sparkland to find a story narrated by a ghost ("He
looked as if he would murder me and he did," a dead
narrator explains), a plot turned by an angel. Yet it is a
measure of Spark's artistry that—in those works where
everything gels—ghosts and angels seem no more (but also
no less) outrageous than rhododendrons. Somehow it is
not a problem that the anonymous telephone calls to the
characters in *Memento Mori* (1959) reminding them of
their doom are without earthly source. Suspending or extending disbelief hardly comes into it: Spark's spare, im-
maculate prose—cool and fatally accurate—does the work,
easing collusion if not, exactly, affirmation. There is a
moral but no catechism.

In this respect, if in few others, her work recalls the
Gothic realism of the American novelist and master of
the short story Flannery O'Connor. For both writers, the
operation of grace is generally a funny but decidedly
astringent affair. The humor comes from regarding the
doings of man *sub specie aeternitatis*, the ultimate prescription for farce. What we might call this cosmic dimension of Spark's comic vision led the novelist Malcolm
Bradbury to speak, admiringly, of her "great gift for being
appalling." The gift is appalling because it grants insight
but tends to discount such homely virtues as warmth,
human attachment, affection. Not everyone finds this attractive. The critic Christopher Ricks, for example, writing
about Spark in 1968, commented that "Perhaps when man
proposes, God disposes with as cool a disposition as Mrs.
Spark's, though if He indeed looks upon His created world
with the same eye with which she looks upon hers, then

thank God I am an atheist." One imagines Spark savored that "thank God."

She was intensely literary from the dawn of reason, setting down poem after poem beginning in grade school. But Muriel Spark did not embark earnestly on fiction until the early 1950s. Since then, she has been unstoppable. Although she has lived for some years in Italy, dividing her time, we are told, between Rome and Tuscany, Spark has not relinquished a Scottish disposition to industry. ("What a wonderful thing it was to be a woman and an artist in the twentieth century," Fleur Talbot, the narrator of *Loitering with Intent* [1981], repeatedly exclaims: despite the irony—Fleur is a bit creepy—the declaration has the air of a credo.) To date, in addition to several early collaborations, Spark has to her credit nineteen novels, an abundance of verse (she continues, she says, to think of herself as "predominantly a poet"), a plump *Collected Stories*, a play, a children's book, biographies of Mary Shelley and John Masefield, and an edition of the Brontë letters. One of her best and most subtle books, *The Prime of Miss Jean Brodie* (1961), was made into a successful play and then, with Maggie Smith in the title role, a successful movie. (Glenda Jackson was signed up for the movie version of *The Abbess of Crewe* [1974], a political potboiler, which seems about right.)

Along the way, Spark has collected much critical admiration—piquantly leavened with the occasional critical dissent—literary awards too numerous to list, endless academic comment, and, in 1967, an O.B.E. from Queen Elizabeth. In 1993, Spark published *Curriculum Vitae*, an autobiography, which sets forth the facts, personages, and occasions of Muriel Spark's life from 1918, when she was born, through 1957, when her first novel, *The Comforters*, was published. It presents the contingencies through which a precocious young woman became Muriel Spark, providing, as she hoped it would, a portrait of the young woman as an artist: a vivid if carefully cropped picture of her "formation as a creative writer." Concluding just as she crosses the threshold into literary maturity, the book ends with a promise of a sequel dealing with the "work, many travels and adventures" as well as "friends, famous and obscure," that have filled her life since 1957.

Various rumors, half-truths, fabrications, and other types of falsehood have collected around Spark as they collect around many well-known writers. Part of her reason for undertaking *Curriculum Vitae*, she tells us, was to "put the record straight." To this end, she has not relied solely on her memory for corroboration of the events she recounts, but has endeavored "to write nothing that cannot be supported by documentary evidence or eyewitnesses." Spark professes a horror of untruth. "Lies," she warns, "are like fleas hopping from here to there, sucking the blood of the intellect." She regards with contempt the writer of a biography who could not understand why Spark should be irritated about the fabrications promulgated in her book since, after all, she had portrayed Spark "in a good light." "Be that as it might," Spark writes, "it was all untrue."

Some of the errors circulating about Muriel Spark can be traced to innocent mistakes that have assumed the patina of plausibility through constant repetition by critics and scholars. Other errors have their source in the animus of certain of Spark's former friends, especially Derek Stanford, with whom she collaborated on several literary projects in the early Fifties. Stanford, Spark tells us, was "bookish with scholarly leanings" but "wildly and almost constitutionally inaccurate." When he got around to writing about Spark in the 1960s (and then again in 1977), he seems to have produced farragoes of error and invention. For example, Stanford claims that Spark was in love with T. S. Eliot (in fact, she had never met him), that her grandmother had gypsy blood (a "picturesque proposition," Spark comments, for which no evidence exists), that he went with her to visit her "Uncle Solly" about money (there was no such relative). He thinks Proust wrote a book called *Recherche dans le temps perdu* and assures readers that the infant Muriel was suckled until she was two. ("How ridiculous!" was her mother's comment: "There must be something wrong with the man.") Spark provides only an incomplete list of Stanford's errors, but we get the point: *caveat lector*. And watch out for the silver, too: Spark reports that Stanford pilfered certain manuscripts of her early work and later tried to sell them back to her through an agent.

Curriculum Vitae opens in Edinburgh, the Morningside district, with Muriel's birth to Bernard and Sarah Camberg. Her father, an engineer, was of Scottish-Jewish descent; her mother, neé Uezzell, was from an English shopkeeping family in Watford. Philip, Muriel's only sibling, was the elder by five and a half years. Financially, the Cambergs were modestly but respectably situated: there were few luxuries, but then who went in for luxuries at that time in Edinburgh? Family life seems to have been chummy and reasonably cheerful. Sarah Camberg had suffered what Muriel describes as a nervous breakdown before her daughter was born, but the only aftereffects mentioned are a tendency to mild superstition and a dislike of being left alone. Religious education at school was standard-issue Presbyterianism, laced at home with a few Jewish observances.

Bernard Camberg's Jewishness presented no social problems for young Muriel—having grown up in Edinburgh, he fit right in—but her mother's Englishness was a recurrent source of small, but memorable, mortifications. "'Foreigners' were something fairly tolerated, but 'the English' were something quite different," she recalls. Everyone knew that the English tended to be "superficial," "hypocritical," and "overdressed." They also talked funny. Not only did Sarah Camberg wear a coat trimmed with beige fox fur when she ought to have worn tweed or (if it was really cold) musquash (i.e., muskrat), but also she was overheard by her daughter to say to another mother at school: "I have some shopping to do." Spark remarks: "I nearly died. She should have said, 'I've got to get the messages.'"

This is a book bursting with such particularities. "Details fascinate me," Spark writes at the beginning of her chronicle. "I love to pile up details. They create an atmosphere. Names, too, have a magic, be they never so humble." Accordingly, the first part of *Curriculum Vitae* is a compilation of childhood details, a building-up of atmosphere. Sights, sounds, tastes, names, personalities, amusements. We learn about the neighborhood bakery, Howden's, and the kinds of bread they made; we visit the Buttercup Dairy where one purchased fresh butter from a pink-and-white complexioned girl; and we rehearse the proper method of making tea. "Everyone who came to the house was offered a cup of tea, as in Dostoyevsky." If served at five o'clock, tea was something one "took"; at six, one "ate" it. High tea, accompanied by kippers, smoked haddock, ham, and eggs, occurred at 6:30. Other details: her grandmother's clothes, for example. The "petticoats were voluminous, gathered at the waist; one in each set was cream-coloured or grey flannel, one was white linen edged with lace and one was black. My grandmother's stockings were black wool. They were kept up by

pink elastic bands, her garters," etc. There are many such
"piles" of detail in this short, relaxed, elegantly written
book. As Miss Jean Brodie put it, in a somewhat different
context: "For those who like that sort of thing . . . that
is the sort of thing they like." (While on the subject of
detail, it may be worth pointing out that aficionados of
detail, and others, are likely to be frustrated by *Curriculum
Vitae*'s lack of an index.)

Spark describes herself as an avid listener and "person-
watcher" from an early age. One believes it. Young Muriel
must have been a formidable creature to have around the
house, listening, watching. When she was about "four or
five," she recalls,

> I had been given a dolls' pram constructed for twins, with a
> folding hood at each end. My dolls, Red Rosie and
> Queenie, sat facing each other. I remember one day I was
> crying and bawling for some reason. My father fetched a
> face-cloth and wiped the faces of my two dolls, bidding
> them not to cry. I was so fascinated by this performance
> that I stopped crying, and I distinctly recall a sensation or
> instinct that, if I could have put it into words, would have
> been "I'm not taken in by his ruse, but at the same time
> what a good child-psychologist he is!"

And what a prodigious child psychologist was she.

Education was held in exceptionally high esteem in
Edinburgh, and rich merchants vied with one another to
found and endow schools. One such worthy was James
Gillespie, snuff merchant, who died in 1797, leaving part
of his fortune to found a school for boys and girls. (When
Gillespie asked a friend for a motto for his carriage, Spark
informs us, the friend proposed: "Wha wad hae thocht it /
That noses had bocht it." Gillespie declined the couplet

and used his initials instead.) Muriel entered the school at the age of five and spent twelve years there, "the most formative years of my life, and in many ways the most fortunate for a future writer." She was a clever student whose grades were good enough to secure a scholarship when she entered the high school. "After the age of twelve," she proudly reports, "I did not involve my parents in school fees."

At a time when allegations of "child abuse" are in the papers daily, it is refreshing to contemplate the relative innocence of social life in a city like Edinburgh in the 1920s. Spark tells a charming story about her history master, a Mr. Gordon. Being fond of her hair, Gordon would have Muriel sit in the front of the class so that he could stroke her hair while teaching. Because of "the universal decency of our school teachers' deportment," she notes, no one thought ill of him for it. "There was nothing whatsoever wrong with Jerry Gordon," she remarks. "The girls tittered quite a lot. I liked it quite a lot."

Among other attainments, James Gillespie's High School for Girls (as it came to be) was the original for the Marcia Blaine School for Girls that provides the setting for *The Prime of Miss Jean Brodie*. An eccentric schoolmistress, Miss Christina Kay, provided the inspiration for Jean Brodie. "I fell into Miss Kay's hands at the age of eleven," Spark writes. "It might well be said that she fell into my hands." Spark started writing about Miss Kay and her adventures even then.

Like her fictional counterpart, Miss Kay adorned her classroom walls with reproductions of paintings by Leonardo, Giotto, Botticelli, and other Italian masters; it was the late Twenties, and this lover of romance, again like her fictional counterpart, also displayed a newspaper clipping of Mussolini's *fascisti* marching along the streets of Rome.

Spark does not say whether Miss Kay, like Miss Jean Brodie, walked with her head "up, *up*"; but Miss Kay did refer to her young charges as the "crème de la crème" and regaled them with stories of her travels in Rome, Egypt, Switzerland as well as the poetry of Wordsworth, Browning, Tennyson, Swinburne, Edmund Blunden, Rupert Brooke, Walter de la Mare, Yeats, and (a favorite of Spark's) John Masefield.

Muriel Camberg was certainly one of Miss Kay's favorites, for she and a schoolmate accompanied her (at Miss Kay's expense) to the theater, to art galleries, and to Anna Pavlova's last tour of Edinburgh. From what Spark says, it seems that Miss Kay displayed the charm and imperiousness but not the deep moral ambiguity that distinguished Jean Brodie. One can imagine Miss Kay believing, with Miss Brodie, that the solution to mathematical problems was all well and good, but "quite useless to Sybil Thorndike, Anna Pavlova and the late Helen of Troy." One cannot imagine her trying to manipulate one of her former students into sleeping with a married man whom she herself loves but has forsaken. Miss Kay, Spark conjectures, would have put Miss Brodie "firmly in her place."

After the James Gillespie's School, the prospect of university was less than wholly appealing. Not only would a university career for the modestly situated Camberg girl be "something of a luxury" but also, Muriel noticed, "many older girls who were studying at Edinburgh University in those days were humanly rather dull and earnest, without adult style or charm, indeed there was a puritanical atmosphere." Instead of university, she took a course in précis writing, a discipline that shows itself in her trim, to-the-point writing to this day. "I love economical prose, and would always try to find the briefest way to express a meaning." She then taught in a small private day school where instead of pay she was given free tuition in shorthand and typing. This stood her in good stead when she put in a brief stint at an exclusive women's department store in Edinburgh working as a secretary to the owner. The department store provided some comic relief—Spark recalls overhearing "some of the most affected and absurd conversation between the clients and the saleswomen that I've ever heard in my life"—but essentially she was biding her time, waiting for the rest of her life to happen.

It began happening later that year, 1936, when Muriel met Sydney Oswald Spark at a club in Edinburgh. Thirteen years her senior, Spark was a teacher who was soon to depart for a three-year appointment in Southern Rhodesia (now Zimbabwe). It is an exquisitely Sparkian detail that Sydney Spark should have been known as s.o.s. He was an emotional wreck and must have been emitting distress signals from the start. Muriel's parents sensed trouble, but she in her eagerness to get on with life—and out of Edinburgh—saw only the prospect of escape. "I thought him interesting, as I generally found 'older men.'" In 1937, Muriel became engaged to Spark and in due course followed him to Southern Rhodesia. She was then nineteen. Being underage, she had to cable her father for permission to marry. Reluctantly, he gave it.

Sydney Spark was, as she now acknowledges, a "disastrous choice." In Africa, he became more and more unbalanced and subject to fits of violence. Within two years Muriel was thinking of leaving him. In a calm and lucid moment, the wretched fellow said "One day this will all appear to you as a bad dream." He was right. "He became a borderline case," Muriel remarks, "and I didn't like what I found on either side of the border." When she became pregnant, Sydney tried to convince her to get an abortion.

This form of murder was not the routine procedure it has become today, and Muriel refused. A son, Robin, was born in July 1938.

Because of her husband's quarrelsomeness, the Sparks were constrained to move around Southern Rhodesia a great deal. Domestically, Muriel admits, this was a "drawback." But a new toughness was dawning, and she points out that "drawbacks can be advantages if you think in the opposite direction." In those years, circumstances provided many occasions for thinking in the opposite direction. It might be said that Muriel Camberg got two good things from her husband, a son and a name: "Spark," as she implies, has more poetry in it than "Camberg." But she also got Africa. As the world tilted toward and finally collapsed into war, Muriel found herself trapped there, unable to arrange transport back to England.

Muriel Spark's sojourn in Africa was the opposite of pleasant: a failed marriage, poverty, little prospect of leaving before the end of the war, few friends with literary interests. (Doris Lessing was living someplace in Rhodesia at the time, but the two writers did not meet until many years later.) Nevertheless, she continued to write, poems mostly, and collected material for some of her best-known stories. Africa, as much as Edinburgh, formed her as a writer. It also made her an adult. It was in Africa, she says, that she "learned to cope with life." "It was there that I learned to keep in mind . . . the essentials of our human destiny, our responsibilities, and to put in a peripheral place the personal sorrows, frights and horrors that came my way."

Horrors there were aplenty. The racial situation was barbaric. The Afrikaner women with whom Muriel mingled were full of smug stories about how uppity blacks had

been "fixed." There was, for example, the farmer who discovered a young black boy standing outside the window of
his wife's room, peeping in at her while she breast-fed her
baby. For this violation, the farmer shot the boy dead. The
woman who told Spark this story only lamented that the
farmer had been sent to prison for three years for killing
the boy. "I was unable to speak," Spark reports. "I simply
stared at the woman."

Racial barbarism took other forms as well. After leaving
her husband, Muriel applied for a job in an Anglican con-
vent school. The Mother Superior took a great liking to
her, especially her fair "complexion and golden hair."
During her second interview—there were four in all—the
nun told her that there might indeed be an opening for her.
"You see," she said, "the trouble with this war is the Jews.
We need more people like you." She went on and on about
the Jews and how right Hitler was. Muriel played along,
fascinated to see how far the woman would go. But before
the fourth interview she said to the woman,

> "Of course, I'm a Jew."
> She said, "It's not so."
> I said, "What isn't so?"
> She said, "What you *just said*."
> I took my fair skin and my golden locks right out of
> there.

Despite warnings about the dangers and privations, Muriel
was aching to return to England before the war ended.
Finally, in February 1944, she found transport on a troop-
ship. She and the thirty or so other women who joined her
were told not to undress for bed and to wear dark trousers.
Dark clothes, a typed instruction sheet informed them,
were advisable in case the boat should be torpedoed:

sharks tended to overlook dark clothes. "I am sure," she writes, "this was a mess-room jollification."

After visiting her family in Edinburgh, Spark went to London to look for work. She stayed at the Helena Club, founded by a daughter of Queen Victoria for "Ladies from Good Families of Modest Means who are Obliged to Pursue an Occupation in London." This of course was the original of the May of Teck Club, the setting for *The Girls of Slender Means* (1963), one of Spark's funniest books. Recalling events in 1945, when "all the nice people in England were poor, allowing for exceptions," the book peeks in on the life of half a dozen girls living at the club. "As they realized themselves in varying degrees, few people alive at the time were more delightful, more ingenious, more movingly lovely, and, as it might happen, more savage than the girls of slender means."

Spark landed a plum job with the Foreign Office after a woman at the employment bureau noticed that she was reading a novel by one of her favorite writers, Ivy Compton-Burnett. Spark became a Duty Secretary in the same division of military intelligence that employed Ian Fleming. Their job was psychological warfare or "black propaganda." "Black propaganda," she explains,

> was distinct from the BBC's white variety. Black took up the position that we were loyal Germans devoted to the Führer. From that point of view the news was presented in such a way that the Germans got the impression that they were listening to a German station. This was a camouflage for subtle and deadly anti-Nazi propaganda.

It was, she concludes, "detailed truth with believable lies" —a phrase that, suitably qualified, might double as a description of Spark's own technique as a writer.

After the war, Spark first worked as an editor and writer at a quarterly magazine called *The Argentor*, the official publication of the National Jewellers' Association. In 1947, she became editor of *Poetry Review*, the journal of the Poetry Society, where she stayed until 1949. It was a difficult job. Spark took the post partly because she was promised a flat. She never got the flat. But she did earn the abiding animosity of certain members of the Poetry Society who could not understand why she hesitated to print their poetic effusions. There was, for example, Robert Armstrong, "a physically and morally twisted, small, dark fellow," who was on the executive committee of the society. Spark published a poem of his which had been accepted by the previous editor, but she neglected to mention his name on the front cover. This brought an outraged letter from him on his business letterhead, H. M. Inspector of Taxes, Willesdon District. A battle ensued that ended only with Spark's departure from the *Poetry Review*.

Spark reserves some of her most delicious malice for another opponent of her innovations at the Poetry Society, Dr. Marie Stopes. Stopes, famous for her proselytizing activities on behalf of birth control, abominated any hint of experimentation in the realm of poetry. She instantly became Spark's bitter enemy and campaigned vigorously to have her removed as editor. Stopes often led meetings of the society, "literally shaking her fist and making inflammatory, wild pronouncements." Among other things, she wrote to ask if it was true that Spark's husband had divorced her. Spark's reply begins: "I have received your outrageously impudent letter. . . . My private affairs are no concern of yours and your malicious interest in them seems to me to be most unwholesome." Spark briskly acknowledges the beneficence of Stopes's prophylactic advocacy. Then she eviscerates her. "I met [Stopes] at one of our meetings and knew she disliked me intensely on sight. I was young and pretty and she had totally succumbed to the law of gravity without attempting to do a thing about it." Spark concludes wistfully, "I used to think it a pity that her mother rather than she had not thought of birth control."[1]

After leaving the Poetry Society, Spark started a short-lived magazine called *Forum* with the financial help of some friends. In 1950, she wrote her study of Mary Shelley—now an overdone subject, but at the time quite out of the ordinary. She met and interviewed John Masefield, whom she also wrote about, and began her rocky collaboration with Derek Stanford. She was writing a great deal of poetry but found herself often entering the word "returned" in the ledger in which she kept track of the publications she sent her work to. Her first notable public success came in 1951 when her story "The Seraph and the Zambesi" won first prize (out of 6,700 entries) in a competition sponsored by *The Observer*. The judges were David Astor, editor of the paper, Philip Toynbee, and

---

[1] Spark was too kind to Marie Stopes. Particularly ironical was Stopes's nasty question about Spark's being divorced. As the philosopher David Stove shows in "O Pioneers! . . . ," an essay about Stopes and that other prophetess of contraception, Margaret Sanger, Stopes, though believing herself an instrument of Divine Will, was hardly a model of marital fidelity. When her husband lost nearly all his money in the Depression, she lost no time in winkling him out of Norbury Park, his beautiful eighteenth-century house and grounds. "She drafted a document (purporting to have been drafted by him) which stated that he released her . . . from any interference on his part with her sexual freedom. She bullied him into signing it, and into staying away henceforth from Norbury Park. He was reduced to living alone in a single room in London, where in due course he died. This saddened Marie, who wrote a little poem about it, deploring the housing shortage."

Terence Kilmartin. First prize was the then-handsome sum of £250. She gave £50 to her son for his bar mitzvah and also generously gave £50 to Derek Stanford, thus illustrating the principle that no good deed goes unpunished. She bought herself a blue velvet dress and a complete set of *A la recherche du temps perdu.*

"The Seraph and the Zambesi" was an important success. But it did not bring financial security. At one point in the early Fifties Spark had only one dress and her shoes had holes in them. In 1954, as a result of undernourishment and too much dexedrine, she fell ill and suffered from mild hallucinations. Graham Greene, who had become an avid admirer of her work, offered to give her £20 a month until she recovered.

The hallucinations, however, turned out to be a godsend. They formed the inspiration for her first novel, *The Comforters* (written in 1955 but not published until 1957), in which the narrator hears voices and believes herself to be a character in the novel she is writing. Evelyn Waugh, noting the similarity between *The Comforters* and his book *The Ordeal of Gilbert Pinfold* (also published in 1957), was full of praise in his review: "I was struck by how much more ambitious was Miss Spark's essay and how much better she had accomplished it."

On May 1, 1954, Spark was received into the Catholic Church at Ealing. Naturally, one recurrent question concerns her conversion. As a youth, she tells us, she had "no specific religion, but a strong religious feeling." What experiences, bafflements, convictions—what terrors, what joys—led this earnest half-Presbyterian, half-Jewish woman to make the turn to Rome in her mid-thirties? The book jacket of the English edition of *Curriculum Vitae* promises Spark's answer to this question. In the event, what she provides is a paragraph or so in the last few

pages of the book. What can one say? Spark is as illuminating as one could be without being illuminating. She
recounts the menu but doesn't attempt to describe the
meal. Perhaps, in anything short of a spiritual *apologia*,
this is as much as one can expect. A precipitating experience, she says, was her absorption in the theological
writings of John Henry Newman in 1953. (Newman's
writings figure, ambiguously, in some of Spark's novels,
especially in *Loitering with Intent*.) But she doesn't divulge
what Newman said or argued that swayed her. This is
what Spark tells us:

> When I am asked about my conversion, why I became a
> Catholic, I can only say that the answer is both too easy
> and too difficult. The simple explanation is that I felt the
> Roman Catholic faith corresponded to what I had always
> felt and known and believed; there was no blinding revela-
> tion in my case. The more difficult explanation would
> involve the step by step building up of a conviction; as
> Newman himself pointed out, when asked about his con-
> version, it was not a thing one could propound "between
> the soup and the fish" at a dinner party. "Let them be to
> the trouble that I have been to," said Newman. Indeed, the
> existential quality of a religious experience cannot be
> simply summed up in general terms.

True, true. But somehow one wants a detail or two about
the beliefs that helped build her conviction, some taste,
some sample of the "existential quality" she has in mind.
Newman, after all, provided the *Apologia pro Vita Sua*.
We have some hints in Spark's novels, to be sure, but
works of fiction are not the same as a statement made *in
propria persona*.

In any event, Spark's religious convictions have played a

powerful, if somewhat elusive, role in her fiction. It might be said that they form the invisible core or center of her work. This has helped to confer depth and psychological complexity to her fiction, but may also account for the disturbing "otherworldly" quality much of it exhibits. Aristotle advised the poet to prefer probable impossibilities to improbable ones. It is an open question whether Spark's impossibilities are always suitably "probable." But *Curriculum Vitae* once again reminds us that she is a paid-up subscriber to another of Aristotle's dictums, that "the perfection of style is to be clear without being mean."

The Qualities
of Robert Musil

*"Why, then, aren't we realists?" Ulrich asked himself. Neither of
them was, neither he nor she: their ideas and their conduct had
long left no doubt of that; but they were nihilists and activists,
sometimes one and sometimes the other, whichever happened to
come up.*

—Robert Musil, The Man Without Qualities

*In the realm of the aesthetic . . . even imperfection and lack of
completion have their value.*

—Robert Musil, "Address at the Memorial Service for Rilke in Berlin"

THE AUSTRIAN NOVELIST Robert Musil (1880–1942)
occupies a peculiar position in the pantheon of great
twentieth-century writers. He is admired by literati for a
handful of astringent modernist fictions, especially for his
first novel, *Die Verwirrungen des Zöglings Törless (The
Bewilderments of the Schoolboy Törless)*. This brutal yet
seductively introspective tale of adolescent cruelty and
sexual exploitation at a German military boarding school
was published to instant critical acclaim in 1906, when
Musil was only twenty-six. (Later, in the 1930s and 1940s,
Törless was hailed as a prescient allegory of the spiritual
deformations of the Nazi era.) Musil's play *Die Schwärmer*

(1921, *The Enthusiasts*) explores that favored modern topic, the collapse of traditional bourgeois ideals; its taut language and intense dramatization won it the Kleist Prize in 1923 and, eventually, a regular spot in the German theatrical repertory. *Drei Frauen* (1924, *Three Women*), a celebrated suite of three novellas, plumbs the relationship between eroticism (generally unhappy) and transcendence—one of Musil's staple themes.

Then there are Musil's essays, some of which are masterpieces of ironic cultural commentary. "Uber die Dummheit" ("On Stupidity"), a lecture that Musil delivered in Vienna in 1937, deserves special mention for its signal contemporary relevance. Particularly pertinent is its withering analysis of "the higher, pretentious form of stupidity"—the "real disease of culture," in Musil's opinion, which infiltrates even "the highest intellectual sphere" and has repercussions throughout society. "The examples," he dryly notes, "are pretty blatant." As indeed they are. Finally, some of Musil's short prose pieces, collected in *Nachlass zu Lebzeiten* (1936, *Posthumous Papers of a Living Author*), rival Kafka's fables in their vertiginous humor and enigmatic creepiness.

All of Musil's works (the German edition of which runs to nine volumes) have their partisans and admirers. But for most of us, Robert Musil is first and foremost the author of *Der Mann ohne Eigenschaften* (*The Man Without Qualities*), a book in which the major themes of his earlier works coalesce to form a novelistic tapestry of extraordinary wit, complexity, and intelligence.

It is worth stressing the wit. *The Man Without Qualities*, the book upon which Musil's claim to greatness chiefly rests, is regularly cited alongside Joyce's *Ulysses*, Proust's *A la recherche du temps perdu*, Thomas Mann's *Der Zauberberg*, and Hermann Broch's *Die Schlafwandler* as a triumph of high modernism. Like those other novels, *The Man Without Qualities* is a book of weighty seriousness and deep erudition. It is also, in parts, an exceptionally funny book. Few readers with any sympathy for Musil's writing will be able to read far without laughing aloud, at least as they make their way through the first volume. Whatever else one can say about it, *The Man Without Qualities* stands as one of the great modern works of satire.

Set in Vienna in 1913, it depicts a world on the edge of a precipice—the moral, cultural, political precipice that was to give way to the abyss of World War I the following year. But it turns out that, in Musil's hands, peregrinations at the brink of disaster are as amusing as they are poignant; and Musil's man without qualities—a gifted, amoral, concupiscent mathematician of good family named Ulrich—is one of the most engaging comic anti-heroes in modern fiction.

It almost goes without saying that *The Man Without Qualities* is a peculiar book, or set of books. Like the other great novels just mentioned, it is monumental—in its literary ambition, its intellectual sophistication, and, not least, in its length. Certainly, as Dr. Johnson said of *Paradise Lost*, "none ever wished it longer than it is." Musil began working on *The Man Without Qualities* in 1924. He published the first volume—some thousand pages—in 1930, and the first part of the second volume in 1933 (for which he was awarded that year's Goethe Prize).

Under pressure from his publisher, who had been steadily advancing him money for years, Musil reluctantly began preparing the second part of the second volume for publication in the late 1930s. By then, Musil and his wife Martha, a painter whose parents were assimilated Jews, were living in penurious exile from the Nazis in Switzerland. An energetic (not to say fanatical) rewriter—a literary perfectionist, really—Musil had retrieved the galleys from the printer and was in the process of extensively reworking them when, in April 1942 at the age of sixty-two, he suddenly collapsed from a cerebral hemorrhage and died. Apparently, he succumbed while performing his morning gymnastics (another activity to which he was fanatically devoted). According to his widow, who found him a short while later, the look on his face was one of "mockery and mild astonishment."

We really have no idea how Musil intended to end *The Man Without Qualities*. Probably, the last section would have been titled "A Sort of Ending" to mirror the opening sequence, "A Sort of Introduction." He once said that he wanted to conclude the book in the middle of a sentence, with a comma. Be that as it may, in addition to the twenty chapters in half-corrected galley proof, there exist dozens of draft chapters as well as voluminous notes, character sketches, alternative chapters, and miscellaneous jottings related to the book. Musil's widow published the second part of the second volume in 1943. The "complete" German edition of this incomplete novel was published in 1951.

The first English translation of *The Man Without Qualities* was by Eithne Wilkins and Ernst Kaiser, who also collaborated on translations of *Törless* and some of Musil's stories. Published in three volumes from 1954 to 1960, this edition included all of the novel that Musil published during his lifetime (that is, all of volume one and the first thirty-eight chapters of volume two). A projected fourth volume was to contain the posthumously published chapters and notes. Although incomplete, the Wilkins–Kaiser translation remains a sound introduction to *The Man Without Qualities*: the translation is fluent, and a prefatory essay provides an excellent précis of Musil's career.

The one clear advantage of the more recent two-volume translation of *The Man Without Qualities* by Sophie Wilkins and Burton Pike (Knopf, 1995) is that it contains Musil's posthumously published chapters. It also contains several hundred pages of Musil's notes, sketches, and alternative versions of chapters. While some of this material will interest readers of the novel (as distinct from those who prefer to dissect it), much of it will command the attention only of Musil specialists. It must be said, too, that shoe-horning all of this material into only two volumes has bloated the second volume to tumid, phone-book proportions: a pity, not only because it makes the book difficult to handle, but also because it seems unfair to the striking and elegant jacket design that the publisher provided.

In an afterword, Burton Pike tells us that "the translator's intention was to have the writing startle the reader in English in the same way it startles a reader in German." He and his co-translator have produced a version of the novel that is generally a bit more literal than the previous translation; whether it is always quite as readable is another question. It is perhaps an improvement in accuracy to translate "Haus und Wohnung des Mannes ohne Eigenschaften" as "House and home of the man without qualities" (Wilkins–Pike) instead of "Abode of the Man Without Qualities" (Wilkins–Kaiser); or to render "ein leichter Geruch von verbranntem Pferdehaar" as "a whiff of burnt horsehair" (W–P) rather than "a faint whiff of brimstone" (W–K)—though given the presence of the devil in the previous clause, there is surely something to be said for "brimstone."

In any event, other decisions in the new translation are more dubious. For example, Wilkins–Kaiser translated the second part of the first volume, "Seinesgleichen geschieht," as "The Like of It Now Happens." If nothing else, this does have the advantage of more or less accurately rendering the German. The Wilkins–Pike alternative is "Pseudoreality Prevails." This may indeed fulfill Mr. Pike's ambition to "startle the reader." The problem is that it would probably have startled the author as well: presumably, if Musil had wanted "Pseudoreality Prevails" he would have written it. Not that translating Musil is an easy task. Indeed, nothing about Musil is easy. Writing some years ago about *The Bewilderments of the Schoolboy Törless*, the critic John Simon noted that whatever Musil touched "was or became difficult. Simplicity was not for him: in style, thought, or life." For readers of an English translation of Musil's magnum opus, the difficulties begin with the book's title. For while *Eigenschaften* can indeed mean "qualities," it carries with it a penumbra of associations that no English word quite captures. "Qualities," "properties," "attributes"— *Eigenschaften* can mean any or all of these things. But it suggests something more. *Eigen* is the German word for "own," as in "for one's own use." Hence the *eigen* in *Eigenschaften* insinuates a sense of self-possession that remains inexplicit in the English approximations. To speak of a man without *Eigenschaften* is therefore not so much to deny that he exhibits any definite qualities but rather to suggest that whatever qualities he displays are not really *his*. To be without *Eigenschaften* is in this sense to be without character—that inscribed residuum of identity that makes us who we are—though to be without character is by no means to be anonymous. As Ulrich admits to himself, "he was, after all, a character, even without having one."

For readers in the habit of opposing the claims of science to those of art, part of what makes Musil difficult is the way that he complicates the Romantic impulse to champion art as a kind of escape or redemption from unpalatable scientific truths. I will have more to say about this subject—a key theme in *The Man Without Qualities*—below. But for now it is enough to note Musil was himself of a scientific bent by temperament and training (or perhaps by temperament because of training). Not for nothing was *Genauigkeit* ("precision," "accuracy," "exactness") one of his favorite words. And Musil was *genau* in everything: dress, speech, manner, and intellectual comportment. As he put it in one essay, "If I want to have a worldview, then I must view the world. That is, I must establish the facts."

Musil had great respect for facts, and for the procedures science had devised for obtaining them. His education was primarily technical, not literary. The only son of the knighted engineer Hofrat Alfred Edler von Musil, Robert was sent at a young age to military school, first at Eisenstadt and then at Weisskirchen, the latter providing the inspiration for the dismal institution that Musil portrayed in *Törless*. (Asked later whether the school was the original for the "W." of *Törless*, Musil laughed and said that the fictional school was as nothing compared to the reality.)

In 1897, the year in which he began writing in earnest, Musil went to study civil engineering. He took a diploma from the Technical University in Brno in 1901, and, after doing his military service, spent a year working in the engineering laboratories in Stuttgart. He then went to Berlin, where he studied psychology, logic, and philosophy (the gloomy Maurice Maeterlinck and, later, Emerson and Nietzsche were particularly important influences). His doctorate, under Karl Stumpf, was on the epistemology of the great Austrian physicist and philosopher Ernst Mach (1838–1916), about whom William James once remarked that he appeared to have read and thought about everything. And although Musil decided against pursuing an academic career, he remained deeply interested in empirical science. He was even something of an inventor. Early on, he invented a chromatometer. This device, an earlier version of which was invented by Newton, resolves all the colors of the spectrum into whiteness—an appropriate invention, as one commentator has observed, for the author of a book called *The Man Without Qualities*.

But the portrait of Robert Musil, technician, is not of course the whole story. If Musil was the son of an engineer, he was also the son of a tempestuous, artistically inclined mother, Hermine. As a boy, he was socially withdrawn, often sickly, but also defiant and—in the schoolyard, anyway—effectively pugilistic. Although he was baptized Catholic, his parents were ardent secularists, and Robert was brought up without religious instruction. Nevertheless, Musil later developed an intense "outsider's" interest in religion. In one place he describes Ulrich as "a religious person who simply happened to believe in nothing at the moment"—not a bad definition of Musil himself—and he lards the second volume of *The Man Without Qualities* with quotations from various classics of mystical literature.

Musil's early family life was calculated to breed complication. Apparently with the acquiescence of her husband, Hermine maintained what amounted to a *ménage à trois* with one Heinrich Reiter, who met the family in 1881, shortly after Robert was born. As he grew older, Musil quite naturally came to resent Reiter and to despise his father. About his mother he seems to have entertained a mixture of indifference and contempt. In view of her notable accomplishments as an amateur pianist, the contempt no doubt continued to show itself in Musil's unusual hostility to music when he was an adult; his indifference seems to have been reciprocated by both parents.

The erotic irregularity of the Musil household later had

profound echoes in Robert's fiction—as did an earlier tragedy. Musil's only sibling, Elsa, died in infancy before he was born. Although he never knew her, the image of this lost sister came to haunt him as the embodiment of an unobtainable unity and wholeness: an alter ego or "other half" such as Aristophanes famously described in his speech about the nature of love in Plato's *Symposium*. She would come back as Agathe, Ulrich's "forgotten sister," in the second volume of *The Man Without Qualities*.

It must also be understood that Musil, born in 1880 in Klagenfurth, southern Austria, was very much a product of the hothouse atmosphere of *fin-de-siècle* Vienna. This was an atmosphere in which, as the historian Carl Schorske put it, "the usual moralistic culture of the European bourgeoisie was . . . both overlaid and undermined by an amoral *Gefühlskultur* [sentimental culture]." As Schorske went on to note, this revolution in sensibility amounted to a crisis of morality—Hermann Broch called it a "value vacuum"—that quickly precipitated a crisis in liberal cultural and political life *tout court*. "Narcissism and a hypertrophy of the life of feeling were the consequence," Schorske continued.

> The threat of the political mass movements lent new intensity to this already present trend by weakening the traditional liberal confidence in its own legacy of rationality, moral law, and progress. Art became transformed from an ornament to an essence, from an expression of value to a source of value.

These transformations were a catalyst for disaster. The resources of civilization—epitomized by the faith in rationality, moral law, and progress that Schorske mentions—were hollowed out from within; weightless, they soon lost the capacity to resist the barbarism of feeling—aesthetic, sexual, social, political feeling—that rushed in to fill the spiritual vacancy of the times. It was, as the Marxists used to say, "no accident" that Nazism and other extreme movements got their start in this narcotic environment. Musil put it in terms of the credit system:

> In love as in business, in science as in the long jump, one has to believe before one can win and score, so how can it be otherwise for life as a whole? However well founded an order may be, it always rests in part on a voluntary faith in it, a faith that, in fact, always marks the spot where the new growth begins, as in a plant; once this unaccountable and uninsurable faith is used up, the collapse soon follows; epochs and empires crumble no differently from business concerns when they lose their credit.

Musil's contemporary Hugo von Hofmannsthal spoke in this context of *das Gleitende*: the slipping away of the world in an access of aestheticized sentimentality. To locate Musil within the folds of *fin-de-siècle* Vienna is not to say that he preferred his spirituality *mit Schlag*, as it were. In many respects, he vigorously rebelled against the *Gefühls-kultur* that Schorske evokes; but he also, in other crucial respects, capitulated to it. *The Man Without Qualities* contains a record of both activities.

There was at any rate a great deal in Musil's background and milieu to complicate and enlarge his "technical" temperament. What he wanted was not *Genauigkeit* alone but rather *Genauigkeit und Seele*, "precision and soul." Rilke ("a poet who leads us into the future") was Musil's favorite poet largely because of the way that he struggled to salvage a sense of man's spiritual dignity from the debris of discredited "Great Ideas," on the one side, and crass ma-

EXPERIMENTS AGAINST REALITY

terialism on the other. Likewise, The supremely empirical Musil emerges as a champion of spiritual values in the face of the twin threats of desiccating rationalism and enthusiastic irrationalism. Which is to say that Musil was both a partisan of "soul," and that he was a sharp and exceedingly entertaining critic of "Soul"—upper case and in scare quotes.

It was in fact the union of his commitment to *Genauigkeit* with a thoroughgoing revulsion to what we might call spiritual sentimentality that fueled his most penetrating observations about the modern condition. In this, as in other respects, Musil sought to emulate the thinker who probably most deeply influenced his understanding of cultural matters, Friedrich Nietzsche. Indeed, *The Man Without Qualities* may be seen as an attempt to continue Nietzsche's anatomy of nihilism in the form of a novel. Its large ambition is to diagnose and, in its way, to treat the "mysterious" even "imponderable" disease of an age that breeds men without qualities.

In his 1924 essay on Oswald Spengler, Thomas Mann observed that "the spiritual essay" or "intellectual novel" was the dominant contemporary form of fiction. His own greatest novels (*The Magic Mountain, Doctor Faustus*) certainly answer to that description, as do many other classics of modernism. Broch's *Sleepwalkers* even has a long essay ("The Disintegration of Values," a very Musilian topic) distributed throughout it in short sections. Yet *The Man Without Qualities* was probably the most self-consciously essayistic of all these novels.

It's not simply that the book often reads like a series of essays, with its short, discursive chapters, its many quotations and allusions, and its wry chapter titles: "4. If there is a sense of reality, there must also be a sense of possibility";

"12. The lady whose love Ulrich won after a conversation about sports and mysticism"; "13. A racehorse of genius crystallizes the recognition of being a man without qualities," etc. Musil mimicked the essay form in order to enjoy something of the *authority* of assertion without incurring all of its responsibilities.

Although potentially disingenuous, this procedure offers the novelist one way to explore that hazy territory between the simple indicative, which outstrips his knowledge, and the frankly fictional, which seems insufficiently urgent. In a 1914 piece on the essay form, Musil defined the genre as "the strictest form attainable in an area where one can*not* work precisely." The essay, he wrote, "takes its form and method from science, its matter from art." In the first volume of *The Man Without Qualities*, the narrator observes that "a man who wants the truth becomes a scholar; a man who wants to give free play to his subjectivity may become a writer; but what should a man do who wants something in between?" The short answer, no doubt, is that he writes *The Man Without Qualities*.

In Musil's mind, the essay form was deeply connected to a major theme of *The Man Without Qualities*, the aestheticized view of the world that results from an inflated sense of possibility. More so even than most novels, *The Man Without Qualities* was written *sub specie possibilitatis*, under the aspect of possibility; its dominant mood is the subjunctive; Ulrich, the man without qualities, is one in whom the sense of possibility is overdeveloped—or, what amounts to the same thing, one in whom the sense of reality is in abeyance. A man with an ordinary sense of reality, Musil explains, nibbles at the "hook" of life without being aware of the line; but "a man with that sense of reality which can also be called a sense of possibility trawls a line through the water and has no idea whether there's any bait on it. His extraordinary indifference to the life snapping at the bait is matched by the risk he runs of doing utterly eccentric things."

Initially liberating, the triumph of possibility over reality is in the end an invitation to despair—something that Musil himself seems to have discovered along with Ulrich. But the pattern of Ulrich's escapades and interactions with others, especially in the first volume, presupposes the supremacy of possibility, as does the form—and, finally, the ultimate formlessness—of *The Man Without Qualities*. Kierkegaard summed up the attractions of this version of aestheticism for connoisseurs of the possible in his book *Either/Or*:

> A completely finished work has no relation to the poetic personality; in the case of posthumous papers one constantly feels, because of the incompletion, the desultoriness, a need to romance about the personality. Posthumous papers are like a ruin. . . . The art, then, is artistically to produce the same effect, the same appearance of carelessness and the accidental, the same anacoluthic flight of thought; the art consists in producing an enjoyment which never actually becomes present, but always has an element of the past in it, so that it is present in the past.

"A man without qualities," one of Musil's characters reflects, "does not say No to life, he says Not yet!"

Although Musil was in the process of veering off in many other directions in the last years he worked on the book, the portions that he actually published center largely around Ulrich. We never learn his last name (one symptom, perhaps, of his lack of qualities), but we do know quite a bit about Ulrich. The only son of a well-to-do lawyer of some scholarly achievement and pronounced pedantic tendencies, Ulrich is an unemployed thirty-two-year-old, who doesn't know what to do with himself. He is capable of great charm, but there is also something a little repulsive, even thuggish about him. He is "no respecter of rights unless he respects the person whose rights they are, which is not very often." In his school days, Ulrich's model was Napoleon, partly because of his "natural admiration for the criminal," partly because his teachers called Napoleon a tyrant. "Passionate and detached at the same time," Ulrich "never needed that overhauling and lubrication that is called probing one's conscience."

Before the story of the novel begins, Ulrich had made three attempts to be a "great man," first through the cavalry, then in civil engineering, and finally in mathematics. He left the army after having been reprimanded for seducing an archduke's wife, quit engineering after concluding that engineers tend to "have that peculiar, stiff, remote, superficial manner that never goes deeper inside than the epiglottis," and was now settled on his own in mathematics, doing respectable but unrewarding work. Ulrich seems to agree with the narrator that mathematics is "the source of an evil intelligence that while making man the lord of the earth has also made him the slave of his machines." Yet he loves mathematics if for no other reason than "the kind of people who could not endure it."

Ulrich gave up on greatness the day he happened to see a racehorse described as "a racehorse of genius." If a racehorse can be a "genius," what then? (What would Ulrich, or Musil, have made of contemporary culture, where every second pop singer is acclaimed a "genius"?) Concluding that "no matter what you do . . . it doesn't make the slightest difference," Ulrich decides "to take a year's leave of absence from his life in order to seek an appropriate application for his abilities." *The Man Without Qualities* is an account of that year's holiday from life.

Ulrich's basic sense of confusion is mirrored in his house, a small château that "had something blurred about it, like a double-exposed photograph." Faced with the prospect of redecorating it, he feels paralyzed by the infinite possibilities that yawn open before him. Free to choose any style "from the Assyrians to Cubism,"

> he was in that familiar state . . . of incoherent ideas spreading outward without a center, so characteristic of the present, and whose strange arithmetic adds up to a random proliferation of numbers without forming a unit. Finally he dreamed up only impracticable rooms, revolving rooms, kaleidoscopic rooms, adjustable scenery for the soul, and his ideas grew steadily more devoid of content.

Ulrich never really finds his vocation, but chance breaks in when his father helps arrange for him to become honorary secretary of a national campaign to celebrate the seventieth jubilee of the Emperor Franz Josef in 1918. Called the "Parallel Campaign" because of a similar celebration being planned in Germany, this was one of those phony endeavors whose aim is everything and nothing. Construed partly as a way of showing up the Germans (whose emperor would be celebrating merely his thirtieth jubilee), the Parallel Campaign was much more than a way of honoring Franz Josef. It was to be a celebration of Great Ideas— peace, patriotism, culture: a "spontaneous" outpouring of good will from the people that would be orchestrated down to the last detail. In short, the Parallel Campaign was the perfect repository for all manner of frustrated idealism, misguided beneficence, and outright charlatanry.

It was also the perfect repository for Musil's wicked

sense of humor. Who could have foretold that Kakania—Musil's name for the Austro-Hungarian Empire—would disappear before those celebrations could take place? In 1913, everything was still so *gemütlich*.

> Of course cars rolled on these roads too, but not too many! The conquest of the air was being prepared here too, but not too intensively. A ship would now and then be sent off to South America or East Asia, but not too often. There was no ambition for world markets or world power. Here at the very center of Europe . . . words such as "colony" and "overseas" sounded like something quite untried and remote. There was some show of luxury, but by no means as in such overrefined ways as the French. People went in for sports, but not as fanatically as the English. Ruinous sums of money were spent on the army, but only just enough to secure its position as the second-weakest among the great powers.

And yet even in cosy Kakania, many strange things were happening:

> Men who once merely headed minor sects have become aged celebrities; publishers and art dealers have become rich; new movements are constantly being started; everybody attends both the academic and the avant-garde shows, and even the avant-garde of the avant-garde; the family magazines have bobbed their hair; politicians like to sound off on the cultural arts, and newspapers make literary history. . . . Persons who would before never have been taken seriously became famous. Harshness mellowed, separations fused, intransigents made concessions to popularity, tastes already formed relapsed in uncertainties. Sharp boundaries everywhere became blurred and some

new, indefinable ability to form alliances brought new people and new ideas to the top.

Plus ça change, plus c'est la même chose.

Throughout the first volume of *The Man Without Qualities*, the Parallel Campaign is the scaffolding upon which Musil hangs his tale and parades his motley cast of characters. There is the Jewish banker Leo Fischel and his daughter Gerda; she takes up with a band of Christian nationalists who

> despised capitalism and maintained that no Jew had yet proved capable of serving as a great symbol of humanity. Leo Fischel called them anti-Semitic louts and would have forbidden them his house, but Gerda said, "You don't understand, Papa, they only mean it symbolically."

There are Ulrich's numerous inamoratas, for example the nymphomaniac he nicknamed Bonadea—"the good goddess"—who we see "stretched out on her back on the divan, her tender maternal belly in white batiste free to breathe unhampered by whalebone and laces. She called this position 'thinking.'" The wife of a prominent man and mother of two, Bonadea's favorite phrase was "highly respectable." "She could utter the words 'truth, goodness, and beauty' as often and as casually as someone else might say 'Thursday.'" No wonder V. S. Pritchett described Musil's sympathy as "tender and deadly."

And then there is Ulrich's cousin Ermelinda Tuzzi, a prime mover of the Parallel Campaign. Her real name is Hermine (like Musil's mother), but Ulrich nicknames her Diotima, after the high priestess of love in Plato's *Symposium*. The beautiful, unhappy wife of a high-ranking civil servant, Diotima was drawn to "Maeterlinck's batik-wrapped metaphysics," Novalis, and "most of all . . . the ineffable wave of anemic romanticism and yearning for God that, for a while, the machine age squirted out as an expression of its spiritual and artistic misgivings about itself." Her contribution to the Parallel Campaign included such assertions as "true Austria is the whole world" and "any feeling that isn't boundless is worthless."

One of Diotima's many admirers is Dr. Paul Arnheim, an immeasurably rich Prussian industrialist who is half-Jewish and speaks five languages. His chief ambition is to bring "ideas into the spheres of power," and he has written many books and pamphlets declaring the union of "soul and economics." Not that Arnheim is a narrow specialist; on the contrary, he also writes extensively on "algebraic series, benzol rings, the materialist as well as the universalist philosophy of history, bridge supports, the evolution of music, the essence of the automobile, Hata 606, the theory of relativity, Bohr's atomic theory, autogenous welding, the flora of the Himalayas, psychoanalysis . . . and all the other achievements that prevent a time so greatly enriched by them from turning out good, wholesome, integral human beings." It seemed to both Arnheim and Diotima that they had been fated by destiny to find true, if unfulfillable, love with each other; but then it turns out that Arnheim's chief interest in the Parallel Campaign had something to do with gaining control of the Galician oil fields.

There are three other characters that deserve to be mentioned. The first two are Ulrich's boyhood friend Walter, a failed pianist, and his young wife of three years, Clarisse, a chilly, neurotic, destructively unnurturing woman. Clarisse "had considered Walter a genius since she was fifteen, because she had always intended to marry only a genius. She would not let him fail her in this." As the daughter of a painter renowned for stage designs, Clarisse rebelled by growing up to hate "everything voluptuary in art." She refuses to sleep with Walter when he plays Wagner, taunting him with his artistic sterility. Walter is a different, more obvious sort of narcissist: "for him, the very act of moving his own arm was fraught with spiritual adventure, or else it was paralyzed in loving contemplation of itself." Walter is one of those people who was full of promise when young but who settled into cruel ordinariness as he got older. His solution to this problem—still a common solution among the terminally disappointed—is to blame his failure on the hopeless decadence of the age.

This tactic has many advantages. "Instead of *his* feeling bad and unable to work, it was now the times that were sick, while he was fine. His life, which had come to nothing, was now, all at once, tremendously accounted for, justified on a world-historical scale." No longer does Walter talk about "contemporary art" and "the art of the future," ideas that Clarrisse has associated with him since she was fifteen. Now, he

> would draw a line somewhere—in music stopping at, say, Bach, in literature at Stifter, in painting at Ingres—and explain that everything that came later was florid, degenerate, over-sophisticated and on the downward path. And he became increasingly violent in his assertion that in a time so poisoned at its spiritual roots as the present an artist of real integrity must abstain from creation altogether. But the treacherous thing was that although such austere opinions issued from his mouth, what issued from his room, as soon as he had locked himself in, was, more and more often, the sound of Wagner's music, that is to say, a kind of music that in earlier years he had taught Clarisse to despise as the

perfect example of a philistine, florid, degenerate era, and to which he himself had now become addicted as to thickly brewed, hot, intoxicating poison.

Finally, some mention must be made of the carpenter Christian Moosbrugger: a huge, physically powerful man who is something of a simpleton. Moosbrugger has "a face blessed by God with every sign of goodness" but he also just happens to be a crazed sex murderer whose trial for brutally slaughtering a prostitute forms one of the many leitmotifs of *The Man Without Qualities*. Whether Moosbrugger is mentally competent to stand trial is a question mooted throughout the book; since he tends to regard his acts as having "perched on him like birds that had flown in from somewhere or other," perhaps not. Although Musil never resolved Moosbrugger's fate, or his exact significance for the novel, it is clear that Moosbrugger represents the dark, unconscious viciousness and irrationalism pulsating underneath Kakania's rancid optimism. "If mankind could dream collectively [*als Ganzes*]," Ulrich reflects, "it would dream Moosbrugger." Ulrich flirts with trying to get Moosbrugger acquitted, and the increasingly deranged Clarisse becomes obsessed with him: "the murderer," she exclaims, "is musical!" In Moosbrugger, Clarisse envisions the eruption of a transforming violence that would sweep away the detritus of her frustrated, rudderless existence.

Musil has great fun playing these characters off one another. As V. S. Pritchett noted in an admiring 1962 essay, one of Musil's great achievements is to have made such exotic characters humanly engaging. Another achievement, in the first volume, anyway, was to have woven his various "essayistic" themes so seamlessly into the novel. As already noted, one of the most important of these themes concerns the Nietzschean question of the value—the human, moral value—of scientific knowledge. Musil ridicules the Romanticism of characters like Diotima who condemn science for disenchanting the world with "facts." And yet he seems to side with Ulrich when he explains that "knowledge is a mode of conduct, a passion. At bottom, an impermissible mode of conduct: like dipsomania, sex mania, homicidal mania, the compulsion to know forms its own character that is off balance."

In one pivotal chapter, Musil reflects on the "peculiar predilection of scientific thinking for mechanical, statistical, and physical explanations that have, as it were, the heart cut out of them." This is the key passage:

> The scientific mind sees kindness only as a special form of egotism; brings emotions into line with glandular secretions; notes that eight or nine tenths of a human being consists of water; explains our celebrated moral freedom as an automatic mental by-product of free trade; reduces beauty to good digestion and the proper distribution of fatty tissue; graphs the annual statistical curves of births and suicides to show that our most intimate personal decisions are programmed behavior; sees a connection between ecstasy and mental disease; equates the anus and the mouth as the rectal and the oral openings at either end of the same tube—such ideas, which expose the trick, as it were, behind the magic of human illusions, can always count on a kind of prejudice in their favor as being impeccably scientific.

Scientific rationality in this sense is not merely disillusioning; it is radically dehumanizing. It replaces the living texture of experience with a skeleton of "causes," "drives," "impulses," and the like. The enormous power over nature that science has brought man, Musil suggests, is only part of its attraction. Psychologically just as important is the power it gives one to dispense with the *human* claims of experience. How liberating to know that kindness is just another form of egotism! That beauty is merely a matter of fatty tissues being arranged properly! That every inflection of our emotional life is nothing but the entirely predictable result of glandular activity! *Just another, merely, nothing but . . .* How liberating, how dismissive are these instruments of dispensation—but how *un*true, finally, to our experience.

Musil presents scientific rationality as a *temptation* as well as an accomplishment because he sees that inherent in its view of the world is an invitation to forget one's humanity. It is this Promethean aspect of science that links it with evil. The feeling that "nothing in life can be relied on unless it is firmly nailed down," Musil writes, is "a basic feeling embedded in the sobriety of science; and though we are too respectable to call it the Devil, a slight whiff of brimstone still clings to it."

At the same time, however, Musil is never willing to side wholeheartedly with the Romantic attack on science. A bit earlier, he reminds his readers that

> One must not forget that basically the scientific cast of mind is more God-oriented than the aesthetic mind, ready to submit to "Him" the moment "He" deigns to show Himself under the conditions it prescribes for recognizing Him, while our aesthetes, confronted with His manifestation, would find only that His talent was not original and that His view of the world was not sufficiently intelligible to rank Him with really God-given talents.

Musil's reflections on the moral significance of scientific rationality are exceptionally subtle and illuminating. Especially impressive is the way that he weaves these reflections into his narrative, adjusting their resonance and implication to each character, and, finally, showing how the passion for reason was powerless to save Kakania from the great irrationality that was poised to engulf it.

Volume one concludes after Ulrich's proposal to establish a General Secretariat for Precision and Soul is (not surprisingly) rebuffed by the organizers of the Parallel Campaign. The machinations of the Campaign now begin to recede and the story of Ulrich and his sister, Agathe, comes to the fore. (Like many of the important female characters, Agathe's name is of some significance: it comes from the Greek word *agathos*, "the good," i.e., that to which we all aspire.) Brought together after many years' separation by the death of their father, the siblings rediscover each other. The mood of the book now changes substantially: gone is the bright, satirical tone of the first volume. This may have been partly due to darkening elements in Musil's life. Since at least the mid-Twenties, Musil's financial condition had been precarious; increasingly, his psychological condition followed suit. In 1929, the year before the first volume of *The Man Without Qualities* appeared, he suffered a nervous breakdown. Friends started a Musil Society to help support the novelist, but he was never really to know financial security again for the rest of his life. In 1933, he and Martha left Germany for Vienna when Hitler came to power; in 1938, they left for Switzerland after the Anschluss delivered Austria into Hitler's hands. In the meantime, in 1936, Musil suffered a stroke, but was able to work again before long.

The later portions of *The Man Without Qualities* have their admirers. But for many they will be slow going. The long conversations between Ulrich and Agathe, and the detailed ruminations on various religious texts, are dramatically static. There are many enlivening episodes and aperçus as the pages accumulate, but accumulate they do; the novel never really recovers its momentum. This is a pity, for Musil clearly invested a great deal in the story of Ulrich and Agathe; there is even some evidence that he regarded the story of their relationship as the centerpiece of the book: when he began working on the novel, in the mid-Twenties, his working title was "The Twin Sister." It is daunting to think of the thousand pages of the first volume of *The Man Without Qualities* as prolegomenon, but there you are. Unfortunately, this is a case in which aspiration did not match achievement. As Musil himself acknowledged in a note, "Volume One closes approximately at the high point of an arch; on the other side it has no support."

It has often been pointed out that, at bottom, Musil was a kind of moralist. Like his beloved Rilke, he wanted his work to communicate the imperative "Du mußt dein leben ändern" ("You must change your life"). He hoped that the relationship between Ulrich and Agathe would furnish a model for that imperative. It is here that Musil's investment in Nietzsche betrays him. The title of the second volume of *The Man Without Qualities* is "Into the Millennium (The Criminals)." The criminals in question were Ulrich and Agathe. Their crime, in the first instance, was to shatter, or attempt to shatter, the traditional bourgeois moral code. Musil signals this by hinting at an incestuous union between them. He hoped that by placing the siblings "beyond good and evil" he could picture a form of life that transcended the many human and cultural deficiencies he had anatomized in the first volume. Musil's term for this state of transcendence was *der andere Zustand*, "the other condition," a species of aestheticized religious experience that Musil summarized in one essay as "the condition of love, of goodness, of renunciation of the world, of contemplation, of vision, of approach to God, of entrancement, of will-lessness, of meditation," etc. One might dismiss such experiences, he wrote, did they not leave traces everywhere and did they "not constitute the marrow of our morality and idealism."

> One finds again and again the presence of another world, like a solid ocean bottom from which the restless waves of the ordinary world have drawn back; and in the image of this world there is neither measure nor precision, neither purpose nor cause: good and evil simply fall away.

Musil's evocation of "the other condition" is attractively poetic; but it does not offer the existential transformation he seeks. As one commentator on *The Man Without Qualities* noted, in the relationship between Agathe and Ulrich there is "the repeated implication . . . that there might be a way to have a permanent vacation *in* reality." But reality will always reassert itself, and with reality come all the moral strictures *this side* of good and evil. At one point, Ulrich confides, "I believe that all our moral injunctions are concessions to a society of savages." In fact, it is only by heeding our moral injunctions that we may be preserved from savagery. Scholars conjecture that the last words Musil wrote the morning he died were those quoted above in an epigraph to this chapter in which Ulrich acknowledges that he and Agathe were "nihilists and activists," not realists. Perhaps Musil was coming around to that realization as well.

Part Two

James Fitzjames Stephen
v. John Stuart Mill

The most mischievous errors on record . . . [have been] half-truths taken as the whole.
—Samuel Taylor Coleridge, *Literary Remains*, 1838

From the winter of 1821, when I first read Bentham, . . . I had what might truly be called an object in life; to be a reformer of the world. My conception of my own happiness was entirely identified with this object.
—John Stuart Mill, *Autobiography*, 1873

Complete moral tolerance is possible only when men have become completely indifferent to each other—that is to say, when society is at an end.
—James Fitzjames Stephen, *Liberty, Equality, Fraternity*, 1873

IT IS A melancholy truth that bad arguments often prevail over better ones, and that very bad arguments sometimes gain a virtual monopoly in the court of public sentiment. In extreme cases, a bad argument so mesmerizes the public that its status *as* an argument—as one, necessarily limited, point of view competing with others—tends to deliquesce. It takes on an aura of inevitability. It seems to present not so much a way of looking at the world as the world itself. When this happens, serious alternatives suffer the handicap of being regarded as mere "partisan" or political gestures, even as the partisan nature of the triumphant argument is increasingly lost to view. Dissent from this new orthodoxy then appears as dissent from the simple reality of the way things are: less a challenge than a perversion.

Liberalism, broadly defined, has long occupied this enviable position. It prescribes not only the terms of debate, but also the rhetorical atmosphere in which any debate must take place. Many of its central doctrines—above all, perhaps, its uncritical celebration of "innovation" in social, political, and moral matters—are taken-for-granted articles of belief. Do not be misled by any renewed attention that may from time to time be lavished on welfare reform, tax cuts, "family values," law and order, civility, or military preparedness. Laudable though they may be, necessary though they often are, these and other remedial initiatives identified as "conservative" today take place in a context saturated by liberal assumptions. For better or worse—no doubt for better and worse—we are all liberals now: by dint of contagion if not conviction. How could it be otherwise? As the English historian Maurice Cowling noted in his book *Mill and Liberalism* (1963, rev. ed. 1990), for many years now "to use liberal language has been taken to be *intelligent*: to reject it evidence of *stupidity*." That conviction has long since been elevated into a fundamental *donnée* of intellectual life: an unspoken assumption that colors every aspect of political and moral deliberation.

No one was more important in bringing about this state of affairs than Cowling's subject, John Stuart Mill (1806–1873). Mill would not have been surprised that to speak as he taught one to speak—to speak in Mill, as it were—was to be thought intelligent, while to speak otherwise was to be thought stupid. He believed it himself; and he did everything in his very considerable powers to encourage the belief in others. "The stupid party" was Mill's own summary description of conservatives (this despite his admiration for Coleridge). For anyone interested in understanding the nature of the modern liberal consensus, the extraordinary success of Mill's rhetoric and the doctrines it advances afford a number of lessons. Above all, it provides an object lesson in the immense seductiveness inherent in a certain type of skeptical moralizing. Together with Rousseau, Mill supplied nearly all of the arguments and most of the emotional weather—the texture of sentiment—that have gone into defining the liberal vision of the world. His peculiar brand of utilitarianism—a cake of Benthamite hedonism glazed with Wordsworthian sentimentality—accounts for part of Mill's appeal: it provides a perfect recipe for embellishing programmatic shallowness with a cosmetic patina of spirituality. It is a recipe that has proven to be irresistible to those infatuated with the spectacle of their own virtue.

Another large part of Mill's appeal rests on his "feminism." I mean his conviction, put forward in *The Subjection of Women* (1869), that differences between the sexes were accidental and that, as Leslie Stephen put it, "women could be turned into men by trifling changes in the law." Both are indispensable elements in the intoxicating potion that constitutes Millian liberalism and that makes much of his thinking seem so contemporary.[1]

Mill was undoubtedly a complex figure. As the historian Gertrude Himmelfarb has shown in *On Liberty and Lib-*

---

1 Mill's "feminism" got an additional boost from his long intimacy with Harriet Taylor—Mrs. John Taylor. After her husband died, Mill married Taylor and then, after her death, adulated her in embarrassingly extravagant terms; it is noteworthy that what Mill himself described as his "lofty minded" relationship with Harriet Taylor was apparently never consummated.

eralism: The Case of John Stuart Mill (1974), the apostle of radical liberalism was matched by a more circumspect figure, the "other Mill" whose ideas about the limits of freedom are often at odds with those of his alter ego. But the Mill who matters for the betrayal of liberalism is the radical Mill, the Mill of *On Liberty*. More than any other work, this brief manifesto provides the intellectual and affective keys to understanding the success of Mill's doctrine. *On Liberty* was published in 1859, coincidentally the same year as *On the Origin of Species*. Darwin's book has been credited—and blamed—for all manner of moral and religious mischief. But in the long run *On Liberty* may have effected an even greater revolution in sentiment. It did an immense amount to codify the way we think, not about the world, exactly—Mill was not a scientist—but about what matters in the way we comport ourselves in the world.

The first thing to be said about *On Liberty* is that it is a masterpiece of liberal polemic. Its core ideas are as the air we breathe: unnoticed because ubiquitous. Mill's arguments and pronouncements about man as a "progressive being," the extent of individual autonomy, the limits of acceptable moral and legal censure, the importance of innovation and (perhaps his most famous phrase) "experiments in living" are all familiar to the point of invisibility. Likewise his corollary insistence on the poverty of custom, prejudice, and tradition. Mill's contentions on these subjects are nowadays less objects of debate than of reverence: moral principles that discussion is expected to presuppose, not challenge. As Professor Himmelfarb put it, "What Mill proposed as a bold new doctrine has come down to us as an obvious, axiomatic truth."

But the success of Mill's teaching in the court of public sentiment says nothing about the cogency of his arguments. In fact, Mill's central arguments are open to—and have from the beginning been subjected to—serious criticism. Yet they have raged like wildfire through the Western world, consuming everything that stands in their path. Which means, among other things, that they exert an appeal quite distinct from any intellectual merit they may possess. (And which in turn may suggest something about the potential liability of being thought "intelligent" by Millians—as well as the possible advantages of what Mill castigated as "stupidity.")

As for the nature of Mill's arguments, consider, for example, his famous plea on behalf of moral, social, and intellectual "experiments." Throughout history, Mill argues, the authors of such innovations have been objects of ridicule, persecution, and oppression; they have been ignored, silenced, exiled, imprisoned, even killed. But (Mill continues) we owe every step of progress, intellectual as well as moral, to the daring of innovators. "Without them," he writes, "human life would become a stagnant pool. Not only is it they who introduce good things which did not before exist; it is they who keep the life in those which already exist." Ergo, innovators—"developed human beings" is one phrase Mill uses for such paragons—should not merely be tolerated but positively be encouraged as beacons of future improvement.

The philosopher David Stove called this the "They All Laughed at Christopher Columbus" argument. In a penetrating essay in his book *Cricket Versus Republicanism* (1995), Stove noted that "the Columbus argument" (as he called it for short) "has swept the world."

With every day that has passed since Mill published it, it has been more influential than it was the day before. In the intellectual and moral dissolution of the West in the twentieth century, every step has depended on conservatives being disarmed, at some critical point, by the Columbus argument; by revolutionaries claiming that any resistance made to them is only another instance of that undeserved hostility which beneficial innovators have so regularly met with in the past.

The amazing thing about the success of the Columbus argument is that it depends on premises that are so obviously faulty. Indeed, as Stove observes, a moment's reflection reveals that the Columbus argument is undermined by a downright glaring weakness. Granted that every change for the better has depended on someone embarking on a new departure: well, so too has every change for the worse. And surely, Stove writes, there have been at least as many proposed innovations which "were or would have been for the worse as ones which were or would have been for the better." Which means that we have at least as much reason to discourage innovators as to encourage them, especially when their innovations bear on things as immensely complex as the organization of society.

The triumph of Millian liberalism shows that such objections have fallen on deaf ears. But why? Why have "innovation," "originality," etc., become mesmerizing charms that neutralize criticism before it even gets started when so much that is produced in the name of innovation is obviously a change for the worse? An inventory of the fearsome social, political, and moral innovations made in this century alone should have made every thinking person wary of unchaperoned innovation. One reason that innovation has survived with its reputation intact, Stove notes, is that Mill and his heirs have been careful to supply a "one-sided diet of examples." It is a technique as simple as it is effective:

Mention no past innovators except those who were innovators-for-the-better. Harp away endlessly on the examples of Columbus and Copernicus, Galileo and Bruno, Socrates and (if you think the traffic will bear it) Jesus. Conceal the fact that there must have been at least one innovator-for-the-worse for every one of these (very overworked) good guys. Never mention Lenin or Pol Pot, Marx or Hegel, Robespierre or the Marquis de Sade, or those forgotten innovators of genius to whom humanity has been indebted for any of the countless insane theories which have ever acquired a following in astronomy, geology, or biology.

Mill never missed an opportunity to expatiate on the value of "originality," "eccentricity," and the like. "The amount of eccentricity in a society," he wrote, "has generally been proportional to the amount of genius, mental vigor, and moral courage it contained." But you never caught Mill dilating on the "improvement on established practice" inaugurated by Robespierre and St. Just, or the "experiments in living" conducted by the Marquis de Sade. (It is hardly surprising that, today, the phrase "experiments in living" is redolent of the fatuous lifestyle "experiments" of the 1960s; whatever else can be said about the phrase, Stove is surely right that it represented "a sickeningly dishonest attempt to capture some of the deserved prestige of science for things that had not the remotest connection with science"—principally "certain sexual and domestic arrangements of a then-novel kind.")

David Stove offers some telling insights into the weaknesses of Mill's liberalism. But in order to understand its world-conquering success, one has to go beyond simple credulity and an abundance of one-sided examples. Flattery comes into it. Mill was exceptionally adroit at appealing to his readers' moral vanity. When he spoke (as he was always speaking) of "persons of decided mental superiority" he made it seem as though he might actually be speaking about *them*. Mill said that there was "no reason that all human existence should be constructed on some one or some small number of patterns." Quite right! Even if persons of genius are always likely to be "a small minority," still we must "preserve the soil in which they grow." Consequently, people have a duty to shun custom and nurture their individual "self-development" if they are not to jeopardize "their fair share of happiness" and the "mental, moral, and aesthetic stature of which their nature is capable."

Mill's blandishments went even deeper. In *On Liberty*, Mill presented himself as a prophet of individual liberty. He has often been regarded as such, especially by liberal academics, who of course have been instrumental in propagating the gospel according to Mill. And "gospel" is the *mot juste*. Like many radical reformers, Mill promised almost boundless freedom, but he arrived bearing an exacting new system of belief. In this sense, as Maurice Cowling argues, *On Liberty* has been "one of the most influential of modern political tracts," chiefly because "its purpose has been misunderstood." Contrary to common opinion, Cowling wrote, Mill's book was

> not so much a plea for individual freedom, as a means of ensuring that Christianity would be superseded by that form of liberal, rationalising utilitarianism which went by the name of the Religion of Humanity. Mill's liberalism was a dogmatic, religious one, not the soothing night-comforter for which it is sometimes mistaken. Mill's object was not to free men, but to convert them, and convert them to a peculiarly exclusive, peculiarly insinuating moral doctrine.

Mill wished to moralize all social activity. . . . Mill, no less than Marx, Nietzsche, or Comte, claimed to replace Christianity by "something better." Atheists and agnostics, humanists and free-thinkers may properly give thanks to Mill.

This tension in Mill's work—between Mill the libertarian and Mill the moralistic utilitarian—helps to account for the vertiginous quality that suffuses the liberalism for which *On Liberty* was a kind of founding scripture. Mill's announced enemy can be summed up in words like "custom," "prejudice," "established morality." All his work goes to undermine these qualities—not because the positions they articulate are necessarily in error but simply because, being customary, accepted on trust, established by tradition, they have not been subjected to the acid-test of his version of the utilitarian calculus. (Mill elsewhere refers to such calculation as "rational self-conscious scrutiny," the implication being that anything else is less than completely rational.) The tradition that Mill opposed celebrated custom, prejudice, and established morality precisely because they had prevailed and given good service through the vicissitudes of time and change; their longevity was an important token of their worthiness. It was in this sense, for example, that Edmund Burke extolled prejudice, writing that "prejudice renders a man's virtue his habit. . . . Through just prejudice, his duty becomes a part of his nature."

Mill overturned this traditional view. Indeed, he was instrumental in getting the public to associate "prejudice" indelibly with "bigotry." For Mill, established morality is suspect first of all *because* it is established. His liberalism is essentially corrosive of existing societal arrangements, institutions, and morality. At bottom, Mill's philosophy is a kind of inversion of Alexander Pope's optimism: "Whatever is, is suspect" might have been Mill's motto. He constantly castigated such things as the "magical influence of custom" ("magical" being a negative epithet for Mill), the "despotism of custom [that] is everywhere the standing hindrance to human advancement," the "tyranny of opinion" that makes it so difficult for "the progressive principle" to flourish. According to Mill, the "greater part of the world has, properly speaking, no history because the sway of custom has been complete."

Such passages reveal the core of moral arrogance inhabiting Mill's liberalism. They also suggest to what extent he remained—despite the various criticisms he made of the master—a faithful heir of Jeremy Bentham's utilitarianism. And I do not mean only the Bentham who propounded the principle of "the greatest happiness for the greatest number," but also the Bentham who applauded the proceedings of the Star Chamber, advocated the imprisonment of beggars, defended torture, and devised the "Panopticon"—a machine, he said, for "grinding rogues honest"—to keep miscreants under constant surveillance.[2] Liberty was always on Mill's lips; a new orthodoxy was ever in his heart. There is an important sense in which the libertarian streak in *On Liberty* is little more than a prophylactic against the coerciveness that its assumption of virtuous rationality presupposes.

Such "paradoxes" (to put it politely) show themselves wherever the constructive part of Mill's doctrine is glimpsed through his cheerleading for freedom and eccentricity. Mill's doctrine of liberty begins with a promise of emancipation. The individual, in order to construct a "life plan" worthy of his nature, must shed the carapace of

---

2 See Richard A. Posner's *The Economics of Justice* (Harvard, 1981), pages 33–35, on this aspect of Bentham's teaching.

inherited opinion. He must learn to subject all his former beliefs to rational scrutiny. He must dare to be "eccentric," "novel," "original." At the same time, Mill notes, not without misgiving, that

> As mankind improve, the number of doctrines which are no longer disputed or doubted will be constantly on the increase; the well-being of mankind may almost be measured by the number and gravity of the truths which have reached the point of being uncontested. The cessation, on one question after another, of serious controversy is one of the necessary incidents of the consolidation of opinion— a consolidation as salutary in the case of true opinions as it is dangerous and noxious when the opinions are erroneous.

In other words, the partisan of Millian liberalism undertakes the destruction of inherited custom and belief in order to construct a bulwark of custom and belief that can be inherited. As Mill put it in his *Autobiography* (posthumously published in 1873),

> I looked forward, through the present age of loud disputes but generally weak convictions, to a future . . . [in which] convictions as to what is right and wrong, useful and pernicious, [will be] deeply engraven on the feelings by early education and general unanimity of sentiment, and so firmly grounded in reason and in the true exigencies of life, that they shall not, like all former and present creeds, religious, ethical, and political, require to be periodically thrown off and replaced by others.

So: a "unanimity of sentiment" (a.k.a. custom) is all well and good as long as it is grounded in the "true exigencies of life"—as defined, of course, by J. S. Mill.

One measure of Mill's triumph is that the "unanimity" of sentiment that he looked forward to has long since been all but achieved. Not that Mill has lacked critics. On the contrary, from the very beginning both his utilitarianism and his doctrine of liberty have been subjected to searching, indeed devastating, criticism. That they not only survived but also thrived is a testament to—among other things—the beguiling power of Mill's rhetoric and the seductive spell of his core doctrines. On the principle that sooner or later reality must vanquish illusion, however, it is worth revisiting certain criticisms of Mill's liberalism. Repetition of an old truth may eventually dislodge even stubborn new falsehoods.

By far the most concentrated and damaging single attack on Mill's liberalism is *Liberty, Equality, Fraternity*, first published serially in the *Pall Mall Gazette* in 1872–1873, and then in book form in March 1873 in the last year of Mill's life. It was written by the lawyer, judge, and journalist Sir James Fitzjames Stephen (1829–1894), Leslie Stephen's older brother and hence—such is the irony of history—Virginia Woolf's uncle. Mill himself never responded to Stephen's book beyond observing, as Leslie Stephen reports in his excellent biography of his brother, that he thought the book "more likely to repel than attract." But several of Mill's disciples responded—the most famous of whom was the liberal politician and journalist John Morley (1838–1923). Stephen brought out a second edition of his book the following year, 1874, in which he reproduces and replies to many criticisms raised by Morley and others. Leslie Stephen described *Liberty, Equality, Fraternity* as "mainly controversial and negative." *Pugnacious* and *devastating* would be equally appropriate adjectives. As one commentator put it, Stephen made "mincemeat" of Mill. And when it appeared, the book sparked a lively controversy, rousing, as Leslie Stephen noted, "the anger of some, the sympathy of others, and the admiration of all who liked to see hard hitting on any side of a great question." And yet for nearly one hundred years *Liberty, Equality, Fraternity* disappeared almost without a trace. After 1874, it was not republished until Cambridge University Press brought out a new edition in 1967.[3]

Writing in the introduction to the Chicago edition of *Liberty, Equality, Fraternity*, Richard Posner described the book as "a magnificent period piece: as vivid and revealing a document of British imperialism in its heyday as John Buchan's novel *Prester John* and Kipling's verse would be a generation later." Judge Posner was at least partly right. Written directly after Stephen completed a stint as Chief Justice of Calcutta, the book is full of the justified confidence of flourishing empire. Stephen saw the great good that the English had brought to India in health and education, in maintaining civic order, in putting down barbaric customs like suttee. He recognized clearly that following Mill's liberal principles would make carrying out that civilizing mandate difficult if not impossible. And he decided forthrightly that the fault lay with Mill's liberalism, not with civilization.

It would be a mistake, however, to regard *Liberty, Equality, Fraternity* merely as a "period piece." As Judge Posner acknowledges, it is also "an audacious and radical challenge to classical liberalism." The challenge is all the

---

3 The Cambridge edition, with notes by R. J. White, has since gone out of print. But that text, edited and with a new introduction by the legal philosopher Richard A. Posner, was reprinted by the University of Chicago in 1991. Another edition, edited and with an introduction by Stuart D. Warner, was published by Liberty Fund in 1993.

more audacious because it emerged from ground very close to Mill. Stephen was himself a Liberal (though one of conservative temperament) and a utilitarian of decidedly undoctrinaire persuasion. He comments at one point that "Bentham's whole conception of happiness as something which could, as it were, be served out in rations, is open to great objection." Stephen was too moral to be a strict utilitarian, too pragmatic to abandon that philosophy altogether. Leslie Stephen described him as "at once a Puritan and a Utilitarian," which seems about right. Stephen was also an ardent admirer of many aspects of Mill's philosophy; early on in *Liberty, Equality, Fraternity* he called Mill "a great man to whom I am in every way indebted." He had even reviewed *On Liberty* warmly in the *Saturday Review* when it first appeared. But in time he came to regard Mill's doctrine of liberty—and the apotheosis of an abstract equality and fraternity that flows from it—as an unmitigated disaster. *Liberty, Equality, Fraternity* explains why.

Judge Posner describes as "naughty" Stephen's decision to adopt the revolutionary motto "Liberty, Equality, Fraternity" as the title of a book about Millian liberalism. But that is perhaps because Posner's sympathies on many issues are closer to Mill's than to Stephen's. In fact, the title is perfect. As Stephen explains in his opening pages, the book is an effort to examine "the doctrines which are rather hinted at than expressed by the phrase 'Liberty, Equality, Fraternity.'" Although that phrase had its origin in the French Revolution, Stephen noted, it nonetheless had come to express "the creed of a religion"—one "less definite than most forms of Christianity, but not on that account the less powerful." Indeed, the motto "Liberty, Equality, Fraternity" epitomized "one of the most penetrating influences of the day," namely the "Religion of Humanity"—the secular, socialistic *alternative* to Christianity put forward in different ways by thinkers like Auguste Comte, Jeremy Bentham, and John Stuart Mill. "It is one of the commonest beliefs of the day," Stephen wrote, "that the human race collectively has before it splendid destinies of various kinds, and that the road to them is to be found in the removal of all restraints on human conduct, in the recognition of a substantial equality between all human creatures, and in fraternity in general." Taking *On Liberty*, *The Subjection of Women*, and *Utilitarianism* (1863) as his primary texts, Stephen shows in tonic detail why these beliefs are mistaken and why, should they be put into practice, they are bound to result in moral chaos and widespread personal unhappiness.

The phrase "Liberty, Equality, Fraternity" suggests the immense rhetorical advantage that liberalism begins with. One can hardly criticize the slogan without arousing the suspicion that one must be a partisan of oppression, servitude, and dissension. "Liberty," Stephen notes, "is a eulogistic word." Therein lies its magic. Substitute a neutral synonym—"permission," for example, or "leave" (as in "I give you leave to go")—and the spell is broken: the troops will not rally. It is the same with *equality* and *fraternity*. The eulogistic aspect of liberalism means that its critics are practically required to begin with an apology. So it is hardly surprising that Stephen stresses at the beginning of his book that he is "not the advocate of Slavery, Caste, and Hatred" and that there is a sense in which he, too, can endorse the phrase "liberty, equality, fraternity."

Stephen begins by pointing out that Mill and other advocates of the Religion of Humanity have exaggerated the advantages and minimized the disadvantages that these qualities involve. For one thing, taken without further specification "liberty, equality, fraternity" are far too abstract to form the basis of anything like a religion. They are also inherently *dis*establishing with regard to existing social arrangements; that indeed is one reason they exert so great an appeal for the radical sensibility. Take Mill's doctrine of liberty, which boils down to the exhortation: Let everyone please himself in any way he likes so long as he does not hurt his neighbor. According to Mill, any moral system that aimed at more—that aimed, for example, at improving the moral character of society at large or the individuals in it—would be wrong in principle.[4] But this view, Stephen notes, would "condemn every existing system of morals."

> Strenuously preach and rigorously practise the doctrine that our neighbor's private character is nothing to us, and the number of unfavorable judgments formed, and therefore the number of inconveniences inflicted by them can be reduced as much as we please, and the province of liberty can be enlarged in corresponding ratio. Does any reasonable man wish for this? Could anyone desire gross licentiousness, monstrous extravagance, ridiculous vanity, or the like, to be unnoticed, or, being known, to inflict no inconveniences which can possibly be avoided?

As Stephen dryly observes, pace Mill, "the custom of looking upon certain courses of conduct with aversion is the essence of morality."

The great pragmatic lesson to be drawn from *Liberty*,

---

4 Not that Mill held to this radical doctrine consistently. In a letter of 1829, for example, Mill writes, in direct contradiction to the position he put forward in *On Liberty*, that "government exists for all purposes whatever that are for man's good: and the highest and most important of these purposes is the improvement of man himself as a moral and intelligent being."

Equality, Fraternity concerns the relation between freedom and power. "Power," Stephen insists, "precedes liberty"— that is, "liberty, from the very nature of things, is dependent upon power; and . . . it is only under the protection of a powerful, well-organized, and intelligent government that any liberty can exist at all." It is for this reason that it makes no sense to ask whether liberty *tout court* is a good thing. The question whether liberty is a good or bad thing, Stephen writes, "is as irrational as the question whether fire is a good or bad thing. It is both good and bad according to time, place, and circumstance." As Gertrude Himmelfarb notes, while we may have learned Lord Acton's dictum that absolute power corrupts absolutely, we have not yet learned that "absolute liberty may also corrupt absolutely." Mill's failure to recognize these truths endows his doctrine of liberty with extraordinary malleability. It also infuses that doctrine with an air of unreality whenever it approaches the problem of freedom in everyday life. It is axiomatic with Mill that "society has no business *as* society to decide anything to be wrong which concerns only the individual." It follows, Mill writes, that "fornication, for example, must be tolerated and so must gambling." But should a person be free to be a pimp? Or to keep a gambling house? Mill thinks these are exceptionally difficult questions:

> Although the public, or the State are not warranted in authoritatively deciding, for purposes of repression or punishment, that such or such conduct affecting only the interests of the individual is good or bad, they are fully justified in assuming, if they regard it as bad, that its being so or not is at least a disputable question: That, this being supposed, they cannot be acting wrongly in endeavoring to exclude the influence of solicitations which are not disin-

terested, of instigators who cannot possibly be impartial—
who have a direct personal interest on one side, and that
side the one which the State believes to be wrong, and who
confessedly promote it for personal objects only.

To which Stephen replies: "There is a kind of ingenuity
which carries its own refutation on its face. How can the
State or the public be competent to determine any question
whatever if it is not competent to decide that gross vice is a
bad thing? I do not," Stephen continues,

> think the State ought to stand bandying compliments with
> pimps. "Without offence to your better judgment, dear sir,
> and without presuming to set up my opinion against yours,
> I beg to observe that I am entitled for certain purposes to
> treat the question whether your views of life are right as
> one which admits of two opinions. I am far from express-
> ing absolute condemnation of an experiment in living from
> which I dissent, . . . but still I am compelled to observe that
> you are not altogether unbiased by personal considerations.
> . . ." My feeling is that if society gets its grip on the collar
> of such a fellow it should say to him, "You dirty rascal, it
> may be a question whether you should be suffered to
> remain in your native filth untouched, or whether my
> opinion about you should be printed by the lash on your
> bare back. That question will be determined without the
> smallest reference to your wishes or feelings; but as to the
> nature of my opinion about you, there can be no question
> at all."

The contrast of tone between Mill and Stephen could not
be more graphic. And here we approach a subject that has
become almost undiscussable. As Stephen noted in his letters, there was a peculiar "want of virility" about Mill. In

part it was a matter of abstractedness: Mill seemed to him "comparable to a superlatively crammed senior wrangler, whose body has been stunted by his brains." He was "too much a calculating machine and too little of a human being." But besides abstractedness, there was also an element of what Leslie Stephen called "feminine tenderness" about Mill: his character, his prose, his doctrines. It is not, I think, coincidental that one senses something similar in Rousseau: a smothering fussiness, grown rancorous and paranoid in Rousseau's case, merely querulous and impertinent in Mill's. The "feminization of society" we occasionally read about is in this sense a coefficient of the triumph of liberalism. Its distrust of masculine directness is the other side of its inveterate impulse to moralize all social activity.

This stereoscopic quality in Mill's doctrine of liberty shows itself in other ways as well. One moment it seems to license unrestrained liberty; the next moment, it seems to sanction the most sweeping coercion. When Stephen says that "the great defect" of Mill's doctrine of liberty is that it implies "too favorable an estimate of human nature," we know exactly what he means. Mill writes as if people, finally awakened to their rational interests, would put aside all petty concerns and devote themselves to "lofty minded" relationships and the happiness of mankind in general. "He appears to believe," Stephen writes with barely concealed incredulity, "that if men are all freed from restraints and put, as far as possible, on an equal footing, they will naturally treat each other as brothers, and work together harmoniously for their common good." At the same time, Mill's estimation of actually existing men and women is very unfavorable. "Ninety-nine in a hundred," he tells us, act in ignorance of their real motives. He is always going on about "wretched social arrangements," the

bad state of society, and the general pettiness of his contemporaries. In this respect, too, he resembles Rousseau,
who late in life confessed that "I think I know man, but as
for men, I know them not."

In fact, when it comes to his view of mankind, Mill
vacillates between the two caricatures: a flattering one and
a repulsive one (actually, they are both repulsive, though in
different ways). The friction between the two produces an
illusion of benevolence; that illusion is at the heart of
liberalism's appeal. Yet what Mill describes is an ideal that,
in proportion as it is realized, tends to grow into its opposite. In *Utilitarianism*, Mill writes that "as between his
own happiness and that of others, justice requires [every-
one] to be as strictly impartial as a disinterested and ben-
evolent spectator." Stephen comments: "If this be so, I can
only say that nearly the whole of nearly every human creature is one continued course of injustice, for nearly
everyone passes his life in providing the means of happiness for himself and those who are closely connected with
him, leaving others all but entirely out of account." And
this, Stephen argues, is as it should be, not merely for
prudential but for moral reasons:

> The man who works from himself outwards, whose con-
> duct is governed by ordinary motives, and who acts with a
> view to his own advantage and the advantage of those who
> are connected with himself in definite, assignable ways,
> produces in the ordinary course of things much more hap-
> piness to others . . . than a moral Don Quixote who is al-
> ways liable to sacrifice himself and his neighbors. On the
> other hand, a man who has a disinterested love of the
> human race—that is to say, who has got a fixed idea about
> some way of providing for the management of the concerns
> of mankind—is an unaccountable person . . . who is

capable of making his love for men in general the ground of all sorts of violence against men in particular.

"The real truth," Stephen concludes, "is that the human race is so big, so various, so little known, that no one can really love it."

Mill's refusal to recognize this is a standing invitation to irony. His attitude reminds one of W. H. Auden's version of the social worker's ethic: "We're all on earth to help others. What on earth the others are here for, we don't know." Truth in advertising should have required *On Liberty* to begin with the words, "Once upon a time. . . ." Although written by a learned man and talented philosopher, there is a sense in which it really belongs more to the genre of fantasy than moral philosophy. It says a number of emollient things about human capabilities, but outlines a moral-political system more or less guaranteed to stymie those capabilities.

Consider Mill's paeans to the value of eccentricity, diversity, and originality as solvents of "the tyranny of opinion." Doubtless he is sincere in his eulogies. But as we can see from looking around at our own society, the growth of Mill's equalizing liberty always tends to homogenize society and hence to reduce the expression of genuine originality and individuality. Mill's philosophy declares originality desirable even as it works to make it impossible. Uniformity becomes the order of the day. In a memorable analogy, Stephen says that Mill's notion of liberty as a politically "progressive" imperative in combination with his demand for originality is "like plucking a bird's feathers in order to put it on a level with beasts, and then telling it to fly." Furthermore, by confounding, as Stephen puts it, the proposition that "variety is good with the proposition that goodness is various," Mill's teaching tends to encourage a shallow worship of mere variety, diversity for its own sake with no regard for value of the specific "diversities" being celebrated. This is obviously a lesson we still have not learned. Notwithstanding the slogans of our cultural commissars, "diversity" itself is neither good nor bad. Signs announcing a "commitment to diversity" that one sees at college campuses and businesses across the country are so nauseating precisely because they are little more than badges declaring the owner's virtue. The odor of political correctness surrounding them them is the odor of unearned self-satisfaction.

In *On Liberty*, Mill says that "exceptional individuals . . . should be encouraged in acting differently from the mass" in order that they might "point the way" for the rest of us. But Stephen is right that

> if this advice were followed, we should have as many little oddities in manner and behaviour as we have people who wish to pass for men of genius. Eccentricity is far more often a mark of weakness than a mark of strength. Weakness wishes, as a rule, to attract attention by trifling distinctions, strength wishes to avoid it. Originality consists in thinking for yourself, not in thinking differently from other people.

It is part of Mill's polemical purpose to claim that society hitherto had persecuted eccentricity out of fear and small-mindedness. But again Stephen is surely right that

> it would be hard to show that the great reformers of the world have been persecuted for "eccentricity." They were persecuted because their doctrines were disliked, rightly or wrongly as the case may be. The difference between Mr.

Mill's views and mine is that he instinctively assumes that whatever is is wrong. I say, try each case on its merits.

Stephen's recourse to the particular—he would have cited his allegiance to utilitarian principles of expediency— infuses his discussion of the relation between liberty and power with robust common sense. It also sets it sharply at odds with Mill's treatment of those issues. In one of the most famous passages in *On Liberty*, Mill outlines what he thinks are the limits of acceptable interference in an individual's "liberty of action."

> The object of this essay is to assert one very simple principle, as entitled to govern absolutely the dealings of society with the individual in the way of compulsion and control, whether the means used be physical force in the form of legal penalties or the moral coercion of public opinion. That principle is that the sole end for which mankind are warranted, individually or collectively, in interfering with the liberty of action of any of their number is self-protection. That the only purpose for which power can be rightfully exercised over any member of a civilized community, against his will, is to prevent harm to others. His own good, either physical or moral, is not a sufficient warrant.

Mill adds various qualifications. He notes, for example, that this license applies only to "human beings in the maturity of their faculties," not to "children or young persons below the age which the law may fix as that of manhood or womanhood." He further notes, in a passage that has caused great hand-wringing among his disciples, that "despotism is a legitimate form of government in dealing with barbarians, provided the end be their improvement." But—and here is the nub of his argument restated—"as soon as mankind have attained the capacity of being guided to their own improvement by conviction or persuasion (a period long since reached in all nations with whom we need here concern ourselves), compulsion is no longer admissible as a means to their own good, and is justifiable only for the security of others." Consequently, for Mill "the appropriate region of human freedom [demands] absolute freedom of opinion and sentiment on all subjects, practical or speculative, scientific, moral, or theological."

Mill's description of his "one very simple principle" shows the extent to which his liberalism rests, as the philosopher Roger Scruton put it in *The Meaning of Conservatism* (1980, rev. ed. 1984), on a "generalization of the first-person point of view." His apotheosis of the "I" is also a movement of abstraction. One of the first things one notices about Mill's "individuals" is how little air there is around them. They exist as flat, abstract cut-outs. Arguing for the relativity of moral values, Mill notes that "the same causes which make [someone] a churchman in London would have made him a Buddhist or a Confucian in Peking." But this is to take an entirely disembodied view of the relevant "causes." Part of what makes (or once made) someone a churchgoer in London is living in London; that is not an "accidental" datum that can be subtracted without cost from an individual's identity. Our culture and history are essential ingredients: remove them and you remove the individual. Individuality is not fungible.

Mill's assumptions about the nature of individuality stand at the heart of his liberalism. They also highlight what is most problematic about it. In the first place, it is by no means clear that we have knowledge (in Stephen's paraphrase) of any "very simple principles as entitled to govern absolutely the dealings of society with the individual in the way of compulsion and control." Mill's bland language conceals an extraordinary, and completely unjustified, presumption. In the second place, Stephen notes, Mill's famous distinction between "self-regarding" and "other-regarding" acts is "radically vicious. It assumes that some acts regard the agent only, and that some regard other people. In fact, by far the most important part of our conduct regards both ourselves and others."

As Stephen observes, "men are so closely connected together that it is quite impossible to say how far the influence of acts apparently of the most personal character may extend." The splendid isolation that Mill's imperative requires is a chimera. Individuals exist not in autonomous segregation but in a network of relationships. Thus it is, as Stephen argues, that

> every human creature is deeply interested not only in the conduct, but in the thoughts, feelings, and opinions of millions of persons who stand in no other assignable relation to him than that of being his fellow-creatures. A great writer who makes a mistake in his speculations may mislead multitudes whom he has never seen. The strong metaphor that we are all members one of another is little more than the expression of a fact. A man would be no more a man if he was alone in the world than a hand would be a hand without the rest of the body.

By broadly excluding the sanctions not only of "legal penalties" but also of "the moral coercion of public opinion," Mill renders his notion of liberty fantastic.

When it comes to education, Mill admits that society must exert a moral influence on the young. But he then argues that, because society enjoys moral authority over the young, it must not presume to dictate the behavior or shape the manners of adults. But how can this be? How, Stephen asks, "is it possible for society to accept the position of an educator unless it has moral principles on which to educate? How, having accepted that position and having educated people up to a certain point, can it draw a line at which education ends and perfect moral indifference begins?" In fact, Stephen argues, "If people neither formed nor expressed any opinions on their neighbours' conduct except in so far as that conduct affected them personally, one of the principal motives to do well and one of the principal restraints from doing ill would be withdrawn from the world."

Some of Mill's qualifications concede something to common sense; but they do so at the cost of turning his "one very simple principle" into a vacuous cliché. "Either," Stephen observes, Mill means that "superior wisdom is not in every case a reason why one man should control another—which is a mere commonplace—or else [he] means that in all the countries which we are accustomed to call civilised the mass of adults are so well acquainted with their own interests and so much disposed to pursue them that no compulsion or restraint" is ever justified, which is incredible. It is precisely this oscillation between the commonplace and the fantastic that has made Mill's liberalism such a durable commodity. Its radical promise is hedged by common-sense qualifications that can be wheeled out when objections are raised and then promptly retired when the work of remaking society is meant to proceed.

Stephen is quick to admit that "if Mr. Mill had limited himself to the proposition that in our own time and country it is highly important that the great questions of morals and theology should be discussed openly and with complete freedom from all legal restraints, I should agree with him." He agrees, too, that "neither legislation nor public opinion ought to be meddlesome," and that "those who have due regard to the incurable weaknesses of human nature will be very careful how they inflict penalties upon mere vice, or even upon those who make a trade of promoting it, unless special circumstances call for their infliction." But he goes on to note that it is "one thing . . . to tolerate vice so long as it is inoffensive, and quite another to give it a legal right not only to exist, but to assert itself in the face of the world as an 'experiment in living' as good as another, and entitled to the same protection from the law." No doubt "the busybody and world-betterer who will never let things alone" is a "contemptible character." But, Stephen continues, "to try to put [him] down by denying the connection between law and morality is like shutting all light and air out of a house in order to keep out gnats and blue-bottle flies."

Mill's "one very simple principle" depends on a variety of questionable assumptions about human nature and the way moral life ought to be conducted. Above all, it depends on a notably anemic view of moral life: one in which the sociocultural fabric that gives body to freedom is redefined as the enemy of freedom and the actual process of moral choice is turned into a process of frigid ratiocination. Mill's view of liberty is at once far too simplistic and far too rigorous. It is simplistic in its demonization of the customary and conventional; it is overly rigorous in its demand that moral choices be arrived at through "the collision of adverse opinions." "On no other terms," Mill says, "can a being with human faculties have any rational assurance of being right."

Mill argues that to deny this—to hold that sanctions, even the sanctions of negative public opinion, ought to be otherwise enjoined—"is to assume our own infallibility." But this is surely not the case. As Stephen points out, "the incalculable majority of mankind form their opinions" not by a process of ratiocination but out of a network of transmitted custom, prejudice, and conventional practice. "Doctrines come home to most people in general, not if and in so far as they are free to discuss all their applications, but if and in so far as they happen to interest them and appear to illustrate and interpret their own experience." Furthermore, on the issue of infallibility, Stephen points out that there are innumerable propositions about which we have rational assurance, even though we may not claim infallibility. The fact that we *might* be wrong says nothing against this, as Mill's own work in logic and probability ought to have reminded him. (Abstract possibility is always a cheap commodity.) Rational assurance is not the same thing as perfect certitude. "There are plenty of reasons," Stephen observes, "for not forbidding people to deny the existence of London Bridge and the river Thames, but the fear that the proof of those propositions would be weakened or that the person making the law would claim infallibility is not among the number." Mill argued that programmatic support for "the collision of adverse opinions" ultimately helps to secure "rational assurance." Its real results, however, have been intellectual and moral anomie. As Gertrude Himmelfarb noted with respect to this side of Mill's teaching, "by making truth so dependent upon error as to require not only the freest circulation of error but its deliberate cultivation, [Mill] reenforced the relativism of later generations."

Mill hoped that his regime of liberty would replace the reign of prejudice with the reign of reason. In fact, it has had the effect of camouflaging prejudices with rational-sounding rhetoric. The effort to unseat customary practice and belief has resulted not, as Mill predicted, in encouraging a drift toward unanimity but in increasing chaos. Nor is this surprising. As Stephen noted, "the notorious result of unlimited freedom of thought and discussion is to produce general scepticism on many subjects in the vast majority of minds." Such are the paradoxes generated by Mill's liberalism.

Today, we are living with the institutionalization of those paradoxes—above all, perhaps, the institutionalization of the paradox that in aiming to achieve a society that is maximally tolerant we at the same time give (in David Stove's words) "maximum scope to the activities of those who have set themselves to achieve the maximally-intolerant society." The activities of the American Civil Liberties Union, for example, daily bear witness to the hopeless muddle of this anchorless liberalism. Maximum tolerance, it turns out, leads to maximum impotence. The refusal to criticize results in a moral paralysis. That paralysis is the secret poison at the heart of Mill's liberalism.

Stephen noted that Mill's "very simple principle"—the principle that coercive public opinion ought to be exercised only for self-protective purposes—was "a paradox so startling that it is almost impossible to argue against." He was right. As Maurice Cowling observed,

> to argue with Mill, in Mill's terms, is to concede defeat. *Rational* does not *have* to mean conclusions reached by critical self-examination. *Prejudice* may reasonably be used to mean commitments about which argument has been declined, but to decline argument is not in itself *irrational*. *Bigotry* and *prejudice* are not necessarily the best descriptions of opinions which Comtean determinism has stigmatized as historically outdated.

Mill claimed a monopoly on the word "rational." So long

as that monopoly remains unchallenged our paralysis will be complete. The antidote to the moral helplessness that Mill's liberalism generates is not to be found by digging deeper in the trench of liberal rationalization. On the contrary, it begins with the forthright recognition that no "one very simple principle" can relieve us of the duties we owe to the inhabited world that we, for this brief while, share with many others.

The Legacy of
Friedrich Nietzsche

*The ideal of morality has no more dangerous rival than the ideal
of supreme strength, of a life of maximum vigor, which has also
been called the ideal of aesthetic greatness. That life is in truth
the ultimate attainment of the barbarian, and unfortunately in
these days of civilization's withering it has won a great many
adherents. In pursuance of this ideal man becomes a hybrid
thing, a brute-spirit, whose cruel mentality exerts a horrible
spell upon weaklings.*
—Novalis

I am no man, I am dynamite.
—Friedrich Nietzsche

O F ALL nineteenth-century thinkers, perhaps only Karl
Marx surpassed Nietzsche in his influence on the
twentieth century. And not even Marx has exercised the
intellectual and spiritual fascination commanded by his
unhappy countryman. Indeed, as more and more of the
political regimes erected under the banner of Marxism
repudiate Marx's ideas, it becomes ever clearer that much
of what makes the modern world modern also makes it
Nietzschean. Nietzsche's glorification of power and his
contention that "there are altogether no moral facts" are

grim signatures of the age. So, too, is his enthusiasm for violence, cruelty, and the irrational. As Erich Heller put it in *The Importance of Nietzsche* (1988), Nietzsche has "drawn the fever-chart of an epoch."

This is not to say that Nietzsche would approve of the societies that his ideas have shaped so profoundly. On the contrary, he would regard both the proliferation of democracy and the triumph of mass media and popular culture with a distaste bordering on horror. He would abominate the widespread attack on rank, hierarchy, and social distinction; the political emancipation of women in particular he would reject as (to quote from *The Genealogy of Morals*) "one of the worst developments of the general *uglification* of Europe." Even the casual atheism, relativism, and hedonism of our time—even, that is, behavior and attitudes that might seem (in Nietzsche's arresting phrase) "beyond good and evil"—would earn his contempt precisely for being adopted casually: it was a first principle with this enemy of first principles to make nothing easy for himself—or for us.

One of Nietzsche's greatest fears was creeping mediocrity. If the *Ubermensch* represented his ideal—the ideal of a being strong enough to create his own values, strong enough to live without the consolation of traditional morality—the opposite of the *Ubermensch* was the timid creature Nietzsche called *der letzte Mensch*, "the last man." In a famous passage near the beginning of *Thus Spoke Zarathustra*, Nietzsche has Zarathustra warn a crowd of followers about this grave spiritual danger:

> "Alas, the time is coming when man will no longer give birth to a star. Alas, the time of the most despicable man is coming, he that is no longer able to despise himself. Behold, I show you the *last man*.

"'What is love? What is creation? What is longing? What is a star?' thus asks the last man, and he blinks.

"The earth is small, and on it hops the last man, who makes everything small. His race is as ineradicable as the flea-beetle; the last man lives longest.

"'We have invented happiness,' say the last men, and they blink. They have left the regions where it was hard to live, for one needs warmth. One still loves one's neighbor and rubs against him, for one needs warmth.

"Becoming sick and harboring suspicion are sinful to them: one proceeds carefully. . . . A little poison now and then: that makes for agreeable dreams. And much poison in the end, for an agreeable death.

"One still works, for work is a form of entertainment. But one is careful lest the entertainment become too harrowing. . . .

"No shepherd and one herd! Everybody wants the same, everybody is the same: whoever feels different goes voluntarily into a madhouse. . . .

"One is clever and knows everything that has ever happened: so there is no end of derision. One still quarrels, but one is soon reconciled—else it might spoil the digestion.

"One has one's little pleasure for the day and one's little pleasure for the night: but one has a regard for health.

"'We have invented happiness,' say the last men, and they blink."

Having heard Zarathustra's description, the crowd shouts: "Give us this last man, O Zarathustra . . . Turn us into these last men!" I have quoted this at such length because it provides an outline of practically everything Nietzsche found contemptible: the last man's lack of striving and ambition, his meekness and absorption in "little pleasures," even his obsession with health.

If much that characterizes the modern world would disgust Nietzsche, little about its spiritual landscape would surprise him. In announcing "the death of God"—something that he described as "the greatest recent event"— Nietzsche foresaw the rise of anomie, the spreading sense of angst and meaninglessness, what the Czech novelist Milan Kundera called "the unbearable lightness of being": the whole existentialist panoply of despair and spiritual torpor. All this Nietzsche diagnosed under the heading of *nihilism*: the situation, he wrote, in which "the highest values devalue themselves" and the question "Why?" finds no answer.

The last man, Nietzsche predicted, would be one response to nihilism, but the full implications of the death of God had yet to unfold. "The event itself is far too great, too distant, too remote from the multitude's capacity for comprehension even for the tidings of it to be thought of having *arrived* as yet." And when they did arrive, what certainties would not suddenly become dispensable!—"for example, the whole of our European morality." Not for nothing, perhaps, did Nietzsche put the first announcement of the death of God in the mouth of a madman. To say that he welcomed this development would be only half true. He thought that it meant liberation, yes: with the death of God, Nietzsche believed that man would be free to create values that accord more generously with human nature than do inherited religious values. But he knew that the loss of religious faith also threatened man with a terrifying rootlessness. What happens when "the highest values devalue themselves"? Who or what will take the place of God? What prodigies will fill the vacuum left by a faltering morality? What unfathomed comforts will man devise for himself in the absence of faith? To a large extent, Nietzsche's philosophy is an attempt to live with these questions: to probe the loss, the temptations, the opportunities that they imply. Nietzsche also seemed to believe that he had fashioned a novel—and honest—response to nihilism, though it is not always clear that his answers are usefully distinguishable from the problems that they are meant to address.

An inventory of the philosophers, writers, and artists whom Nietzsche influenced would form a compendious tour of twentieth-century culture. Heidegger, Sartre, and the other existentialists are inconceivable without Nietzsche; so indeed is Max Weber's theory of value; writers from Rilke, Yeats, Gide, and George Bernard Shaw, to Thomas Mann, W. H. Auden, and Wallace Stevens were all deeply influenced by aspects of his thought; ditto for D. H. Lawrence, Hermann Broch, Robert Musil, André Malraux; Oswald Spengler, author of *The Decline of the West*, wrote that he owed "almost everything" to Goethe and Nietzsche; Nietzsche's most famous book, *Also sprach Zarathustra*, provided Richard Strauss with inspiration and a title for a symphonic tone poem; Freud acknowledged that Nietzsche's insights about human motivation "agree in the most amazing manner" with the findings of psychoanalysis; and on and on.

Nietzsche snidely remarked that Christianity was just "Platonism for the masses." In the academy today we have what we might call Nietzscheanism for the masses, as squads of cozy nihilists parrot his ideas and attitudes. Nietzsche's contention that truth is merely "a moveable host of metaphors, metonymies, and anthropomorphisms," for example, has become a veritable mantra in comparative literature departments across the country. But even if Nietzsche's corrosive beliefs about truth, morals, and religion seem custom-made for fashionable academics, in other respects he is hardly what one would call politically

EXPERIMENTS AGAINST REALITY

correct. "When a woman has scholarly inclinations," Nietzsche tells us in *Beyond Good and Evil* (1886), "there is usually something wrong with her sexually." "What is truth to woman? From the beginning nothing has been more alien, repugnant, and hostile to woman than truth— her great art is the lie, her highest concern mere appearance and beauty." Of course, since Nietzsche insisted that truth is "ugly" and exalted "mere appearance," it might be possible to give a positive interpretation of this statement. But I doubt that any hermeneutical legerdemain can salvage his remark that a man who has "depth" should think about woman as "Orientals" do: "as a possession."

More even than with most thinkers, people have taken very different sorts of things from Nietzsche. This is partly a function of his style, which is epigrammatic, literary, and sometimes elusive to the point of enigma. Many of his central ideas and doctrines—the Eternal Recurrence, the *Ubermensch* (which Shaw slyly translated as "superman," thus giving the idea a slightly comic aura), even the Will to Power—have functioned more as suggestive metaphors than as arguments. Indeed, while it cannot exactly be said that Nietzsche spurned arguments, one has the sense that he resorted to them reluctantly: how much better—more dramatic, more convincing—to present an unforgettable image instead of stooping to develop an argument! "Alles, was tief ist, liebt die Maske": "Whatever is profound," Nietzsche wrote, "loves masks." Certainly, Nietzsche loved masks. He was a philosopher, but he often wrote like a poet; and poets, he proclaimed in *Zarathustra*, "lie too much." Is Zarathustra, too, he wondered, a poet? And, we wonder, is Nietzsche?

He is, at any rate, rightly regarded as one of the great masters of German prose. Because of serious eye trouble— Nietzsche was often close to blindness for much of his

194

adult life—he could neither read nor write for extended periods. He tended to compose in his head during long daily walks. "[G]ive no credence to any thought," he advised, "that was not born outdoors while one moved about freely." Hence his preference for the aphorism or very short essay. Most of Nietzsche's books are really a series of aphorisms or extended aphorisms strung together. The contention that such a form is unsuitable to serious philosophical reflection was something Nietzsche rejected: "It is aphorisms! Is it aphorisms?—May those who would reproach me thus reconsider and then ask pardon of themselves." For Nietzsche, the aphorism was the favored medium of insight: nimbler and more eloquent than discursive argumentation. "I approach deep problems like cold baths," he confided: "quickly into them and quickly out again. That one does not get to the depths that way, not deep enough down, is the superstition of those afraid of the water, the enemies of cold water; they speak without experience. The freezing cold makes one swift." Nietzsche's particular speciality was the psychological aphorism: the scalpel-like exposure of motives. Here are a few from *Beyond Good and Evil*:

> He who does not *wish* to see what is great in a man, has the sharpest eye for that which is low and superficial in him, and so gives away—himself.

> Anyone who has looked deeply into the world may guess how much wisdom lies in the superficiality of men.

> One begins to mistrust very clever people when they become embarrassed.

> When we have to change our mind about a person, we hold the inconvenience he causes us very much against him.

The abdomen is the reason why man does not easily take himself for a god.

"I have done that," says my memory. "I cannot have done that," says my pride, and remains inexorable. Eventually—memory yields.

Despite Nietzsche's virtues as a stylist, however, it is worth noting that he did not always write well. *Thus Spoke Zarathustra*, for example, is a pretentious rhetorical swamp, punctuated here and there with glittering observations. (Nietzsche, who believed that with *Zarathustra* he had "given mankind the greatest present that has been given to it so far," obviously thought otherwise: "Having understood six sentences from it," he remarked in *Ecce Homo*, "would raise one to a higher level of existence than 'modern' man could attain.") Nietzsche himself admitted that *The Birth of Tragedy* was often "badly written, ponderous, embarrassing, image-mad and image-confused, sentimental, in places saccharine to the point of effeminacy, uneven in tempo, without the will to logical cleanliness." It is an irony that many of Nietzsche's admirers have been most beguiled by elements of his work—the idea of the artist as purveyor of "metaphysical comfort" in *The Birth of Tragedy*, for example, or the quasi-biblical rhetoric of Zarathustra—that Nietzsche himself later rejected or refused to acknowledge.

Nietzsche's style puts a premium on expression; coherence is another matter. Many critics have endeavored to show that, taken as a whole, his work reveals considerably more unity than is at first apparent; it also undoubtedly reveals a more systematic character that one might initially suspect: epistemology, ethics, metaphysics, aesthetics—Nietzsche had distinctive things to say about all the traditional philosophical topics, albeit he often said them in an untraditional way. It may well be true, as one commentator suggested, that Nietzsche's books are easier to read and harder to understand than those of almost any other thinker. A trip through Nietzsche's books will reveal wildly disparate claims about truth, chastity, the Germans, Wagner, the Jews, morality, science, art, and Christianity— to mention a few topics that absorbed his attention. It is easy to quote Nietzsche to almost any purpose, and it is not surprising that his work has been mined to support ideas that he would radically oppose. Given his insistence that "one does not only wish to be understood when one writes, one wishes just as surely *not* to be understood," this is hardly surprising. The existentialist philosopher Karl Jaspers offered the excellent advice that one should not rest content with any assertion in Nietzsche's works until finding a passage that contradicted it: only then would one be in a position to decide what he really meant.

While those influenced by Nietzsche fall into many categories, one useful dividing line is between those who came to Nietzsche before Nazism and those who came later. The former can seem remarkably innocent. Typical is the American writer H. L. Mencken. In his book *The Philosophy of Friedrich Nietzsche* (first published in 1908), Mencken presents us with a bluff, irascible Nietzsche who sounds a good deal like . . . H. L. Mencken. "Broadly viewed," he writes, Nietzsche's ideas "stand in direct opposition to every dream that soothes the slumber of mankind in the mass. . . . They are pre-eminently for the man who is *not* of the mass, for the man whose head is lifted, however little, above the common level"—in short, you understand, they are for men a lot like *us*. Mencken praises Nietzsche's work as a "counterblast to sentimentality"; but what is most likely to strike a contemporary reader is precisely Mencken's own sentimentality: his description of Nietzsche's "noble, and almost holy" sister, Elisabeth, for example, when in fact Elisabeth shamelessly exploited her brother's reputation for her own ends. Even more striking is his sentimentalization of Nietzsche's ideas about morality. For Mencken, Nietzsche was a free-thinking iconoclast, a prickly but not utterly disagreeable ally in the war against what Mencken elsewhere calls the "booboisie."

Nietzsche liked to think of himself as *unzeitgemäss*, "untimely." He believed that his solitary wanderings and meditations had brought him insights far too advanced and devastating for most of his contemporaries. And indeed, some of Nietzsche's writings on truth, language, and morality seem extraordinarily prescient—or at least extraordinarily contemporary. But Mencken's fondness for his thought suggests that Nietzsche was also very much a product of his time, that he was strikingly "timely" as well as untimely. His apotheosis of art, his "immoralism," his celebration of instinct at the expense of reason, his attack on the middle-class, religion, etc.: all this was part of the heady intellectual atmosphere of the *fin de siècle*, in England and America as well as in France and Germany. Even as Nietzsche was suggesting that "to tell the truth is to lie according to a fixed convention," so, for example, Oscar Wilde was bemoaning the "decay of lying" and warning readers not to be led astray "into the paths of virtue." It is worth remembering, however, that attacks on virtue are most attractive when virtue remains well established, just as the homage to power, violence, cruelty, and the like seems amusingly bracing only so long as one doesn't suffer from them oneself.

Nietzsche railed against "Shopkeepers, Christians, cows, females, Englishmen, and other democrats" in a way that

Mencken and others could admire and emulate. But Mencken's bluster, alternately amusing and obnoxious, *presupposed* the society and basic values he attacked; Nietzsche's polemic challenged both in the most fundamental way. Where Mencken pronounced anathema on teetotalers, the YMCA, and chiropractic, Nietzsche sought to overturn the very foundation of Western morality. He summed it up this way in *The Will to Power*: "*My purpose*: . . . to demonstrate how everything praised as moral is identical in essence with everything immoral." What would this mean? As always, there are conflicting passages in Nietzsche. In *Dawn* (1881), he concedes that "It goes without saying that I do not deny—unless I am a fool—that many actions called immoral ought to be avoided and resisted, or that many called moral ought to be done and encouraged—but I think the one should be encouraged and the other avoided *for reasons other than hitherto.*"

Since for Nietzsche "there are altogether no moral facts," there are no actions that are good or bad *in themselves*; if one ought to pursue a course of action traditionally called moral, it is not because it is *good*, but purely for pragmatic reasons. The consequences of this anti-moral view of morality become clearer when one considers Nietzsche's notorious distinction between "master morality" and "slave morality." In *The Genealogy of Morals*, where Nietzsche elaborates the distinction, he reminds us that "One cannot fail to see at the bottom of all these noble races the beast of prey, the splendid *blond beast* prowling about avidly in search of spoils and victory." Once given free rein, Nietzsche writes, his "nobles"

> are not much better than uncaged beasts of prey. They
> savor a freedom from all social constraints, they compen-

sate themselves in the wilderness for the tension engendered by protracted confinement and enclosure within the peace of society, they go *back* to the innocent conscience of the beast of prey, as triumphant monsters who perhaps emerge from a disgusting procession of murder, arson, rape, and torture, exhilarated and undisturbed of soul.

In 1887, such glorification of violence and "the voluptuousness of victory and cruelty" may have been merely piquant; by the 1930s, when the Nazis appropriated Nietzsche's rhetoric as a garland for their murderous deeds, it had become impossible to view such passages neutrally. Nietzsche's sympathetic commentators are no doubt correct that he would have been horrified by Nazism and the Third Reich. They are also right that he regarded himself as an ardent "anti-anti-Semite." But, as Nietzsche himself recognized, part of what makes him "dynamite" is the inextricable link between his attack on morality and the immoralism of his "blond beasts." Insofar as someone accepts this, he notes, "his belief in morality, in all morality, falters."

Nietzsche's attack on morality flows directly from his understanding of the nature of man. The chief philosophical influence on Nietzsche's worldview was undoubtedly Arthur Schopenhauer, "the one teacher and severe taskmaster of whom I boast," as Nietzsche put it in *Schopenhauer as Educator* (1874), the third of his *Untimely Meditations*. At the center of Schopenhauer's philosophy is the revolutionary contention that the traditional understanding of man as the "rational animal" is all wrong. In a move that anticipated Nietzsche and Freud, Schopenhauer inverts the Platonic-Christian view of man, claiming that man is essentially *will*, not reason. According to Schopenhauer, reason, consciousness, morality, judgment—all the properties that we associate with the ego—are mere epiphenomena of the essentially unfathomable and purposeless striving that animates all nature.

Where traditional philosophy had spoken of reason as the "pilot" of the soul, for Schopenhauer reason was the will's prop: a puppet buffeted by inexplicable and fundamentally amoral urgings. Schopenhauer believed that man's bondage to the will condemned him to permanent suffering and unhappiness. "*Willing,*" he wrote, "springs from lack, from deficiency, and thus from suffering." Every apparent satisfaction is merely a prelude to boredom or fresh desire. Hence Schopenhauer's inveterate pessimism. "Existence is certainly to be regarded as an error or mistake," he concluded, "to return from which is salvation." Schopenhauer placed such a high value on art and aesthetic experience precisely because in art he found a temporary refuge from the imperatives of the will. Aesthetic experience "raises us out of the endless stream of willing. . . . [F]or the moment we are delivered from the miserable pressure of the will. We celebrate the Sabbath of the penal servitude of willing; the wheel of Ixion stands still."

Schopenhauer's teaching made an indelible impression on Nietzsche, as it did on so many of his contemporaries. Both the idea that man—that all of nature—is essentially will and his almost religious view of aesthetic experience became permanent features of Nietzsche's thought. Nietzsche at first also accepted Schopenhauer's pessimism. But in his mature work, he inverted Schopenhauer's ethics just as Schopenhauer had inverted the traditional anthropology. Not only was the tradition wrong in seeing man as primarily a rational animal, Nietzsche argued, it was wrong in valuing being over becoming, permanence over evanescence, timelessness over time. Making a virtue of a necessity, Nietzsche came to exalt willing —and hence suffering—as the source of all joy and power. This was his essential innovation on Schopenhauer. Where Schopenhauer saw art as a kind of propaedeutic to renunciation, for Nietzsche art was an alternative to renunciation and the pessimism it presupposed. Instead of disparaging the will, Nietzsche celebrated it. For him, Schopenhauer's repudiation of existence was evidence of a "rancor against time" that we must learn to overcome. In *Zarathustra*, Nietzsche criticizes those who "encounter a sick or an old man or a corpse, and immediately they say, 'Life is refuted.' But only they themselves are refuted, and their eyes, which see only one face of existence." Paradoxically, in order to affirm himself in his entirety, man must learn to affirm himself in his incompleteness: as mortal and essentially time-bound. Man must learn to say "yes" to time. Whether Nietzsche believed he had achieved the radical affirmation of mortality that he championed is open to question. Although time and again he speaks of himself as a "yea-sayer," he portrays even *Zarathustra* as being bitten by the "tarantula" of revenge; and in one note he confesses that "I have tried to affirm life *myself*—but ah!"

There is a tremendous pathos in Nietzsche's struggle to affirm life. As Erich Heller observed, Nietzsche "had the passion truth and no belief in it. He had the love of life and despaired of it. This is the stuff from which demons are made—perhaps the most powerful secret demon eating the heart out of the modern mind." In his investigation into the origin of values, Nietzsche always asked what lack, what need, what deficiency could have prompted the creation of a given value. In *The Gay Science* (1887), for example, he boasts that "my eye grew ever sharper for that most difficult and captious form of . . . backward inference from the work to the maker, from the deed to the doer,

The Legacy of Friedrich Nietzsche

from the ideal to those who *need it*." Yes, indeed: what need could have created the chilly ideal that Nietzsche erected for himself?

Friedrich Wilhelm Nietzsche was born on October 15, 1844, in Röcken, Saxony. The eldest of three children, he was named for Friedrich Wilhelm IV, king of Prussia, whose birthday he shared. The man who would later declare that Christianity was "the calamity of millennia" and who would sign himself "The Antichrist" was swaddled in religion when a child. His father, Karl Ludwig, was a Lutheran preacher and son of a cleric. He was a cultivated man: musical, bookish, and not a little worldly. In the late 1830s he served as a minor courtier, tutoring the three Prussian princesses at Altenburg. He obviously made a favorable impression on the king, for his pastorate at Röcken was in the gift of the crown. Nietzsche's mother, thirteen years her husband's junior, was also a parson's child, brought up to be dutiful and pious. When she married, in 1843, the seventeen-year-old bride joined her husband in a household that included his widowed mother and two unmarried stepsisters. The family of the future apostle of "overflowing health" also featured a potpourri of ailments. Early on the myopic young Friedrich began suffering from the migraines that would plague him throughout his life, while his aunts and grandmother chronically battled a variety of nervous and gastric complaints: these, too, would come to plague Nietzsche. His father was even more unlucky. In 1848 he began suffering from a mysterious brain disease. The diagnosis—a diagnosis that haunted Nietzsche in later life—was "softening of the brain." He was thirty-six when he died the following July.

More tragedy was to come. In 1850, Nietzsche's youngest sibling, Joseph, died. Unable to provide for her family on a widow's pension, Frau Nietzsche soon moved with Friedrich and his doting sister Elisabeth to Naumburg to rejoin her mother- and sisters-in-law who had moved there shortly after Karl Ludwig's death. The serious, exceedingly fastidious youth seemed destined for the cloth. His chief interests were music and theology, and his grave demeanor and absorption in religion inspired his schoolmates to dub him "the little pastor." In 1858, Nietzsche won a full scholarship to Schulpforta, the Eton and Winchester of German boarding schools. He did poorly in mathematics but excelled in languages and literature. By all accounts, Nietzsche became the mildest of men: quiet, unassuming, infallibly courteous and correct. Yet there can be no doubt that he possessed a will of iron. Even as a youth he practiced "self-overcoming" with terrifying severity. Ronald Hayman, one of Nietzsche's many biographers, recounts a revealing episode from the philosopher's schooldays. Nietzsche got into an argument about Gaius Mucius Scaevola, the legendary Roman soldier who, captured by the enemy, is said to have thrust his right hand unflinchingly into a fire to prove his indifference to pain. Not to be outdone, the young Nietzsche took a handful of matches, lighted them, and held the burning sticks steadily in his outstretched palm until a prefect knocked them to the ground. The boy had already been badly burned.

Although he continued to be drawn to theology and music—Nietzsche would go on to compose a good deal of piano music, which is of approximately the same quality as his mature theology—he decided to study classical philology. He went first to Bonn, and then followed his mentor, the eminent philologist Friedrich Ritschl, to the University of Leipzig in 1865. It was soon after arriving in Leipzig that Nietzsche stumbled upon an edition of Schopenhauer's chief philosophical work, *The World as Will and Representation*, in a second-hand book shop.

It was in 1865, too, that the distinctly unworldy Nietzsche visited Cologne. Having asked his guide to take him to a restaurant, he was taken instead to a brothel. Stunned by the gauze-clad whores, Nietzsche stood transfixed for a moment. "Then I made instinctively for the piano as being the only soulful thing present," he reported in a letter. "I struck a few chords, which freed me from my paralysis, and I escaped." Whether Nietzsche later returned to this or similar establishments is a matter of dispute. Many commentators think that Nietzsche died a virgin; Freud speculated that he had contracted syphilis at a male brothel in Genoa; and Thomas Mann believed it "incontestable" that Nietzsche's madness was the product of tertiary syphilis. He made Adrian Leverkühn—the protagonist of *Doctor Faustus* whom he modeled on Nietzsche—seek out the prostitute Esmeralda and, despite her warnings, deliberately infect himself: a prelude to his pact with the devil. Nietzsche himself, shortly after he went mad, claimed that he had twice infected himself in 1866, though he was by then an unreliable witness. It is worth noting, in any event, that if his mental collapse was caused by syphilis, the disease took an irregular course: he did not become incontinent, his speech was not slurred, and he retained some control over his memory.

In 1867 Nietzsche embarked upon his two years' compulsory military service but was discharged after a few months because of an injury he sustained falling off a horse. Returning to Leipzig, he made up in philology what he lacked in horsemanship. "He will simply be able to do anything he wants to do," Ritschl wrote, noting that Nietzsche was "the first from whom I have accepted any contribution at all while he was still a student." The future looked bright: in 1868 he met and became intimate with Wagner and his wife, Cosima. The following year, although lacking his doctorate, he was appointed to the chair of philology at the University of Basel on Ritschl's recommendation. Leipzig hastily conferred the missing degree. In 1870 he was promoted to full professor and became a Swiss citizen. At the beginning, at least, Nietzsche seems to have been an effective and popular teacher. A series of public lectures he delivered in 1871 each drew a crowd of about three hundred. Nietzsche's older colleague at Basel, Jacob Burckhardt, the great historian of the Renaissance, noted that "in places they were quite enchanting, but then a profound melancholy would make itself heard."

When the Franco-Prussian War broke out in 1870, Nietzsche volunteered to serve as a hospital steward at the front, in order, as he put it, to contribute his "small share to the Fatherland's alms box." The delicate scholar soon fell prey to diphtheria and dysentery. There is some conjecture—generally rejected—that he may have also contracted syphilis from tending wounded soldiers. Mencken's claim that Nietzsche was "a slave to drugs" is something of an exaggeration, though it is true that around this time he acquired the life-long habit of dosing himself with various drugs. In addition to indulging in other specifics, in later years he regularly resorted to such potent sedatives as veronal and chloral hydrate to combat the nightmare of chronic insomnia.

Although he occasionally boasted of his strong constitution, the truth is that by the mid-1870s Nietzsche was a physical wreck and had to be extremely careful about his diet. "Alcohol is bad for me," he confided in the second section of *Ecce Homo*, "Why I Am So Clever": "a single glass of wine or beer in one day is quite sufficient to turn my life into a vale of misery." In 1876 he had to take a leave from teaching, and by 1879 his health had so far degenerated that he was forced to resign from Basel altogether. Given his battery of ailments, what is extraordinary is not that he finally went mad, but that he remained lucid and productive for so long. "My existence is a frightful burden," he wrote to a physician in 1880.

Constant pain, a sensation akin to seasickness for several hours a day, semi-paralysis in which speech is difficult for me, by way of change furious convulsions (in the throes of the last I vomited for three days and nights; I thirsted for death). . . . If only I could describe to you the continuousness of it, the constant pain and pressure in the head and on the eyes. . . .

Although he had earlier made two proposals of marriage (one to Lou Salomé, who later became Rilke's mistress and a friend of Freud's), by the time he came to publish *The Genealogy of Morals* in 1887, Nietzsche believed that "the philosopher abhors *marriage*, . . . marriage being a hindrance and calamity on his path to the optimum." From 1879 until his collapse, Nietzsche lived an increasingly isolated, peripatetic existence, subsisting largely on an exiguous pension granted him by Basel. A single room in modest boarding houses in Rome, Sils Maria, Nizza, Mentone, Genoa, Turin: Nietzsche became an itinerant scholar, ever in search of salubrious climate for his wretched health. As the Eighties progressed, he found himself with few friends and scarcely more readers. In 1886 he subsidized the publication of *Beyond Good and Evil*, perhaps his most brilliant book. He wrote to his friend Peter Gast that he would have to sell three hundred copies to recoup his expenses. A year later the book had sold 114 copies. "I am *solitude* become man," he wrote in one mournful note.

While a few critics, including Hippolyte Taine, wrote admiringly of Nietzsche's books, his later work was almost completely ignored until the very end of his mentally competent life. In 1888, the Danish critic Georg Brandes delivered a popular series of lectures on his work in Copenhagen, signaling the beginnings of fame. Alas, early in January 1889 Nietzsche collapsed on the street in Turin, throwing his arms around the neck of a mare that had just been flogged by a coachman. Over the next few days, he managed to dispatch a handful of raving letters signed "Dionysus," "The Crucified," etc. His letter to Jacob Burckhardt, for example, begins by assuring his old colleague that

> In the end I would much rather be a Basel professor than God; but I have not dared push my private egoism so far as to desist for its sake from the creation of the world. You see, one must make sacrifices however and wherever one lives.

To his friend Franz Overbeck he confided that "I am just now having all anti-Semites shot." After conferring with Burckhardt, Overbeck came and removed Nietzsche to a clinic in Basel. Some of Nietzsche's friends claimed to suspect that his madness was just one more mask, one more bit of feigning; in fact his situation was hopeless. After the attentions of various specialists, Nietzsche was released in the care of his mother. He had moments of relative lucidity, but he never regained his faculties.

Nietzsche lingered on in mental twilight for a decade, unaware of his rapidly growing notoriety. His sister, however, was quick to capitalize on it. Fresh from her failed attempt to establish an *echt* German colony in Paraguay with her husband, Bernhard Förster, a rabid anti-Semite who had recently committed suicide, she soon managed to obtain sole jurisdiction over her brother's unpublished writings. Changing her name to Förster-Nietzsche to compound the effect, she appointed herself chief guardian and privileged interpreter of his ideas. In order to exploit the burgeoning Nietzsche cult more effectively, she eventually moved her brother to Weimar—the city of Goethe and Schiller—and set about controlling access to his papers, forging letters, and publishing contrived books from miscellaneous notes. She took particular care to emphasize those passages that accorded with her own nationalistic and anti-Semitic inclinations, thus helping to pave the way for the Nazi's glorification of Nietzsche's philosophy. By the time that he died in August 1900, Nietzsche was world famous. But he had long since been unable to appreciate or even comprehend his triumph.

In 1872 Nietzsche published his first book, *The Birth of Tragedy Out of the Spirit of Music* (revised in its 1886 edition to *The Birth of Tragedy: Or, Hellenism and Pessimism*). Far from justifying the academic establishment's lavish faith in a young unknown, Nietzsche's book seemed calculated to inspire the wrath of the philological establishment. The sharpest barb came from Nietzsche's contemporary at Berlin, Ulrich von Wilamowitz-Möllendorf, who went on to become the most distinguished philologist of his generation. Slyly entitled *Zukunftsphilologie!*—"Philology of the Future," a disparaging allusion to Wagner's "Music of the Future"—Wilamowitz's pamphlet did indeed catch Nietzsche out in a number of factual errors. And it is probably the case that many of

Nietzsche's ideas about the origin of Greek tragedy are, in point of fact, mistaken.

But in an important sense, Wilamowitz's attack was beside the point. For whatever else it is, *The Birth of Tragedy* is not a contribution to academic philology. Completely lacking in scholarly apparatus, it is a bold, speculative inquiry not only into the birth of tragedy, but also into its death and promised rebirth in the operas of Richard Wagner. In part the book is a polemic against the sunny, rationalistic view of Greek culture epitomized by Johann Winckelmann's epithet "noble simplicity and quiet grandeur." For Nietzsche, the neo-classical view of classical culture was shallow and naïve. In its craving for order, it entirely missed the underworld of Dionysian suffering and chaos that stood behind the stately Apollonian figures of the Greek gods and heroes. "The Greek knew and felt the terror and horror of existence," Nietzsche wrote. "That he might endure this terror at all, he had to interpose between himself and life the radiant dream birth of the Olympians." Tragedy was the name of this interposition: Apollo becomes the medium of Dionysus, beguiling suffering by aestheticizing it. Indeed, in one of his most famous lines —repeated three times in the course of *The Birth of Tragedy*—Nietzsche insists that "it is only as an *aesthetic phenomenon* that existence and the world are eternally *justified.*"

But *The Birth of Tragedy* was much more than an interpretation of Greek culture. It was also the beginning of Nietzsche's criticism of modernity for its allegiance to rationalism and science. In the opposition he drew between Socrates as the embodiment of reason and the Dionysian wisdom of tragedy, Nietzsche was writing as much about nineteenth-century Europe as he was about fifth-century Athens. Modernity has been definitively shaped by Socrates' "audacious reasonableness," as the triumph of science and technology reminds us daily. Yet perhaps Socrates' commitment to reason at the expense of the irrational elided reality rather than revealed it? Perhaps, as Nietzsche said, it was "a sign of decline, of weariness, of infection, of the anarchical dissolution of the instincts"? Truth vs. life: it was Nietzsche's startling conclusion that science was at bottom allied with nihilism because of its uncompromising commitment to truth. "All science," he wrote, "has at present the object of dissuading man from his former respect for himself." In order to salvage life from science "the value of truth must for once be experimentally *called into question.*" It is one of the curious features of Nietzsche's mature thought that he wished to question the value of truth while upholding honesty as his one remaining virtue. Traditionally, the moral virtues have been all of a piece. For example, Aquinas observes that "nearly all are agreed in saying" that the moral virtues are interconnected, that "discernment belongs to prudence, rectitude to justice," and so on. It is worth asking whether honesty, sundered from the family of virtues, remains a virtue—whether, in the end, it even remains honest. Untempered by other virtues, honesty functions not so much to reveal truth as to expose it. Is that honest?

Nietzsche clung to honesty after abandoning the other virtues because it allowed him to fashion the most ruthless instrument of interrogation imaginable. Difficulty, not truth, became his criterion of value. Thus he embraced the horrifying idea of the Eternal Recurrence primarily because he considered it "the hardest possible thought"—whether it was also true didn't really matter.

Nietzsche opposed honesty to truth. He looked to art as a "countermovement to nihilism" not because he thought that art could furnish us with the truth but because it accustomed us to living openly with untruth. "Truth is ugly," Nietzsche wrote in *The Will to Power.* "We possess *art* lest we *perish from the truth.*" Of course, there is also such a thing as dishonest art: art that offers not an affirmation of existence but promises an escape from it. Just that, for Nietzsche, was the problem with Wagner and all romanticism: by "counterfeiting . . . transcendence and beyond" Wagner abandoned honesty for the illusion of redemption. What Nietzsche wanted was art that recognized and embraced its status as art, that reveled in appearance *as* appearance. "If we had not welcomed the arts and invented this cult of the untrue," he wrote in *The Gay Science,*

> then the realization of the general untruth and mendaciousness that now comes to us through science—the realization that delusion and error are conditions of human knowledge and sensation—would be utterly unbearable. *Honesty* would lead us to nausea and suicide. But now there is a counterforce against our honesty that helps us to avoid such consequences: art as the *good* will to appearance.

Ultimately, Nietzsche's ideal asks us to transform our life into a work of art. Accepting Schopenhauer's inversion of the traditional image of man, Nietzsche no longer finds human life dignified in itself: if man is essentially an expression of irrational will, then in himself he is morally worthless. This is the dour irony that attends Nietzsche's effort to burden man with the task of *creating* values rather than *acknowledging* them. And it is here, too, that Nietzsche's aestheticism and his rejection of morality intersect. For Nietzsche, man is not an end in himself but only "a bridge, a great promise." In order to redeem that promise, man must treat life with the same imperiousness and daring that the artist brings to his work. If, as Nietzsche argued, "life itself is *essentially* appropriation, injury, overpowering what is alien and weaker; suppression, hardness, . . . and at least, at its mildest, exploitation," then it is hardly surprising that the perfect aesthete will also be the perfect tyrant.

Nietzsche never tired of pointing out that the demands of traditional morality fly in the face of life. One might say, Yes, and that is precisely why morality is so valuable: it acknowledges that man's allegiance is not only to life but also to what ennobles life—that, indeed, life itself is not the highest court of appeals. But for Nietzsche the measure of nobility is the uninhibited pulse of life: hence his penchant for biological and physiological metaphors, his invocation of "ascending" and "descending" forms of art and life. He defines the good as that which enhances the feeling of life. If "to see others suffer does one good, to make others suffer even more," then violence and cruelty may have to be granted the patent of morality and enlisted in the aesthete's palette of diversions. In more or less concentrated form, Nietzsche's ideal is also modernity's ideal. It is an ideal that subordinates morality to power in order to transform life into an aesthetic spectacle. It promises freedom and exaltation. But as Novalis points out, it is really the ultimate attainment of the barbarian.

The World
According to Sartre

JEAN-PAUL SARTRE, anti-bourgeois philosopher *par excellence*, was born to a solidly bourgeois family in Thiviers in June 1905. His father, Jean-Baptiste, was an officer in the French navy and had been educated at the Ecole Polytechnique; his mother, Ann-Marie Schweitzer (cousin of the great doctor and humanitarian, Albert), came from an old and well-to-do Alsatian family. Jean-Baptiste died in 1906, when Jean-Paul was fifteen months old, and Anne-Marie soon took her infant son to live with her father Charles Schweitzer, whom Sartre evokes in largely affectionate terms in *The Words*, the autobiography of his early years. Though Sartre claims to have "loathed" his childhood, he remembers his time in the Schweizter household as years of coddled freedom and happiness when he was the clever center of everyone's world.

The center was displaced in 1917 when his mother married Joseph Mancy, a former schoolmate of the unfortunate Jean-Baptiste, and moved with him to La Rochelle. Sartre remembers his stepfather—when he bothers to recall him at all—with a mixture of contempt and bitterness; not that Mancy was cruel or worthy of contempt, but he had committed the unpardonable sins of disrupting Sartre's world and dividing his mother's attentions.

From the beginning, Sartre enjoyed the privileged education of his class. Early on, his grandfather Schweitzer encouraged his curiosity and interest in reading. Sartre was precocious, adept at music, acting, and languages, though indifferent at best in mathematics. At the Ecole Normale Supérieure, he studied philosophy, taking first place in his *agrégation* in 1929. (A fellow philosophy student he met that year, Simone de Beauvoir, took a close second.) If the future philosopher was a brilliant student, he was hardly a model one. At school, as Annie Cohen-Solal shows in *Sartre* (Pantheon, 1985), Sartre was the "fearsome instigator of all the revues, all the jokes, all the scandals"— "scandals," it seems, that were hardly confined to the harmless expression of youthful high spirits. Once, for example, Sartre took it upon himself to send a letter to the police accusing a fellow student of having murdered a woman, the wife of a diplomat, whose body had recently been found; another of his "pranks" resulted in the principal of the school resigning. As Cohen-Solal notes, "this image of a provoking, disrespectful, subversive Sartre recurs again and again, like a leitmotif, throughout his life."

Reading *Sartre*, one gathers that coming to terms with the philosopher turned out to be far more difficult than Cohen-Solal had reckoned. In one typical passage, she tells us that

> Sartre's life had been more or less equally divided between, on the one hand, intense socializing—trips, rich meals, heavy drinking, drugs, and tobacco—and, on the other, the monastic austerity of a rigid work schedule. Work till noon at Rue Bonaparte. Twelve-thirty: one hour appointments, scheduled by his secretary. One-thirty: back at Rue Bonaparte, with Beauvoir, Michelle, or some other woman. . . . Two hours over a heavy meal, washed down with a quart

of red wine. Punctually, at three-thirty, he would stop in midsentence, push away the table, get up, and run back to his desk at Rue Bonaparte. . . . When he felt really sick, and the doctor prescribed rest, he would opt for a compromise: less tobacco and fewer drugs for a week. . . . His diet, over a period of twenty-four hours included two packs of cigarettes and several pipes stuffed with black tobacco, more than a quart of alcohol—wine, beer, vodka, whisky, and so on—two hundred milligrams of amphetamines, fifteen grams of aspirin, several grams of barbiturates, plus coffee, tea, rich meals.

Such a routine is of course a prescription for disaster, and one is surprised only that it wasn't until 1954 that Sartre suffered his first collapse, the result of acute arterial hypertension. A few years later, he reportedly almost killed himself by taking ever-increasing doses of the then-fashionable stimulant corydrane to help him finish the reader-proof *Critique of Dialectical Reason*. And by the time that Sartre died in 1980, at the age of seventy-five, he had already been leading a posthumous existence for several years. Since childhood, writing had been Sartre's obsession, his raison d'être, his life. Yet after 1973 he was almost totally blind and could neither read nor write. In short order, a series of strokes and a battery of other ailments reduced him to the pathetic, devastated creature that Simone de Beauvoir describes in such excruciating detail in *Adieux: A Farewell to Sartre* (Pantheon, 1981), her memoir of the philosopher's last years.

In the spate of memoirs, interviews, and recollections about Sartre that have appeared since his death, Sartre's friends are at pains to proclaim his generosity and kindness. There is no doubt that he could be both kind and generous, especially to the female members of what Cohen-

Solal calls his "family." But he was also capable of what can only be called wanton viciousness. As extraordinary as Sartre's circle of friends and acquaintances was, even more extraordinary is the catalogue of people with whom he quarreled and broke. From Raymond Aron and Alberto Giacometti to Maurice Merleau-Ponty and Albert Camus, Sartre seems to have delighted in the drama of breaking friendships.

Perhaps the most notorious rift came in 1952 when Sartre ran an exceedingly hostile review of Camus's *The Rebel* in *Les Temps modernes*. Camus, understandably upset by the review, wrote his old friend a chilly letter that opened with the formal salutation: "Monsieur le Directeur." Instead of responding to Camus privately, Sartre published an open letter in the magazine, a letter that Cohen-Solal is surely correct in describing as one of the "most cruel and violent texts he had ever written." "My dear Camus," Sartre began, "Our friendship was not easy, but I will miss it. If you end it today, that doubtless means it had to end."

> Your combination of dreary conceit and vulnerability always discouraged people from telling you unvarnished truths. . . . Tell me, Camus, for what mysterious reasons may your works not be discussed without taking away humanity's reasons for living? . . . How *serious* you are, and yet, to use one of your old words, how frivolous! And suppose you are wrong? Suppose your book simply attested to your ignorance of philosophy? Suppose it consisted of hastily assembled and secondhand knowledge? . . . Are you so afraid of being challenged? . . . But I don't dare advise you to consult *Being and Nothingness*. Reading it would seem needlessly arduous to you: you detest the difficulties of thought.

None of this, however, prevented Sartre from penning a fulsome eulogy when Camus died in 1960: his friends remained enemies only so long as they were capable of being rivals.

From an early age, Sartre was convinced he would become a great writer, enjoying a "great writer's life, as it appears from books." And "as for the content of that life," Sartre wrote in his notebook in 1939,

> it can be easily imagined: there were solitude and despair, passions, great undertakings, a long period of painful obscurity (though I slyly shortened it in my dreams, in order not to be too old when it ended), and then glory, with its retinue of admiration and love. . . . In a word, I'd have liked to be sure of becoming a great man later on, so as to be able to live my youth as a great man's youth. . . . [T]hough I couldn't be sure, I behaved as if I must become one—and was extremely conscious of being the young Sartre, in the same way that people speak of the young Berlioz or the young Goethe.

Yet despite his conviction of potential greatness, Sartre's success was not immediate. His literary career began to blossom only in 1938 when *Nausea*—which many consider his best and most original novel—and *The Wall* were published by the *Nouvelle Revue Française*. As Cohen-Solal informs us, it was Sartre's publisher, Gaston Gallimard, who came up with the title *Nausea*. The book was published to great critical acclaim. Epitomizing the temper of the times, it helped to inaugurate that dour literary-philosophical amalgam that came to be called "existentialism." The title "Nausea" is perfect, of course, for no other word sums up so graphically the hero Roquentin's generalized disgust at existence; and one cannot help wondering if the book's—and Sartre's—career would have been different had he published it under any of the titles he adopted when working on the manuscript: *Factum on Contingency, Essay: On the Loneliness of the Mind, Melancholia,* or finally—when asked for a more descriptive title—*The Extraordinary Adventures of Antoine Roquentin.* Somehow, none has the makings of a literary vogue.

Sartre was thirty-four years old when Germany attacked Poland on September 1, 1939. Having done his military service a decade before in the meteorological corps, Sartre suddenly found himself torn away from his self-possessed life as a teacher and writer, and was engaged once again as an army weatherman. "I was quite comfortably ensconced in my situation as an individualist, anti-bourgeois writer," he recalled later in "Self-Portrait at Seventy."

> What exploded all that was the fact that one fine day in September 1939 I received a call-up paper, and was obliged to go off to the barracks at Nancy to meet fellows I didn't know who'd been called up like me. That's what introduced the social into my life. . . . Up till then I believed myself sovereign; I had to encounter the negation of my own freedom—through being mobilized—in order to become aware of the weight of the world. . . .

But as his first response to life was always to write about it, Sartre did not abandon literary activities in his new situation; the world had not become that weighty. Immediately after he was called up, he conceived the idea of keeping a journal. "Reflecting upon the world of war and its nature," he wrote to Simone de Beauvoir, "I hatched the project of writing a journal. Please include in your parcel a stout black notebook—thick but not too tall or wide, cross-ruled of course."

In fact, Sartre discovered that his new routine afforded him even more time to write than he had had in civilian life. The change of scene and the portentous atmosphere of the times seemed to act as a tonic to his imagination. Stationed just behind the front in a succession of small towns near Strasbourg, Sartre had the sense of being close to great happenings but endured very few actual distractions. His duties, which consisted mostly of taking weather readings, were neither taxing nor time-consuming, and he was usually left to his own devices.

Still, however propitious the situation, Sartre's productivity in the five months that he was writing these notebooks was staggering. First, he managed to fill fourteen notebooks and begin a fifteenth. He also wrote hundreds of letters, most of his novel *The Age of Reason*, and tinkered with several other literary projects. In his translator's introduction to *The War Diaries* (Pantheon, 1983), a selection of Sartre's wartime notebooks, Quentin Hoare estimates that Sartre wrote a total of some one million words during this period.

As the original title of *The War Diaries* indicates (*Les Carnets de la drôle de guerre: Novembre 1939–Mars 1940*), what we have here are not really "war diaries" but notebooks of the "phony war," that strange interregnum after France declared war on Germany when French and German troops sat ensconced in their respective positions along the Alsatian border, eyeing one another with hostility but not fighting. Sartre never saw combat, and while his notebooks occasionally discuss the phenomenon of war, his reflections on the subject tend to be saturated with the kind of abstract, Hegelian logic that dissolves the exigencies of lived experience into a battle of purely conceptual antagonists. "War, when all's said and done," Sartre mused in one typical passage, "is a concrete idea that contains within itself its own destruction and that accomplishes this by an equally concrete dialectic. . . . The essence of war will be *realized* concretely the day war becomes impossible." How consoling would be the thought that war becomes what it really is only when it becomes impossible—if only the unfolding of its "concrete dialectic" weren't such a messy affair.

One instance of such messiness occurred in May, 1940, when the Germans abruptly put an end to the phony war. They outflanked the "impregnable" Maginot line and, in a matter of weeks, had occupied France. Sartre was taken prisoner in June as his company retreated before the German onslaught. He used his time in captivity to study Heidegger and to compose a good portion of what would become his major philosophical work, *Being and Nothingness* (1943). He was released the following year and returned to Paris, where he continued writing and was tangentially involved in the Resistance.

Hoare enthusiastically introduces the war diaries as a "masterpiece"—"without question . . . a marvelously successful work." But despite their historical interest, Sartre's notebooks really do not succeed as a "work." The whole is simply too desultory, sketchy, and uneven to merit Hoare's praise. Yet they surely are an extraordinary set of documents. And it is worth noting, too, that Sartre always assumed that they would be published one day. "I am giving myself short shrift in my little black notebook," he wrote to de Beauvoir. "Whoever reads it after my death—for you will publish it only posthumously—will think I was a dreadful character, unless you accompany it with explanatory annotations of a kindly sort." De Beauvoir did not, alas, provide the requested annotations, but a glance through the notebooks certainly does enable one to appreciate the point of Sartre's veiled request.

Ostensibly the testimony of an "average" soldier caught up in the moment, these notebooks are in fact no more average than was Jean-Paul Sartre himself. Though they include something of an abridged chronicle of Sartre's life at this time—his observations on daily events, relations with his new-found army colleagues, his sundry amours—their chief interest is as a diary of his intellectual obsessions and the peculiar sensibility that nurtured them. We see Sartre discovering, elaborating, reformulating themes that we have come to identify as distinctively Sartrean. Anyone familiar with the basic tenets of his particularly austere brand of existentialism will at once recognize that these notebooks exhibit the entire range of its defining preoccupations: the agonized struggle for authenticity, the insistence on absolute freedom and responsibility, rejection of any transcendent measure for values or morals, minute analyses of one's relations with other people, an ill-defined but thoroughgoing anti-conventional, anti-bourgeois stance ("You're all bourgeois," Sartre snaps at his colleagues near the beginning of the volume, "I wouldn't put myself out for bourgeois people"). In short, as Hoare rightly observes, the war diaries "both prefigure and map out the virtual entirety of the author's subsequent oeuvre."

Especially noteworthy are the many passages that rehearse material that would come to occupy a central place in the argument of *Being and Nothingness*. For example, the notebooks contain lengthy and often quite technical discussions of the concept of Nothingness, the nature of the will, the problem of authenticity, the structure of consciousness, and other specialized matters. Some of these discussions recur almost verbatim in *Being and Nothingness*; often, though, we follow along as Sartre gropes his way to a preliminary understanding and expression of his ideas. Given the level of abstraction at which *Being and*

Nothingness proceeds, such drafts are welcome interpretive aids: their very hesitations and digressions often help to elucidate Sartre's more finished argument in *Being and Nothingness.*

Also of philosophical interest is Sartre's account of his debt to Husserl and Heidegger. Sartre had studied Husserl when he was in Berlin in 1931–33, and philosophically he is in many ways closer to Husserl's phenomenology, with its obvious roots in the Cartesian tradition, than he is to Heidegger. But temperamentally Sartre has much more in common with Heidegger. He did not read Heidegger's major work, *Being and Time* (1927), until a German soldier provided him with a copy when he was a prisoner of war. But by September, 1939, he was acquainted with *What Is Metaphysics?* and other of Heidegger's works, and the existential twist that characterizes Heidegger's philosophy had already begun to exert a deep influence on his thinking.

In addition to indulging in such philosophical reflections, Sartre uses his notebooks to keep a running dialogue with his reading, quoting from and reflecting copiously on whatever he happened to be engaged with at the moment. André Gide, St.-Exupéry, Kierkegaard, Stendhal, Flaubert, Koestler, and Emil Ludwig's biography of Kaiser Wilhelm II figure prominently in these pages, as do a host of lesser characters. Gide and Stendhal already emerge as among Sartre's heros, but Flaubert is severely criticized for inexact writing and stylistic poverty. "How clumsy and disagreeable it is," Sartre writes of *L'Education sentimentale.* "How silly that constant hesitation between stylization and realism in the dialogues and portrayals." He then devotes several pages to a detailed criticism of what he considers Flaubert's ineffective and cliché-ridden use of verbs.

Sartre regarded this period of his life as a time of transition—at one point he compares himself to a snake that has sloughed off its old skin—and his notebooks abound in the kind of autobiographical recollections and self-analyses that such moments are wont to elicit. (Autobiography, of course, became a speciality of Sartre's: *The Words*, his much admired exercise in the genre, won him the Nobel prize in 1964—which, characteristically, he refused.)

Sartre's political enthusiasms, which later bulked so large in his work and personality, show themselves in these notebooks only obliquely. He cites a contemporary critic, one Emile Bouvier, who was dubious about the likelihood of Sartre's becoming "a great novelist." "It is to be feared," Bouvier wrote, "lest . . . he may leave literature for philosophy, mysticism or social preaching." Sartre responded that he was "flabbergasted" by Bouvier's remark: "I'd never have believed that anyone would consign me to mysticism like that. And as for social preaching, M. Bouvier can set his mind at ease."

Sartre was correct about mysticism; but as for philosophy and social preaching—well, here M. Bouvier would seem to have been closer to the mark. One thinks for example of Sartre's preachy denunciations of the United States after the war, his support of Soviet Russia during the last years of Stalin's reign, and the steady stream of left-wing manifestoes, pamphlets, and pronouncements that he issued in the Sixties and Seventies.

Sartre described himself as a Communist. In fact, though, his politics were anything but systematic or even coherent. Despite the friendly visits to Mao, to Khrushchev, to Castro, to Tito, to Che Guevara, despite his declaration after returning from Russia in 1954 that "there is a total freedom of criticism in the USSR," despite his endless proselytizing for Communist causes, Sartre was motivated primarily not by a commitment to the Party but by what de Beauvoir proudly described as "anti-bourgeois anarchism." In the Fifties, Sartre himself assured his readers that he had sworn to the bourgeoisie "a hatred that would die only with me." As Leszek Kolakowski observed in *Main Currents of Marxism*, Sartre oscillated

> between identification with the Communists and violent hostility towards them. . . . At every stage, however, he endeavored to preserve his own reputation as a "Leftist," and even to represent himself and his philosophy as the embodiment of "Leftism" *par excellence*. Consequently, even when attacking the Communists and reviled by them he made a point of directing far more vehement attacks against the forces of reaction, the bourgeoisie, or the United States Government. . . . His whole political activity was vitiated by fear of being in the typical situation of an intellectual condemning events that he has no power to influence; in short, his was that of a politician *manqué*, cherishing unfulfilled ambitions to be on the "inside."

By the Sixties, being "inside" politically meant proclaiming solidarity with the Third World. It was then that Sartre became widely identified with radical causes from Mao's China to Latin America. But here, too, Sartre's commitment to the causes he championed was largely a matter of posturing. He had no scruples about writing a glowing preface for Frantz Fanon's *The Wretched of the Earth*—a book that the historian Paul Johnson called "the most influential of all terrorist handbooks"—or blithely declaring "I believe in illegality" in *La Cause du peuple*, a self-described "revolutionary, proletarian, Communist paper." In 1973, he even admitted his deep interest in the Baader-Meinhof Group: "a real revolutionary group," though one that had "started a little too soon."

But what did all Sartre's sympathy for the dispossessed amount to? As the French writer Pascal Bruckner observed in *The Tears of the White Man* (Free Press, 1983), his brilliant study of Western attitudes toward the Third World, some of Sartre's political activism—most notably, his opposition to the French government during the Algerian conflict—demanded real courage; but for the most part Sartre's "solidarity" with the Third World was a merely rhetorical solidarity, self-congratulatory but impotent. "Sartre's attitude toward the Third World was a strange mixture of masochism and indifference," Bruckner writes.

> Sartre declared that the West was rotten, but after this beginning, was concerned only with the West. He made peace with his conscience after paying a little tithe of guilt. . . . He wasted a great part of his talent in the esthetics of violence and Stalinism, and with regard to the Third World, ended up showing himself to be not only dogmatic, but inconsequential. The hard-liner was in reality a deserter. Let us remember that he came close to justification of the massacre of Israeli athletes by members of the PLO in 1972. He gave way before revolutionary regimes, just as he gave way to the Maoists, giving his name to ideas and actions that went against his innermost convictions. But, deep down, he did not take them seriously. This follower of the Third World did not accept it unless it fulfilled the familiar role of the victim from whom he had nothing to learn. This preacher of universal involvement, this maniacal devotee of petitions, had no real affection for anyone but members of his own tribe.

The real key to Sartre's character is his intellectualizing aestheticism, his tendency to dissolve reality in a play of abstract philosophical or political categories. It is in this sense, for example, that we must understand his admission that he tended to regard words as "the quintessence of things." "The truth is," Sartre wrote in a revealing passage from *The War Diaries*, "I treat my feelings as ideas: with an idea, one pushes it till it cracks—or finally becomes 'what it really was.'" And in fact, Sartre could be quite ruthless about exposing his own failings and selfish motives. But there is pretense, even here, as noted in *The Words*: "I am always ready to criticize myself, provided I'm not forced to." The *game* of self-examination—for it was never more than a game—is merely part of the cynical, anti-bourgeois charade. Again, *The Words* offers sterling examples of the procedure:

> At the age of thirty, I executed the masterstroke of writing *Nausea*—quite sincerely, believe me—about the bitter unjustified existence of my fellowmen and exonerating my own. I *was* Roquentin; I used him to show, without complacency, the texture of my life. . . . Later, I gaily demonstrated that man is impossible; I was impossible myself and differed from the others only by the mandate to give expression to that impossibility, which was thereby transfigured and became my most personal possibility, the object of my mission, the springboard of my glory. I was a prisoner of that obvious contradiction, but I did not see it, I saw the world through it. Fake to the marrow of my bones and hoodwinked, I joyfully wrote about our unhappy state. Dogmatic though I was, I doubted everything except that I was the elect of doubt. I built with one hand what I destroyed with the other, and I regarded anxiety as the guarantee of my security; I was happy.

As Cohen-Solal's biography makes clear, Sartre regarded such confessional exercises as a form of exoneration, as if cleverly analyzing one's failings somehow absolved one of their consequences.

For Sartre, life was essentially an agenda for reflection. No feeling, no sensitivity, no impression was left unencumbered by interpretation; no interpretation was left undisciplined by further scrutiny. Not even the humble struggle against corpulence was exempt from elaborate speculative embroidery. "Every four or five months," Sartre wrote, "I look at my stomach and get unhappy." Yet having then resolved to abstain from bread and wine, he found himself tempted by a carafe of wine one day at lunch:

But, precisely, if Nothingness is introduced into the world through man, anguish at Nothingness is simply anguish at freedom, or if you prefer, freedom's anguish at itself. If, for example, I experienced a slight anguish yesterday before the wine which I *could* but *should not* drink, it's because the "I shouldn't" was already in the past . . . and *nothing* could prevent me from drinking. It was before that particular *nothing* I was so anguished; that nothingness of my past's means of acting on my present. . . . *[N]othing* allows me to foresee what I shall do and, even if I were able to foresee it, *nothing* could prevent me from doing it. So anguish is indeed the experience of Nothingness, hence it isn't a psychological phenomenon. It's an existential structure of human reality, it's simply freedom becoming conscious of itself as being its own nothingness.

Sartre's notebooks are full of such meditations. Taken together, they reveal a mind that does not so much *practice* philosophy as *exude* it; anything and everything, the whole range of his experience, was immediately taken up and digested by reflection. The smallest detail of his or his colleagues' behavior, the most trivial news report: for Sartre they were "understood" only when translated out of their native element and subjected to systematic philosophical probing.

Sartre's tremendous appetite for abstraction and his suspicion of the life of feeling is particularly evident in his uncompromising, absolutist approach to the cardinal existentialist virtues of authenticity and freedom. In *Being and Nothingness*, for example, Sartre defines freedom as a spontaneous "upsurge" that is "beyond causes, motives, ends." Sartre's discussion of freedom, both in the notebooks and in *Being and Nothingness*, is elusive to say the least. It is worth noting that without "causes, motives, or ends," the idea of freedom must remain empty. For if it is to be more than mere accident or spontaneity, if it is not to be arbitrary, then freedom must be limited by particular choices that are based on intelligible criteria—criteria that are in some sense given, not (as Sartre would have it) "freely produced." In default of such criteria, freedom can be little more than an invigorating slogan. (Compare Raymond Aron's description of "the dullness of real emancipation" in *The Opium of the Intellectuals*: how much more pedestrian it sounds, but how much more substantial it turns out to be.) Sartre claims to value freedom above all else; but freedom for him is more man's fate and burden than choice; ineradicable, freedom is yet too absolute to be fully grasped or realized; hence one is not so much privileged as "condemned to be free."

It is the same with Sartre's notion of authenticity. Anything like a definition of authenticity is hard to come by in Sartre's work. Yet it is clear that he understood it to be characterized chiefly by the individual's defiant assertion of unqualified freedom in the face of an essentially absurd reality. Since unqualified freedom entails unqualified responsibility, authenticity, as Sartre insisted in the notebooks, meant being "totally responsible for one's life." "In short," he wrote, "I was seeking the absolute, I wanted to be an absolute, and that's what I called morality."

The problem is that the absolute, by nature completely abstract, is too empty to serve as a criterion for morals or a cue for authenticity. But as a rhetorical trope, allegiance to the absolute can exert a powerful appeal. And Sartre's understanding of authenticity, tinged as it was with Romantic longing, exploits that appeal to the hilt: "In relation to Gauguin, Van Gogh and Rimbaud," he noted in an early notebook entry, "I have a distinct inferiority complex because they managed to destroy themselves. . . . I am more and more convinced that, in order to achieve authenticity, something has to snap."

It follows that, in Sartre's view, authenticity flourishes best in extreme situations. After a brief leave in Paris, for example, he remarked that "it's much easier to live decently and authentically in wartime than in peacetime." Like so much in Sartre's notebooks—indeed, like so much in his work generally—this statement is at once arresting yet open to serious question. What gives it an air of plausibility is the truth that exceptional situations can call forth exceptional virtues. Plunged into crisis, men and women often experience moments of moral clarity that are rare in everyday life. And they sometimes respond to such situations with uncommon selflessness and valor.

But does this mean that it is easier to live "decently and authentically" during war than in peacetime? On the contrary, hasn't wartime generally been the occasion of profound moral degradation and anarchy? The notion that it is somehow easier to live "authentically" in wartime than in the "bourgeois" stability of peace will suggest itself seriously only to someone who discounts the importance of ordinary social life in forming our ideas of authenticity, someone for whom "the authentic" is paradigmatically a lonely battle of an aloof and isolated self. "I rather think I was authentic before my leave," Sartre wrote. "Probably," he explained, "because I was alone."

Just how aloof and isolated Sartre conceived the self to be is exemplified in his contention "the first value and first object of will is: to be its own foundation." Or, as he put it—somewhat more bluntly—in *Being and Nothingness* "the best way to conceive the fundamental project of human reality is to say that man is the being whose project is to be God." This is not to suggest that Sartre believed that God exists. On the contrary, he remarked in the notebooks that he had been an atheist since the age of twelve. And he proceeded, in a later passage, to describe God as an "impossible synthesis of in-itself and for-itself, of total opacity and total freedom, the *causa sui.*" Nevertheless, according to Sartre, the idea of God, though self-contradictory, functions as the ineluctable (if usually unacknowledged) ideal to which we all aspire. Mankind, he writes in *Being and Nothingness*, is "perpetually haunted by a totality . . . without being able to be it."

The thought that man's "fundamental project" is to be his own foundation—that is, to be God—stands at the center of Sartre's philosophy. And this is also to say that Sartre's philosophy is saturated with pride, with hubris. Pride, as St. Augustine put it in *City of God*, is at bottom "a perverse kind of exaltation" in which one seeks to "abandon the basis on which the mind should be firmly fixed" and seeks instead to become self-created. It is pride, for example, that underlies the famous conclusion to the main text of *Being and Nothingness*, in which Sartre contends that "man is a useless passion"—"useless" because his every action is haunted by a desire that for a mortal, finite creature is essentially self-contradictory: the desire to be completely sovereign, autonomous, self-sufficient, the desire to be God. And pride also provides the philosophical conviction that justifies Sartre's constitutional uneasiness with anything that threatens to compromise his sense of mastery and control. "I am nothing but pride and lucidity," he confesses at one point in the notebooks; whatever impinges on that pride or obscures that lucidity will be a source of anguish.

The situation that Sartre outlines takes on tragic dimensions when one realizes that the catalogue of threats to humanity's pride includes the whole of existence: anything organic, mutable, uncertain—anything *real* that exists independently of one's will and thought is immediately suspect. "The essential thing," Sartre's Antoine Roquentin explains in *Nausea*, "is contingency. I mean that one cannot define existence as necessity." Hence the "horrible ecstasy" that Roquentin experiences when he contemplates the roots of a chestnut tree:

> The chestnut tree pressed itself against my eyes. Green rust covered it half-way up; the bark, black and swollen, looked like boiled leather. . . . I realized that there was no half-way house between non-existence and this flaunting abundance. If you existed, you had to *exist all the way*, as far as mouldiness, bloatedness, obscenity were concerned. In another world, circles, bars of music keep their pure and rigid lines. But existence is a yielding. . . .

Like Sartre himself, Roquentin finds the organic world, unwieldy and subject as it is to change and decay, a frightening and vertiginous affront to pride. This revulsion in the face of the organic obviously parallels Sartre's curious and well-known scruples about roots, "the slimy" (*le visqueux*), and so forth in *Being and Nothingness*. What

Roquentin craves is a pristine, necessary world of pure abstraction, a world where everything is subject to the dictates of thought. His "circles and bars of music," rather like the stable beauty of geometrical figures ("something straight or round") that Plato praises in the *Philebus,* answer to this desire: completely abstract, they are also completely comprehensible. They do not frustrate his demand for mastery and control.

Even language is a source of anguish. Roquentin dreams of a language that can "catch the secret smiles of things seen absolutely without men," that can articulate "a discreet, tenacious meaning—very precise, but escaping from the words for ever." But this means that he seeks (impossible thing) a language *without* words, a language that would be fully commensurate with what it describes, a language *beyond* any merely human language, which never captures things just as they are; what Roquentin seeks, in short, is the language of God.

Sartre's understanding of man's "fundamental project" also has profound implications for his view of relations with other people. If one desires to be God, then the very existence of others will be felt as a threatening infringement on one's sovereignty. Because man's pride demands complete self-sufficiency, relations with other people are from the beginning cast into the essentially antagonistic mold of power relations, the mold of a Hobbesean *bellum omnium contra omnes.* It follows that, as Sartre wrote in *Being and Nothingness,* "conflict is the original meaning of being-for-others." As Garcin exclaimed near the end of *No Exit,* "*L'Enfer, c'est les Autres*": "Hell is other people." Not without reason is this oft-quoted line so widely identified with the Sartrean philosophy. Sartre's basic view of "Concrete Relations with Others," as he put it in the title of one of the most influential chapters of *Being and Nothingness*, is evident even in his rhetoric. Sartre speaks throughout his work—even in the more or less private pages of his notebooks—not of "other people" or "human relations" but always of "the Other," as if this strangely impersonal, dehumanizing locution named our most common experiences of other people.

Given all this, it is hardly surprising that sexuality, which continually reminds us of our lack of self-sufficiency and fundamental neediness, is especially problematic for Sartre. It offers an unparalleled field for the exercise of power; but, at the same time it constitutes a tremendous threat to autonomy. Hence Sartre's notorious description of female sexuality in *Being and Nothingness*:

> The obscenity of the feminine sex is that of everything which "gapes open." It is an *appeal to being* as all holes are. In herself woman appeals to a strange flesh which is to transform her into a fullness of being by penetration and dissolution. . . . Beyond any doubt her sex is a mouth and a voracious mouth which devours the penis—a fact which can easily lead to the idea of castration.

Similar passages abound in the notebooks: "the hole is often resistance. It must be forced, in order to pass through. Thereby it is already feminine. It is resistance by Nothingness, in other words modesty. This is obviously why it attracts sexuality (will to power, rape, etc.)."

"Obviously"? Sartre offers these observations as phenomenologically rigorous descriptions of "one of the most fundamental tendencies of human reality—the tendency to fill." But are they really anything more than symptoms of Sartre's own psychopathology, based in the end on his obsession with autonomy and dressed up in the language of philosophy? Whatever insight into sexuality and human relations such meditations may provide, they surely give weight to Iris Murdoch's description of Sartre as "a connoisseur of the abnormal."

Sartre's existentialist rhetoric bristles with condemnations of "reification" and treating people as objects—as "means" rather than "ends." But his writings everywhere reveal that both his temperament and his underlying view of man incline him to do just that. "Nothing is dearer to me than the freedom of those I love," Sartre writes in a passage about seduction, "but the fact is this freedom is dear to me provided I don't respect it at all. It's a question not of suppressing it, but of actually violating it. . . . that's what the desire to be loved means: to hit the Other in the Other's absolute freedom." He goes on to note the "impossibility . . . of conceiving a happy love *after* the seduction. Once the woman has been conquered, I no longer had any idea what to do with her." Sartre admits that this view of love is "utterly inauthentic," but at the same time he insists that it is "the commonest and strongest form of love" and he fails, either in the notebooks or in *Being and Nothingness*, to provide a convincing description of what a more "authentic" version of love would look like.

Without the erotic charge that allows for seduction, Sartre finds that he is basically uninterested in people. Friendship "bores" him, he tells us, and his relations with men tend to be tenuous and superficial. "In short, there's one half of humanity that hardly exists for me." The ideal of self-sufficiency renders the pleasures of ordinary friendship superfluous. "I think I have no *need* of friends," Sartre writes, "because, basically, I don't need anybody. . . . I prefer to derive everything from myself."

Most of us would describe Sartre's view of human relations as grim. But Sartre himself would have rejected the characterization. He proclaimed that "seriousness" was his great enemy. In the concluding pages of *Being and Nothingness*, in a section entitled "Existentialist Ethics," Sartre attacks "the spirit of seriousness," primarily because it compromises freedom by affirming values that are in some sense "transcendent"—that is, given independently of human subjectivity. And near the end of the notebooks Sartre reflects that he has "never wanted to live seriously. I've been able to put on a show—to know pathos, and anguish, and joy. But never, never have I known seriousness. My whole life has been just a game: sometimes long and tedious, sometimes in bad taste—but a game. And this war is just a game for me."

Sartre defines "game" as "the happy metamorphosis of the contingent into the gratuitous," and alludes for support to Friedrich Schiller's famous contention, in *On the Aesthetic Education of Man,* that "Man plays only when he is in the full sense of the word a man, and *he is only wholly Man when he is playing*." But it is important to note that Sartre ignores the caveat with which Schiller immediately precedes this passage: "Man shall *only play* with Beauty, and he shall play *only with Beauty*." Though man is "serious with the agreeable, the good, the perfect," writes Schiller, "with Beauty he plays." In other words, Schiller did not want to subvert seriousness, but only to insure that the realm of beauty and aesthetics remain free from the intrusion of moralistic imperatives. Sartre, however, refused such distinctions. Instead, he embraced a deep, self-centered aestheticism and regarded the whole of existence —even his lovers, even war—as an untoward eruption of contingency that can be disarmed only by being mastered and transformed into a game of his own making. No doubt Jean-Paul Sartre was one of the most gifted writers of his generation; he was also one of its greatest monsters.

The Perversions
of Michel Foucault

*Since it is difficult, or rather impossible, to represent a man's life
as entirely spotless and free from blame, we should use the best
chapters in it to build up the most complete picture and regard
this as the true likeness. Any errors or crimes, on the other hand,
which may tarnish a man's career and may have been committed
out of passion or political necessity, we should regard rather as a
lapse from a particular virtue than as the products of some
innate vice. We must not dwell on them too emphatically in our
history, but should rather show indulgence to human nature for
its inability to produce a character which is absolutely good and
uncompromisingly dedicated to virtue.*
—Plutarch, in the "Life of Cimon"

*I am no doubt not the only one who writes in order to have no
face. Do not ask who I am and do not ask me to remain the
same: leave it to our bureaucrats and our police to see that our
papers are in order.*
—Michel Foucault, *The Archaeology of Knowledge*

LOOKING BACK on our arrogantly skeptical age, future
historians are likely to regard the rebirth of hagiog-
raphy in the 1980s and 1990s with bemused curiosity. For
one thing, these decades witnessed a notable dearth of

likely *hagioi* or saints available for the honor of such commemoration. Then, too, the debunking temper of our times is ill suited—or so one would have thought—to the task of adulation. Yet *The Passion of Michel Foucault* (Simon & Schuster, 1993), James Miller's ambitious biography of the French historian-philosopher, demonstrates that the will to idolize can triumph over many obstacles.

Foucault, who died of AIDS in June 1984 at the age of fifty-seven, has long been a darling of the same super-chic academic crowd that fell for deconstruction, Jacques Derrida, and other aging French imports. But where the deconstructionists specialize in the fruity idea that language refers only to itself (*il n'y a pas de hors-texte*, in Derrida's now-famous phrase), Foucault's focus was Power. He came bearing the bad news in bad prose that every institution, no matter how benign it seems, is "really" a scene of unspeakable domination and subjugation; that efforts at enlightened reform—of asylums, of prisons, of society at large—have been little more than alibis for extending state power; that human relationships are, underneath it all, deadly struggles for mastery; that truth itself is merely a coefficient of coercion; etc. "Is it surprising," Foucault asked in *Surveiller et punir* (English translation: *Discipline and Punish*, 1977), "that prisons resemble factories, schools, barracks, hospitals, which all resemble prisons?" Such "interrogations" were a terrific hit in the graduate seminar, of course. And Miller may well be right in claiming that by the time of his death Foucault was "perhaps the single most famous intellectual in the world" —famous, at least, in American universities, where hermetic arguments about sex and power are pursued with risible fecklessness by the hirsute and untidy. In all this, Foucault resembled his more talented rival and fellow left-wing activist, Jean-Paul Sartre, whose stunning career

Foucault did everything he could to emulate, beginning with a stint in the French Communist Party in the early 1950s. He never quite managed it—he never wrote anything as original or philosophically significant as *Being and Nothingness*, never had the public authority that Sartre, alas, enjoyed in the postwar years. Yet he had eminent and devoted cheerleaders, including such well-known figures as the historian Paul Veyne, his colleague at the Collège de France, who declared Foucault "the most important event in the thought of our century."

Be that as it may, he remains an unlikely candidate for canonization. But the very title of Miller's biography— *The Passion of Michel Foucault*—puts readers on notice that, in Miller's opinion, anyway, his subject presents us with a life of such exemplary, self-sacrificing virtue that it bears comparison with the Passion of Jesus Christ. (Nor is the reference to the Passion adventitious: Miller makes the connection explicit.) The eager reception of *The Passion of Michel Foucault* suggests that Miller, a prolific cultural journalist who teaches at the New School for Social Research, is not alone in his estimation. To be sure, there have been a few dissenting voices, mostly from academic homosexual activists who feel that Miller was insufficiently reverential. But most critics, including such luminaries as Alexander Nehamas, Richard Rorty, and Alasdair Mac-Intyre, have been falling over themselves to express their admiration and "gratitude" for Miller's performance.

What is novel about that performance is Miller's neglect of Plutarch's admonition, quoted above, that one ought to concentrate on "the best chapters" of a life and cover over "any crimes or errors" when writing about a great man. While this might be questionable advice for a biographer, for a hagiographer it would seem to be indispensable. Not that anyone familiar with the outlines of Foucault's life is

EXPERIMENTS AGAINST REALITY

likely to think him an angel. Miller describes him as a "new type of intellectual," "modest and without mystifying pretense." But this is at best disingenuous. True, Foucault occasionally indulged in some ritualistic false modesty before delivering a lecture or when disparaging earlier work in favor of his present enterprises. But as the French journalist Didier Eribon has shown in an earlier biography (and as Miller unwittingly shows in his own), arrogance and mystification were two hallmarks of Foucault's character and writing. Eribon notes that at school, where Foucault decorated his walls with Goya's horrific etchings of the victims of war, the future philosopher was "almost universally detested." Schoolmates remember him as brilliant, but also aloof, sarcastic, and cruel. He several times attempted—and even more often threatened—suicide. Self-destruction, in fact, was another of Foucault's obsessions, and Miller is right to underscore Foucault's fascination with death. In this, as in so much else, he followed the lead of the Marquis de Sade, who had long been one of his prime intellectual and moral heroes. (Though, as Miller notes, Foucault felt that Sade "had not gone far enough," since, unaccountably, he continued to see the body as "strongly organic.") Foucault came to enjoy imagining "suicide festivals" or "orgies" in which sex and death would mingle in the ultimate anonymous encounter. Those planning suicide, he mused, could look "for partners without names, for occasions to die liberated from every identity."

Miller describes Foucault as "one of the representative men—and outstanding thinkers—of the twentieth century." But his great innovation in this book is to seize what was most vicious and perverted about Foucault—his addiction to sadomasochistic sexual practices—and to glorify it as a courageous new form of virtue—a specifically *philosophical* virtue, moreover. Note well: Miller does not attempt to excuse or condone or tolerate Foucault's vices; he does not, for instance, claim that they were the human, all-too-human foibles of a man who was nevertheless a great thinker. Such attitudes, after all, carry an implied criticism: we excuse only what requires exculpation; we tolerate only what makes demands upon our patience or broad-mindedness.[1] What we fully approve of we certify and celebrate; and celebration of Foucault and all he stood for is at the top of Miller's agenda in this book.

Miller claims that Foucault's penchant for sadomaso-chistic sex was itself an indication of admirable ethical adventurousness. In his view, we should be grateful to Foucault for his pioneering exploration of hitherto forbidden forms of pleasure and consciousness. In his preface, Miller suggests that Foucault, "in his radical approach to the body and its pleasures, was in fact a kind of visionary; and that in the future, once the threat of AIDS has receded, men and women, both straight and gay, will renew, without shame or fear, the kind of corporeal experimentation that formed an integral part of his own philosophical quest." In other words, Miller attempts to enroll in the ranks of virtue behavior and attitudes that until fifteen minutes ago were universally condemned as pathological.

Many of his critics have cheerfully followed suit. For example, the prominent Nietzsche scholar Alexander Nehamas, in the course of his long and fulsome review of Miller's book for *The New Republic*, readily agreed that

1 The eclipse of tolerance as a liberal virtue, by the way—the widespread belief that tolerance must now be considered a symptom of reaction—is one of the most insidious by-products of the campaign for political correctness. Among other things, it sharply narrows the space for open debate by requiring allegiance to values or ideas one had hitherto had the luxury of acknowledging without affirmation.

"sadomasochism was a kind of blessing in Foucault's life. It provided the occasion to experience relations of power as a source of delight." Consequently, Nehamas concludes, "Foucault extended the limits of what could count as an admirable human life." Again, Isabelle de Courtivron, head of the department of foreign languages and literatures at MIT, assured readers in a front-page review for *The New York Times Book Review* that Foucault "expanded modern knowledge in profoundly important and original ways." She then commends Miller "for dismissing cliché-ridden concepts about certain specific erotic practices, and for offering a clear and nonjudgmental (even supportive) analysis of the tools and techniques of what he considers a mutually consensual theater of cruelty."

A great deal might be said about this effort to welcome sadomasochism as a bracing new "lifestyle" option. Above all, perhaps, it demonstrates the kind of spiritual and intellectual wreckage that can result, even now—and even for the most educated minds—from the afterwash of the radicalism of the 1960s. Make no mistake: behind Professor de Courtivron's anodyne commendation of a "non-judgmental" approach to human sexuality and Miller's dream of "corporeal experimentation" that proceeds "without shame or fear" stands the vision of polymorphous emancipation that helped turn the 1960s into the moral and political debacle it was. Among the many articulations of false freedom that were published in those years, none was more influential than Herbert Marcuse's Marxist-Freudian tract, *Eros and Civilization* (1959; rev. ed., 1966). Eagerly embraced by countercultural enthusiasts who wanted to believe that heating up their sex lives would hasten the demise of capitalism and bring forth the millennium, it outlines a portentous struggle between "the logic of domination" and the "will to gratification," attacks "the established reality in the name of the pleasure principle," and fulminates against "the repressive order of procreative sexuality."

Very Foucauldian, all that. As indeed is Marcuse's splendid idea of "repressive tolerance," which holds that "what is proclaimed and practiced as tolerance today" (Marcuse was writing in 1965 and had in mind such institutions as freedom of speech and freedom of assembly) "is in many of its most effective manifestations serving the cause of oppression." In plain Orwellian language: Freedom is tyranny, tyranny is freedom.

The aroma of such Sixties radicalism pervades Miller's biography and everywhere undergirds his sympathy for Foucault. With this in view, it seems only natural that among Miller's other credits are *The Rolling Stone Illustrated History of Rock and Roll,* which he edited, and *"Democracy Is in the Streets": From Port Huron to the Siege of Chicago* (1987). I am unfamiliar with the former work, but *"Democracy Is in the Streets"* is a straightforward paean to the New Left and its "collective dream" of "participatory democracy." In that book, Miller was already memorializing crucial "breakaway experiences"— "during sit-ins, in marches, at violent confrontations"— and the Sixties' "spirit of ecstatic freedom." In some ways, *The Passion of Michel Foucault* is a revival of that earlier book, done over with a French theme and plenty of black leather.

Hence it is not surprising that when Miller gets around to *les événements,* the student riots of 1968, his prose waxes dithyrambic as gratified nostalgia fires his imagination. It is as if he were reliving his lost—or maybe not-so-lost—childhood.

The disorder was intoxicating. Billboards were ripped

apart, sign posts uprooted, scaffolding and barbed wire pulled down, parked cars tipped over. Piles of debris mounted in the middle of the boulevards. The mood was giddy, the atmosphere festive. "Everyone instantly recognized the reality of their desires," one participant wrote shortly afterward, summing up the prevailing spirit. "Never had the passion for destruction been shown to be more creative."

Foucault himself, unfortunately, had to miss out on the first wave of riots, since he was teaching at the University of Tunis. But his lover Daniel Defert was in Paris and kept him abreast of developments by holding a transistor radio up to the telephone receiver for hours on end. Later that year, Foucault was named head of the department of philosophy at the newly created University of Vincennes outside Paris. The forty-three-year-old professor of philosophy then got a chance to abandon himself to the intoxication. In January 1969, a group of five hundred students seized the administration building and amphitheater, ostensibly to signal solidarity with their brave colleagues who had occupied the Sorbonne earlier that day. In fact, as Miller suggests, the real point was "to explore, again, the creative potential of disorder." Miller is very big on "the creative potential of disorder." Foucault was one of the few faculty who joined the students. When the police arrived, he followed the recalcitrant core to the roof in order to "resist." Miller reports proudly that while Foucault "gleefully" hurled stones at the police, he was nonetheless "careful not to dirty his beautiful black velour suit."

It was shortly after this encouraging episode that Foucault shaved his skull and emerged as a ubiquitous countercultural spokesman. His "politics" were consistently foolish, a combination of solemn chatter about "transgression," power, and surveillance, leavened by an extraordinary obtuseness about the responsible exercise of power in everyday life. Foucault was dazzled by the thought that the word "subject" (as in "the subject who is reading this") is cognate with "subjection." "Both meanings," he speculated, "suggest a form of power which subjugates or makes subject to." Foucault posed as a passionate partisan of liberty. At the same time, he never met a revolutionary piety he didn't like. He championed various extreme forms of Marxism, including Maoism; he supported the Ayatollah Khomeini, even when the Ayatollah's fundamentalist cadres set about murdering thousands of Iranian citizens. In 1978, looking back to the postwar period, he asked: "What could politics mean when it was a question of choosing between Stalin's USSR and Truman's America?" It tells us a great deal that Foucault found this question difficult to answer.

One thing that is refreshing about Foucault's political follies, however, is that they tend to make otherwise outlandish figures appear comparatively tame. In a debate that aired on Dutch television in the early Seventies, for example, the famous American radical and linguist Noam Chomsky appears as a voice of sanity and moderation in comparison to Foucault. As Miller reports it, while Chomsky insisted "we must act as sensitive and responsible human beings," Foucault replied that such ideas as responsibility, sensitivity, justice, and law were merely "tokens of ideology" that completely lacked legitimacy. "The proletariat doesn't wage war against the ruling class because it considers such a war to be just," he argued. "The proletariat makes war with the ruling class because . . . it wants to take power."

This has been the standard sophistical line since Socrates

encountered Thrasymachus, but these days one rarely hears it so bluntly articulated. Nor were such performances rare. In another debate, Foucault championed the September Massacres of 1792, in which over a thousand people suspected of harboring royalist sympathies were ruthlessly butchered, as a sterling example of "popular justice" at work. As Miller puts it, Foucault believed that justice would be best served "by throwing open every prison and shutting down every court."

Although he came of age in the 1940s and 1950s, the "public" Foucault was fundamentally a child of the Sixties: precocious, spoiled, self-absorbed, full of jejune political sentiments, wracked by unfulfillable fantasies of absolute ecstasy. He became expert at straining the narcissistic delusions of the Sixties through the forbidding, cynical argot of contemporary French philosophy. And it is primarily to this, I believe, that he owes his enormous success as an academic guru. In Foucault's philosophy, the "idealism" of the Sixties was painted a darker hue. But its demand for liberation from "every fixed form," as Miller repeatedly puts it, remained very much in force. In an interview from 1968, Foucault suggested that "the rough outline of a future society is supplied by the recent experiences with drugs, sex, communes, other forms of consciousness and other forms of individuality. If scientific socialism emerged from the *utopias* of the nineteenth century, it is possible that a real socialization will emerge in the 20th century from *experiences*."

Drugs, in fact, were one aid that Foucault freely availed himself of in his search for "experiences." He battened on hashish and marijuana in the Sixties, but it was not until 1975 that he had his first encounter with LSD. Miller considers it crucial to the philosopher's development, and so apparently did Foucault, who described it in what were clearly his highest words of praise. "The only thing I can compare this experience to in my life," he is reported to have said at the time, "is sex with a stranger. . . . Contact with a strange body affords an experience of the truth similar to what I am experiencing now." "I now understand my sexuality," he concluded.

In light of Foucault's subsequent death from AIDS, it seems grimly significant that this pharmacological fête took place in Death Valley. In any event, so galvanizing was Foucault's first experience with hallucinogens that he set aside drafts of the unpublished volumes of *The History of Sexuality*—what a loss! As Miller notes, there were hundreds of pages "on masturbation, on incest, on hysteria, on perversion, on eugenics": all the important philosophical issues of our time.

Nineteen seventy-five was clearly Foucault's *annus mirabilis*. It marked not only his introduction to the pleasures of LSD, but also his first visit to California's Bay Area and introduction to San Francisco's burgeoning sadomasochistic subculture. Foucault had "experimented" with S&M before—indeed, his proclivities in this matter cost him his relationship with the composer Jean Barraqué. But he had never encountered anything so exorbitant as what San Francisco had to offer. According to Miller, the philosopher, now nearing his fiftieth birthday, found it "a place of dumbfounding excess that left him happily speechless." The city's countless homosexual bathhouses, he explained, allowed Foucault to grapple with his "lifelong fascination with 'the overwhelming, the unspeakable, the creepy, the stupefying, the ecstatic,' embracing 'a pure violence, a wordless gesture.'"

As always, Miller presents Foucault's indulgence in sexual torture as if it were a noble existential battle for greater wisdom and political liberation. Thus while sadomasochism is a topic that Miller discusses early and often, his fullest exploration of the subject comes in a chapter called, after the title of one of Foucault's books, "The Will to Know." "Accepting the new level of risk," Miller writes, Foucault

> joined again in the orgies of torture, trembling with "the most exquisite agonies," voluntarily effacing himself, exploding the limits of consciousness, letting real, corporeal pain insensibly melt into pleasure through the alchemy of eroticism. . . . Through intoxication, reverie, the Dionysian abandon of the artist, the most punishing of ascetic practices, and an uninhibited exploration of sadomasochistic eroticism, it seemed possible to breach, however briefly, the boundaries separating the conscious and unconscious, reason and unreason, pleasure and pain—and, at the ultimate limit, life and death—thus starkly revealing how distinctions central to the play of true and false are pliable, uncertain, contingent.

Much of the time, Miller appears as a sober investigative journalist. But just mention the word "transcendence" and he goes all gooey. I suspect it's a reflex, acquired from too much Alan Watts and other quasi-mystical confections of the 1960s. Just as Pavlov's dog could not help salivating when he heard a bell ring, so Miller can't help spouting nonsense whenever anyone mentions Dionysus.

Noting sadly that we may "never know" exactly what Foucault did while exploding the limits of consciousness and effacing the boundaries between pleasure and pain, Miller is nevertheless gruesomely particular in his descriptions of the sadomasochistic underworld that Foucault frequented, a world that featured, among other attractions, "gagging, piercing, cutting, electric-shocking, stretching on racks, imprisoning, branding. . . ." "Depending on the club," he dutifully reports, "one could savor the illusion of bondage—or experience the most directly physical sorts of self-chosen 'torture.'" Foucault threw himself into this scene with an enthusiasm that astonished his friends, quickly acquiring an array of leather clothes and, "for play," a variety of clamps, handcuffs, hoods, gags, whips, paddles, and other "sex toys."

Miller's discussion of sadomasochism is certainly grotesque; it is also comical at times. Despite everything, Miller is a careful scholar, and so he feels obliged to supply readers with a full list of sources. In his compendious notes, he informs us that his discussion is based on such works as "The Catacombs: A Temple of the Butthole," *Urban Aboriginals: A Celebration of Leathersexuality*, and *The New Leatherman's Workbook: A Photo Illustrated Guide to* SM *Sex Devices.* "For the techniques of gay SM in these years," he explains, "I have relied on Larry Townshend, *The Leatherman's Handbook II.*" It's the deadpan delivery that does it.

Unintended comedy aside, however, Miller's whole depiction of sadomasochism is a maze of contradictions, veering wildly between the worst sort of pop psychobabble and pompous pseudo-philosophical sermonizing. Addicted to countercultural platitudes about sexual liberation and psychic emancipation, he can't understand why "SM is still one of the most widely stigmatized of sexual practices." Still, after all these years! On the one hand, to help overcome the stigma, he is desperate to de-toxify the subject, to make the perversion seem "generally benign" and normal. On the other hand, he also feels constrained to present the practice of sexual torture as something brave, "exploratory," and "challenging." The whips and chains are really just "props"; the encounters are "consensual"; the pain is "often mild"; the devotees of s&m are, "on the whole, . . . as nonviolent and well-adjusted as any other segment of the population." But even as he is telling us about the pillows he found in an s&m "dungeon" to make it cozy, he also quotes the expert who, while insisting that "the real trip is mental," freely acknowledges that "there is certainly pain and sometimes a small amount of blood." Only a small amount, though.

One of Miller's frequent explanatory strategies involves a trip down the slippery slope. When was the last time you had a violent impulse? Well, then: aren't we all closet sadists? "After all," Miller argues, "sm on one level merely makes explicit the sadistic and masochistic fantasies implicitly at play in most, perhaps all, human relationships."

Ah yes, "on one level." It never seems to occur to Miller that, even if it were true that such fantasies were "implicitly" at play in most human relationships (itself a dubious proposition), the difference between "implicit" and "explicit" is exactly the difference upon which the entire world of moral behavior is based. Furthermore, the question of "relationships" hardly enters, for as Foucault himself stressed, the anonymity of the encounters formed a large part of their attraction: "You meet men [in the clubs] who are to you as you are to them: nothing but a body with which combinations and productions of pleasure are possible. You cease to be imprisoned in your own face, in your own past, in your own identity."

Even Miller recognizes—though he doesn't come right out and say it—that at the center of Foucault's sexual obsessions was not the longing for philosophical insight but the longing for oblivion. "Complete total pleasure," Foucault correctly observed, is "related to death." The unhappy irony is that this apostle of sex and hedonism should have wound up, like the Marquis de Sade before him, exiling pleasure from sex. In one of the innumerable interviews that he gave in later years, Foucault praised sadomasochism as "a creative enterprise, which has as one of its main features what I call the desexualization of pleasure." What is pathetically revealing is Foucault's belief that this was an argument *for* sadomasochism. He continued: "The idea that bodily pleasure should always come from sexual pleasure, and the idea that sexual pleasure is the root of *all* our possible pleasure—I think *that's* something quite wrong."

Well yes, Michel, there is something quite wrong about that. But who believes that "bodily pleasure should always come from sexual pleasure"? Had a good meal lately? Enjoyed a walk in the sunshine? It is part of the relentless logic of sadomasochism that what begins as a single-minded cultivation of sexual pleasure for its own sake ends by extinguishing the capacity for enjoying pleasure altogether. Indeed, it might be said that the pursuit of ever more extreme sensations of pleasure, which stands at the heart of the sadomasochistic enterprise, drains the pleasure out of pleasure. The desire for oblivion ends up in the oblivion of desire.

Foucault's sexual adventures in the early 1980s also inevitably raise the question of AIDS. Did Foucault know he had the disease? Miller engages in a fair amount of hand-wringing over this question. He begins by saying no, Foucault probably didn't know. But he also quotes Daniel Defert, who thought his friend "had a real knowledge" that he had AIDS. "When he went to San Francisco for the last time, he took it as a *limit experience*." This puts Miller in a tough position. He thinks that "limit experiences" are by definition a good thing. "It is not immoral to be convulsed by singular fantasies and wild impulses," he writes, summarizing the "ethical" point of Foucault's book *Mad-*

ness and Civilization: "such limit-experiences are to be valued as a way of winning back access to the occluded, Dionysian dimension of being human." But what if pursuing the limit involves infecting other people with a deadly disease? What if the pursuit of some "limit experiences" implicates one in what amounts to homicidal behavior? In the end, Miller waffles. He is all for allowing those who "think differently" to engage in "potential suicidal acts of passion" with consenting partners. But homicidal acts? It is pretty clear, in any event, what Foucault himself thought. As he put it in Volume 1 of *The History of Sexuality*, "The Faustian pact, whose temptation has been instilled in us by the deployment of sexuality, is now as follows: to exchange life in its entirety for sex itself, for the truth and the sovereignty of sex. Sex is worth dying for."

Foucault is admired above all for practicing an exemplary suspicion about the topics he investigated. He is supposed to have been a supreme intellectual anatomist, ruthlessly laying bare the hidden power relations, dark motives, and ideological secrets that infect bourgeois society and that fester unacknowledged in the hearts and minds of everyone. It is curious, though, that Foucault's acolytes bring so little suspicion to the master's own claims. Consider the central Foucauldian contention that objective truth is a "chimera," that truth is always and everywhere a function of power, of "multiple forms of constraint." Some version of this claim is propagated as gospel by academics across the country. But wait: is this startling contention *true*? Is it in fact the case that truth is always relative to a "regime of truth," i.e., to politics? If one says: "Yes, it is true," then one plunges directly into contradiction—for haven't we just dispensed with this "naïve" idea of truth?—and the logical cornerstone of Foucault's epistemology crumbles.

Or consider the proposition that Michel Foucault is a kind of latter-day avatar of Friedrich Nietzsche. It is not so much argued as taken for granted that Foucault, like Nietzsche, was the very epitome of the lonely but profound philosophical hero, thinking thoughts too deep—and too dangerous—for most of us. (Except of course for Foucault's followers: for *them* it is the work of a moment to dispense with "Western metaphysics," "bourgeois humanism," and a thousand other evils.) Foucault himself assiduously promoted the idea that he was a modern-day Nietzsche, and Miller has elevated the comparison into a central interpretive principle. In his preface, he announces that his book is not so much a biography as an account "of one man's lifelong struggle to honor Nietzsche's gnomic injunction, 'to become what one is.'" Never mind that thirty pages later we find Foucault insisting that "One writes to become someone other than who one is": the Foucault industry thrives on such "paradoxes." Anyway, who has time for such niceties as logic when engaged on a risky "Nietzschean quest," something we find Foucault pursuing in Miller's book every fifty pages or so?

In fact, the comparison between Foucault and Nietzsche is a calumny upon Nietzsche. As we have seen, Friedrich Nietzsche has a lot to answer for, including the popularity of figures like Foucault. But whatever one thinks of Nietzsche's philosophy and influence, it is difficult not to admire his courage and single-minded commitment to the philosophical life. Wracked by ill health—migraines, vertigo, severe digestive complaints—Nietzsche had to quit his teaching position at the University of Basel when he was in his mid-thirties. From then on he led an isolated, impoverished, celibate life, subsisting in various cheap *pensioni* in Italy and Switzerland. He had but few friends. His work was almost totally ignored. As noted earlier, *Beyond*

Good and Evil, one of his most important books, sold a total of 114 copies in a year. Yet he quietly persevered.

And Foucault? After attending the most elite French schools—the lycée Henri IV, the Ecole Normale Supérieure, the Sorbonne—he held a series of academic appointments in France, Poland, Germany, Sweden, and Tunisia. The jobs were low-paying, but the budding philosopher was aided in his program of resistance by generous subsidies from his parents. In the 1950s, when he was a lowly instructor at the University of Uppsala, he acquired what Didier Eribon calls "a magnificent beige Jaguar" (it is white in Miller's book) and proceeded to drive "like a madman" around town, shocking staid Uppsalian society. Talk about challenging convention! Eribon reminds us, too, that Foucault was an accomplished academic politician, adept at securing preferment for himself and his friends. This is not to say that he concealed his contempt for narrow, bourgeois scruples, however. Attempting suicide and hurling stones at the police were hardly his only efforts to "transgress" accepted academic protocol. While he was teaching at Clermont-Ferrand in the early 1960s, for example, he gave an assistantship to his lover, Daniel Defert. In response to a faculty-council query about why he had appointed Defert rather than another applicant, a woman who was older and better qualified, he replied: "Because we don't like old maids here." Moreover, Foucault enjoyed the esteem of gullible intellectuals everywhere. His book *Les Mots et les choses* (*The Order of Things* in English) became a best-seller in 1966, catapulting him to international fame. The crowning recognition came in 1970 when, at the unusually young age of forty-four, Foucault was elected to the Collège de France, the very pinnacle of French academic culture. Miller, like most academics who write about Foucault, praises Foucault's philosophical daring and willingness to put himself at risk for his ideas. "For more than a decade," Miller writes about Foucault's reputation at the time of his death, "his elegant shaved skull had been an emblem of political courage—a cynosure of resistance to institutions that would smother the free spirit and stifle the 'right to be different.'" What brave resistance to bourgeois society!

But Foucault differed from Nietzsche in more than such outward trappings. The fundamental world outlooks of the two men were radically different. Basically, Foucault was Nietzsche's ape. He adopted some of Nietzsche's rhetoric about power and imitated some of his verbal histrionics. But he never achieved anything like Nietzsche's insight or originality. Nietzsche may have been seriously wrong in his understanding of modernity: he may have mistaken one part of the story—the rise of secularism—for the whole tale; but few men have struggled as passionately with the problem of nihilism as did Nietzsche. Foucault simply flirted with nihilism as one more "experience." Miller is right to emphasize the importance of "experience," especially extreme or "limit" experience, in Foucault's life and work; he is wrong to think that this was a virtue. Foucault was addicted to extremity. He epitomized to perfection a certain type of decadent Romantic, a type that Nietzsche warned against when he spoke of "those who suffer from the *impoverishment of life* and seek rest, stillness, calm seas, redemption from themselves through art and knowledge, or intoxication, convulsions, anaesthesia, and madness." Foucault's insatiable craving for new, ever more thrilling "experiences" was a sign of weakness, not daring. Here, too, Nietzsche is a far better guide than Foucault. "All men now live through too much and think through too little," Nietzsche wrote in 1880. "They suffer at the same time from extreme hunger and from colic, and therefore become thinner and thinner, no matter how much they eat.—Whoever says now, 'I have not lived through anything'— is an ass."

Miller is not entirely uncritical. About *Madness and Civilization* (English translation, 1971), for example, he acknowledges that "the author's own convictions are insinuated more than argued." About *The Order of Things*, he points out that the writing is "awkward, disjointed, elliptical to a fault." But such local criticisms do not go nearly far enough. As the Australian historian Keith Windschuttle showed in his brilliant book *The Killing of History* (1994; rev. ed. 1996), Foucault's scholarship is riddled with errors and deliberate obfuscations. In *Madness and Civilization*, for example, Foucault contrasts the happy time of the Middle Ages when the insane supposedly wandered freely from town to town or traveled on a literal Ship of Fools up and down the Rhine. The birth of the asylum, according to Foucault, was a dark day for the insane, for not only were they now incarcerated, but also they were denied the status of human beings. Foucault makes similar claims about hospitals and penal policy. As Windschuttle shows in devastating detail, in every case Foucault's account is wildly inaccurate. There was no Ship of Fools as Foucault describes; his dates are often wrong by a century or more; and as for the treatment of the insane, Windschuttle quotes the historian Andrew Scull to set the record straight: "Where the mad proved troublesome, they could expect to be beaten or locked up; otherwise they might roam or rot. Either way, the facile contrast between psychiatric oppression and an earlier, almost anarchic toleration is surely illusory." Windschuttle makes the more general case: "Madness became an issue of public policy with the rise of democratic, egalitarian societies, primarily because these societies accepted the madman not as *the other*, or as someone outside humanity, but as *another human being*, as an individual with the same basic status as everyone else."

At the beginning of his book, Miller mentions in passing J. G. Merquior's incisive critical study, *Foucault* (1985). Readers acquainted with that book know that Merquior, who is identified as "a Brazilian diplomat who studied with Ernest Gellner," has politely but definitively exploded almost every significant claim that Foucault made. Merquior typically begins each chapter with a ritual nod to Foucault's brilliance. He then proceeds to show that his arguments rest on shoddy scholarship, distorted history, and untenable generalizations. Whatever "new perspectives" Foucault's work may have opened up, Merquior concludes, its "conceptual muddles and explanatory weaknesses . . . more than outweigh its real contribution." The truth is, Foucault specialized in providing obfuscating answers to pseudo problems. "We have had sexuality since the eighteenth century, and sex since the nineteenth," he writes in *The History of Sexuality*. "What we had before that was no doubt flesh." Yes, and "Sexual intercourse was invented in 1963," as Philip Larkin memorably put it.

Foucault once described his writing as a "labyrinth." He was right. The question is, why should we wish to enter it? It may be the case that, as Miller insists, Foucault's writing expresses "a powerful desire to realize a certain form of life." But is it a *desirable* form of life? Foucault's personal perversions involved him in private tragedy. The celebration of his intellectual perversions by academics continues to be a public scandal. The career of this "representative man" of the twentieth century really represents one of the biggest con jobs in recent intellectual history.

The Anguishes
of E. M. Cioran

What a torment to be ordinary, a man among men!
—E. M. Cioran

THERE ARE certain cultural figures who manage to make
metaphysical gloominess the centerpiece and inspiration of their life's work. Though vigorously atheistic, they
often resort to a quasi-religious terminology to express
their obsession with the transience and absurdities of life,
man's capacity for evil and cruelty, and the ubiquity of
suffering in this imperfect and ephemeral world. Capitaliz-
ing on mankind's hearty appetite for self-dramatization
and self-pity, they expatiate, often with considerable eloquence, on the pointlessness and corruption of all human
endeavors and institutions, elaborating a seductive vision
of doom. The darker strains of Romanticism—one thinks
especially of a figure like Novalis—provide one important
source for this tendency; Schopenhauer's philosophical
pessimism provides another. In modern times, most
devotees of the genre have also injected a heavy dose of
irony into their pathos, transforming Romantic despair
into a species of hyper-conscious self-mockery even as they
pursue their love affair with the void; misguided idealism
gives way to a brittle, nihilistic cynicism. It is only natural

that the title of Oswald Spengler's dour masterpiece, *Der Untergang des Abendlandes, The Decline of the West,* should emerge as the insistent rallying cry of these fervent partisans of disillusionment.

The Rumanian-born essayist and aphorist Emile M. Cioran is a minor but thoroughly typical contemporary representative of this tradition of metaphysical futility. The son of a Greek Orthodox priest, Cioran was born in a village in the Carpathians in 1911. He studied philosophy at Bucharest University, winning a scholarship from the French Institute there in 1937. This took him to Paris, where he lived and worked until his death in 1995. He began writing in French only in 1947, apparently expending great efforts to master the language: "It would be the narrative of a nightmare," he confesses with characteristic understatement, "were I to give you a detailed account of the history of my relations with this borrowed idiom." He published his first book, *Précis de décomposition* (translated as a *A Short History of Decay*), in 1949 and went on to publish several volumes of essays and aphorisms.[1]

While hardly a household name, Cioran attracted a staunch coterie of admirers in both Europe and the United States. In this country, his popularity, such as it is, was sparked largely by the early efforts of that unparalleled impresario of the new, Susan Sontag. In 1968, she contributed an introductory essay to *The Temptation to Exist,* Cioran's first book translated into English. Describing him as "one of the most *delicate* minds of real power writing today," Sontag touts Cioran as the "most distinguished figure" now writing in the anti-systematic tradition of

---

1 Cioran's other collections include *Syllogismes de l'amertume* (1952), *La Tentation d'exister* (1956), *Histoire et utopie* (1960), *La Chute dans le temps* (1964), and *De l'Inconvenient d'être né* (1973).

"Kierkegaard, Nietzsche, and Wittgenstein"—a tradition, she tells us, for which "thinking" (the quotation marks are hers) "is redefined as worthless unless it is an extreme act."

Be this as it may, Sontag's estimation of Cioran's importance is by now commonplace among readers with a taste for his brand of high-pitched, deliberately provocative intellectual marauding. "Thinking Against Oneself" and "On a Winded Civilization": the titles of the opening two essays of *The Temptation to Exist* epitomize the mood and general outlook not only of this volume but all of Cioran's work. Here as elsewhere, what Cioran offers are not reasoned arguments or sustained reflections but a series of highly charged *aperçus* on the *debâcle* of Western civilization, the fate of the intellectual in contemporary society, the end of the novel, the virtues of tyranny, the future of utopia, and other edifying topics. Yet behind these ostensible themes lies his one real abiding concern, a concern that Sontag sums up admirably. "Cioran's subject: on being a *mind*, a consciousness tuned to the highest pitch of refinement. . . . In Cioran's writings," she adds, "the mind is a voyeur. But not of 'the world.' Of itself." With these last characterizations, especially, we come close to the center of Cioran's thought.

Was Cioran the embattled intellectual hero that Sontag presents: a lonely mind of "real power" courageously recording important truths that are too unpalatable for the majority of thinkers to acknowledge? Or was he more in the way of an intellectual *poseur*, a metaphysical aesthete who anatomizes his self-inflicted agonies not for the sake of any presumed truth but merely in order to provide himself with ever more exquisite spectacles of disbelief? Almost everything Cioran wrote points to the latter.

Of course, Cioran's appeal does not rest only on the substance of his position; equally—if not more—important is his style, his epigrammatic tautness. His self-advertised labors with the French language resulted in a style that blends an almost Olympian coolness and intellectuality with the appearance of passion bordering, at times, on hysteria. Like so much about Cioran, it is essentially an adolescent style: highhanded, confessional, histrionic, but nevertheless full of energy. His habitual use of the editorial We—one of his most obvious rhetorical borrowings from Nietzsche—helps invest his writing with a patina of authority; and if one discounts context and forgets about picayune things like meaning and coherence, Cioran can be eminently quotable. But he clearly values the *effect* of his style over consistency of argument. One does not have to read far in his work before understanding Susan Sontag's enthusiasm: in Cioran she found a kindred spirit, an inspiration, a writer who preserved the appearance of serious intellectual inquiry while giving absolute priority to rhetorical gestures, verbal extravagances, and modishly provocative poses. Nor are English readers denied much of the spectacle. Cioran was extremely well served by his main English translator, the poet Richard Howard, who has a remarkable feel for the appropriate cadences and vocabulary with which to render Cioran's self-consciously "brilliant," over-worked prose.

It was obviously terribly important for Cioran to present himself as a Romantic figure *manqué,* a kind of Rimbaud with a degree in philosophy and more staying power. He casually described himself as "prowling around the Absolute" and informed us that "The only minds which seduce us are the minds which have destroyed themselves trying to give their lives a meaning." He liked to see himself as an intellectually inclined aesthete who had the courage and lucidity to see through everything, especially his former ideals. For example, while he came to find poetry "a vision of singsong and nullity, of fetid mysteries and affectations," it is essential that we understand that he was also once a great lover of poetry: "I have loved it at the expense of my health; I anticipated succumbing to my worship of it." His superior insight and tenacity, we are meant to understand, competing with a passionate aesthetic sensibility, allowed him to occupy this lonely aerie above the illusory blandishments of poetry.

Cioran's favorite rhetorical gambit—his predominate bid for attention—is disarmingly simple: he takes conventional wisdom about politics, culture, or ethics and inverts it. In the hallowed tradition of *épater la bourgeoisie*, he sets out to shock, to unsettle, to provoke. Not that there is anything particularly new in Cioran's painstakingly contentious statements; for the most part, they read like formulaic declarations of existentialist angst and venom. True, when one first dips into his work, it can seem brashly outrageous. How extraordinary to be told that philosophy is the "privilege of . . . *biologically* superficial peoples," to discover that "we spend the prime of our sleepless nights in mentally mangling our enemies, rending their entrails, wringing their veins, trampling each organ to mush," or to learn that at the age of twenty Cioran supposed "that to become the enemy of the human race was the highest dignity to which one might aspire."

Similarly, one cannot help being brought up short when Cioran looks back to his native Rumania only to tell us that "I owe it not only my finest, my surest failures, but also this talent for masking my cowardice and hoarding my compunctions," or summarizes his feelings about Paris with the observation that "this city, which I would exchange for no other in the world, is for that very reason the source of my misfortunes. . . . I often regret that wars have spared it, that it has not perished like so many others.

Destroyed, it would have rid me of the happiness of living here. . . . I shall never forgive Paris for having bound me to space, for making me *from somewhere*."

After two or three essays, such displays lose whatever novelty they originally had; and after slogging through several books, one realizes that Cioran's pose of intellectual provocateur is little more than a mask for a series of repetitious clichés. Thus he is everywhere at pains to extol dreams and madness as bastions of freedom and genius. In "Thinking Against Oneself" he writes that "We are all geniuses when we dream, the butcher the poet's equal there. . . . Only the madman enjoys the privilege of passing smoothly from a nocturnal to a daylight existence." And a bit later: "It is the madman in us who forces us into adventure; once he abandons us, we are lost. . . . We cannot be *normal* and *alive* at the same time."

Beggars, too, are favored objects of Cioran's admiration, for in his view the beggar's "thought is resolved into his being and his being into his thought. He *has* nothing, he *is* himself, he endures: to live on a footing with eternity is to live from day to day, from hand to mouth." It's the old image brought up to date of the poor fool turning out to be wiser than the educated philistine. Cioran treats us to this one a good deal. In an essay entitled "Beyond the Novel," he admonishes us to dispense with the genre because it is too bookish and mundane to deal with what really matters.

> What interest can a mere life afford? What interest, books inspired by other books or minds dependent on other minds? Only the illiterate have given me that *frisson* of being which indicates the presence of truth. Carpathian shepherds have made a much deeper impression upon me than the professors of Germany, the wits of Paris. I have seen Spanish

beggars, and I should like to have become their hagiographer. They had no need to invent a life for themselves: they *existed*; which does not happen in civilization.

What *does* happen in civilization? Cioran never really says. Indeed, one wonders if it really matters to him. As his quasi-metaphysical, yet nowhere defined, use of the term "existence" here suggests, he is not against using words primarily as emotional embroidery. And what about the "truth" that these illiterate Spanish peasants are said to possess? In another essay he scornfully summarizes his feelings about that dinosaur with a phrase: "The Truth? An adolescent fad or symptom of senility."

Clearly, Cioran's thought rests largely on a Romantic opposition of instinct to intellect, on a *preference* for instinct over intellect. "Whatever emanates from the inferior zones of our nature," he writes, "is invested with strength, whatever comes from below stimulates: we invariably produce and perform better out of jealousy and greed than out of nobility and disinterestedness." Hence his suspicion of reason as "the rust of our vitality," and his claim that "we are born to exist, not to know; to be, not to assert ourselves. Knowledge, having irritated and stimulated our appetite for power, will lead us inexorably to our ruin. . . . [K]nowledge taints the economy of a human being." No arguments are provided for these sentiments, possibly because, as he notes elsewhere, he is convinced that "the dynasty of intelligibility" is drawing to a close. What use are arguments in a realm of chaos and unintelligibility?

But though Cioran appears as an intellectual campaigning against the hegemony of the intellect, he is by no means given to a worship of the body or man's physical life. His paean to instinct does not preserve him from vituperative expressions of contempt for the body.

In what grease, what pestilence the spirit has taken up its abode! This body, whose every pore eliminates enough stench to infect space, is no more than a mass of ordure through which circulates a scarcely less ignoble blood, no more than a tumor that disfigures the geometry of the globe. Supernatural disgust! No one approaches without revealing to me, despite himself, the stage of his putrefaction, the livid destiny which awaits him.

It cannot be said that Cioran has improved or particularly matured with age. *The Trouble with Being Born* (1976), a collection of aphorisms published in French in 1973, strikes one as a series of rambling, disconnected thoughts culled from the journal of a well-read but deeply troubled teenager—that, or a collection of rejected entries from Woody Allen's parody of Kafka. Here are a few more or less randomly chosen tidbits:

Three in the morning. I realize this second, then this one, then the next: I draw up the balance sheet for each minute. And why all this? *Because I was born.* It is a special type of sleeplessness that produces the indictment of birth.

Physical need of dishonor. How I should have liked to be the executioner's son!

If disgust for the world conferred sanctity of itself, I fail to see how I could avoid canonization.

The right to suppress everyone that bothers us should rank first in the constitution of the ideal State.

A book is a postponed suicide.

Sometimes I wish I were a cannibal—less for the pleasure of eating someone than for the pleasure of vomiting him.

It is easy, is it not, to see why Susan Sontag describes this man as "one of the most *delicate* minds of real power writing today"?

Cioran's attitude—not to say attitudinizing—toward violence and disaster epitomizes his efforts at self-dramatization. Often, he pauses to vent his spleen on himself. "I have hated myself in all the objects of my hatreds, I have imagined miracles of annihilation, pulverized my hours, tested the gangrenes of the intellect." But he saves most of his energy for others. In "Odyssey of Rancor" we are told that by nature man is saturated with murderous resentment. Hate is presented as mankind's guiding principle, yet most men, especially in the civilized West, "are not equal to their hatred." Only this keeps them from destroying one another at once. The "need to kill, inscribed in every cell," has been stymied by civilization, and this has vitiated man's primitive vigor and led to decadence and decline. For Cioran, "we become *good* only by destroying the best of our nature," and, similarly, "our imaginations function only in hope of others' misfortune." "We"? "Our"? How easily grammar insinuates complicity!

In essays like "Russia and the Virus of Liberty" and "Learning from the Tyrants" (both of which, with "Odyssey of Rancor," appear in *History and Utopia*), Cioran elevates the themes of violence and hatred from the individual to the social and political level. Democratic liberalism appears not as a social and political achievement of the first order but as a concession to weakness and decay. "Freedoms prosper only in a sick body politic: tolerance and impotence are synonyms." Since he believes that "the passion to reduce others to the status of objects" is the key to understanding politics, he has profound respect for political tyrants. Reflecting on the Russian tradition from the time of the tsars down through Lenin and Stalin, for example, he tells us that "they were, as are these more recent tyrants who have replaced them, closer to a geological vitality than to human anemia, despots perpetuating in our time the primordial sap, the primordial spoilage, and triumphing over us all by their inexhaustible reserves of chaos."

Although he assures us that he "abominates tyrants," Cioran also admits that he "harbors a weakness for tyrants"—largely, one suspects, because he thinks that "a world without tyrants would be as boring as a zoo without hyenas." Indeed, he seems to believe that we all would behave as tyrants if only we had the courage, lucidity, and forcefulness. Hence tyrants are said to "reveal us to ourselves, they incarnate and illustrate our secrets." And hence Cioran regards the asperity and violence of his writing as a substitute for the physical violence he has been incapable of perpetrating: "Unable to render myself worthy of [tyrants] by action, I hoped to do so by words, by the practice of sophism and enormity: to be as odious with the means of mind as they were with those of power, to devastate by language, to blow up the word and with it the world, to explode with one and the other, and finally to collapse under their debris." Moreover, he envisions a great tyrant on the horizon, one who will forge the nations of the earth into a single entity. "The scattered human herd will be united under the guardianship of one pitiless shepherd, a kind of planetary monster before whom nations will prostrate themselves in an alarm bordering on ecstasy." Somehow, though, the decidedly unecstatic alarm one feels reading such professions is not assuaged by his blithe identification of Hitler as "the rough draft of our future," the harbinger of this envisioned "planetary monster."

Given his infatuation with exile, alienation, and historical catastrophe, one could have predicted that Cioran
would sooner or later find himself moved to write about
Judaism and the Jews. Among other things, "A People of
Solitaries," his essay on the Jews in *The Temptation to
Exist* is a perfect example of his simplifying hostility
toward religion.

> For them, eternity was a pretext for convulsions, a spasm:
> vomiting imprecations and anthems, they wriggle before
> the eyes of a God insatiable for hysterias. This was a
> religion in which man's relations with his Creator are ex-
> hausted in a war of epithets, in a tension which keeps him
> from pondering, from emphasizing and thereby from
> remedying his differences, a religion based on adjectives,
> effects of language, and in which style constitutes the only
> hyphen between heaven and earth.

Not, one hastens to add, that he is much better on Christianity. "[W]e"—that inveigling plural again—"yawn over
the Cross . . . To attempt to save Christianity, to prolong
its career, would not occur to us; on occasion it awakens
our . . . indifference." (The ellipses are Cioran's.)

But of course his chief interest in Judaism is not in its
religious dimension but in the stereotype of the Jew as vic-
tim and scapegoat. And here, as in his frequent invocation
of "biological capital" in other essays, Cioran betrays a
species of race thinking that is tantamount to racism. For
him, the Jews occupy a distinct ontological category that
makes them different *toto genere* from "ordinary" human
beings: "Let someone else do them the insult of making
'meaningful' statements about them! I cannot bring myself
to do so: to apply our standards to them is to strip them of
their privileges, to turn them into mere mortals, an ordi-

nary variety of the human type." Professed admiration becomes a cloak for an extraordinarily patronizing presumptuousness. Did the Jews suffer untold barbarities at the hands of the Nazis? Cioran airily dismisses the question, advising us to "leave aside regrets, or delirium. . . . The instinct of self-preservation mars individuals and collectivities alike." Perhaps it was this last observation that led even Susan Sontag to admit that Cioran's discussion of the Jews "displays a startling moral insensitivity to the contemporary aspects of his theme."

Sontag described Cioran's politics as "conservative." But even the briefest glimpse at his political animadversions shows that this is a complete misnomer. Cioran has no more desire to conserve or preserve traditional social and political arrangements than—well, than the tyrants he so lovingly eulogizes. Not that it is easy to determine what Cioran's politics are. "Tradition," "heritage," "democracy," "liberalism": these are terms of abuse for Cioran. But he is a a connoisseur of inconsistency, capable of castigating Marxism on one page for "the sin of optimism" while later championing Communism as "the only reality to which one might still subscribe, if one harbors even a wisp of illusion as to the future." He declares in one place that "life without utopia is suffocating" yet insists in another that "we shall never praise utopias sufficiently for having denounced the crimes of ownership, the horror property represents, the calamities it causes. Great or small, the owner is corrupted, sullied in his essence: . . . To own even a broom, to count anything at all as *our* property, is to participate in the general infamy."

But if there is a wild inconsistency of argument in Cioran's work, there is nonetheless an almost rigid consistency of attitude; Cioran's positions and opinions shift from page to page; contradictions abound; but throughout it all he maintains his stance as an extreme philosophical anarchist: "Bluntly: my rebellion is a faith to which I subscribe without believing in it," he writes, reasoning that "since the Absolute corresponds to a meaning we have not been able to cultivate, let us surrender to all rebellions: they will end by turning against themselves, against us." And this, you understand, is meant as a recommendation.

In a writer as unsystematic and (one assumes) deliberately inconsistent as Cioran, it will perhaps seem idle to look for the presuppositions of his position. But lurking behind much of his writing is the essentially Romantic glorification of absolute freedom—the *confusion*, that is to say, of indeterminate spontaneity with genuine freedom, which has meaning only when limited and determined by particular choices and commitments. Throughout Cioran's work one encounters the idea that *any* definite thought or action is an encroachment upon freedom that ought ideally to be resisted. "The sphere of consciousness shrinks in action," he writes in the lead essay of *The Temptation to Exist*.

> No one who acts can lay claim to the universal, for to act is to cling to the properties of being at the expense of being itself, to a form of reality to reality's detriment. . . . If we would regain our freedom, we must shake off the burden of sensation, no longer react to the world by our senses, break our bonds. . . . The only free mind is the one that, pure of all intimacy with beings or objects, plies its own vacuity.

Elsewhere he speaks of "the illusory character, the nullity of all action" and concludes that "freedom can be manifested only in the void of beliefs, in the absence of axioms, and only where the laws have no more authority than a hypothesis." In other words, according to Cioran, freedom can be manifested only where it is impossible. For him, freedom is the elusive corollary of "Being" or "the Absolute," terms whose emptiness is not remedied simply by being capitalized.

At bottom, Cioran's main theme, the theme to which he returns again and again, the theme that more than any other has endeared him to Leftist intellectuals like Sontag and allowed them to overlook his otherwise unacceptable politics, is hatred of the West, its institutions, heritage, and future. Describing the West as "a sweet-smelling rottenness, a perfumed corpse," Cioran asserts that, having shed brutality, the West has also lost its strength. "Once subjects, they [the nations of the West] have become objects, forever dispossessed of that luminescence, that admirable megalomania which had hitherto protected them from the irreparable." Again and again he proclaims the end of Western culture. Even now the the West is "preparing for its end," he tells us, "let us envisage chaos. Already, most of us are resigned to it."

Predictably, bourgeois society, being an enclave of liberal democratic thought, comes in for special criticism. In "Letter to a Faraway Friend," the opening essay in *History and Utopia,* Cioran enlarges on the "lacunae of bourgeois society," assuring his "faraway friend" that such a society is not "entirely and absolutely displeasing to me—you know my weakness for the horrible—but the expenditure of insensitivity it requires to be endured is out of all proportion to my reserves of cynicism." Expatiating on the "curse" that has fallen upon the liberal West, he asks why the West "produces only these businessmen, these shopkeepers, these racketeers with their blank stares and atrophied smiles, to be met with everywhere, in Italy as in France, in England as in Germany? Is it with such vermin as this that a civilization so delicate and complex must come to an end?" Anti-Western animus has been a stock-in-trade of fashionable intellectuals at least since the middle of the nineteenth century. But Cioran's vitriol attains a rare level of savagery and contempt. And one cannot help wondering if there isn't something in the rejoinder that Cioran quotes from an unnamed friend in "Some Blind Alleys: A Letter": "'The West—you aren't even part of it.'"

Especially in his earlier work, Cioran's rhetoric recalls no one so much as Friedrich Nietzsche, and one is not surprised to find that Sontag observes—not without embarrassment, one suspects, for the observation cannot but dim her subject's claim to originality—that Nietzsche "set down almost all Cioran's positions almost a century ago." In fact, though, this is only half-true. There is no doubt that Cioran was deeply impressed by Nietzsche; his writing is permeated by the philosopher's themes, his perfervid prose, even his distinctive locutions and images. Nietzsche's infatuation with violence and power, his use of physiological metaphors to explain art and other cultural phenomena, his deliberate inversion of inherited moral categories, his vision of an existential stance "beyond good and evil": all this and more reappears predigested in Cioran's works.

But, like Foucault, Cioran was less Nietzsche's disciple than his ape. He adopted the extravagant rhetorical gestures, gloried in shocking conventional wisdom, and clearly would liked to have described himself, as did Nietzsche, as intellectual "dynamite." But when one comes to examine the substance of Cioran's thought, one discovers that on almost every issue his position—insofar as he adopts a consistent position—was completely at odds with Nietzsche's teaching. Sontag herself admits that "What's missing in Cioran's work is anything parallel to

Nietzsche's heroic effort to surmount nihilism." Since the effort to surmount nihilism forms the core of Nietzsche's mature work, its utter absence in Cioran's work already marks an important divergence from Nietzsche.

More generally, Cioran's gloomy flirtations with the void are diametrically opposed to Nietzsche's efforts to overcome the life-poisoning pessimism of (as he put it in *The Gay Science*) the man who "revenges himself on all things by forcing his own image, the image of his torture, on them, branding them with it." Cioran's work proceeds from a disgust—or at least the pretense of a disgust—with life, especially the life of civilized man. Despite his own excesses, at the center of Nietzsche's thought is the ambition to woo modern man back from his disenchantment with life. "I should very much like," Nietzsche writes, "to do something that would make the thought of life even a hundred times more appealing." For Cioran, revenge is the lugubrious tonic that provides life with its chief fascination; for Nietzsche "the spirit of revenge" constitutes the main impediment to man's self-affirmation. Behind all the bravura, there is something terribly pathetic about Cioran. "What a torment to be ordinary, a man among men!" he has exclaimed. But, as he put it in one of his most insightful observations, "Nothing is more commonplace than the *ersatz* troubled soul, for everything can be learned, even *angst*."

Part Three

The Trivialization
of Outrage

*Today everybody innovates. Deliberately, methodically. And the
innovations are deliberately and methodically made startling.
Only it now turns out not to be true that all startling art is
necessarily innovative or new art. . . . It has become apparent
that art can have a startling impact without really being or
saying anything startling—or new. The character itself of being
startling, spectacular, or upsetting has become conventionalized,
part of safe good taste.*
—Clement Greenberg

*The artist used to be at war with the Philistine. Today, for fear of
being tainted with élitism or with failing to meet the elementary
requirements of the democratic outlook, your intellectual abases
himself before the power-hungry world of show-business, or
fashion, or advertising.*
—Alain Finkielkraut

A MONG THE MANY peculiarities affecting our cultural
life today, perhaps none is more peculiar, or more
fateful for the practice and enjoyment of art, than the fact
that virtually anything can be put forward *and accepted* as
a work of art. "Virtually" anything? An unnecessary caution, surely. Let your imagination run riot: whatever gro-

tesquerie you conjure up—from the numbingly banal and commonplace to the repulsively pathological—rest assured that it has been eagerly proffered and just as eagerly embraced as art. And if by some fluke you named something that has not yet done duty as art—no matter: it is merely an oversight and will be corrected within a season or two.

Item: In January, 2000, Jonathan Yegge, a twenty-four-year-old student at the San Francisco Art Institute performed "Art Piece No. 1" on an open-air stage in front of some twenty fellow students, two professors, and various passersby. The full details of this performance are too loathsome to merit describing here; suffice it to say that, in the words of an Associated Press wire story, it "involved unprotected oral sex and exchanging excrement with a bound and gagged classmate."

The extreme repulsiveness of Jonathan Yegge's behavior —not to mention the health hazard it posed—earned him a few headlines. Nervous school officials, worried about law suits and negative publicity, required him to be tested for AIDS and imposed other sanctions. But within a few days a story in the *San Francisco Examiner* epitomized the hoary liberal response under the headline "'Shocking' Art a Venerable Tradition."

It is worth pausing to consider the significance of those scare quotes. Are they meant to suggest that Mr. Yegge's behavior performance was *not* shocking? "What is going on here," the writer of that story told us, "is part of a long and rich tradition." Right on cue, he wheeled on Edouard Manet's "Olympia." Defenders of the so-called "cutting edge" in art always cite that nude by Manet. Never mind that Manet's painting was a technical masterpiece and was at least as shocking in formal terms as it was in content. Mr. Yegge's performance, in contrast, was merely an exhibition of sexual psychopathology leavened by bad-boy bravado. Nevertheless, the writer of the *Examiner*'s story firmly embraced the embarrassing logical solecism that because some great art of the past has been shocking, everything that manages to get itself called art and is also shocking must therefore be great.

The very existence of phenomena like "Art Piece No. 1" tells us something about our culture. The fact that such a piece should have been offered as part of a course in art at a reputable school tells us something about what has happened to our conception of art and to our educational institutions. And the fact that writers for reputable newspapers respond by defending such displays by marshalling the rhetoric of "innovation" and "transgression" tells us something about the state of contemporary criticism.

The reporter for the *San Francisco Examiner* was right about one thing: that Mr. Yegge's performance, though disgusting, was not really new. Indeed, recourse to the repellent has been a stock-in-trade of certain artists at least since Surrealism. We've all seen it before countless times: the pornography, the pathological fascination with decay and mutilation, the toying with blasphemy (dressed up, occasionally, as a new religiosity). Consider this statement:

> I "made up" the putrefaction of the donkeys with great pots of sticky glue which I poured over them. Also I emptied their eye-sockets and made them larger by hacking them out with scissors. In the same way I furiously cut their mouths open to make the rows of teeth show to better advantage, and I added several jaws to each mouth, so that it would appear that although the donkeys were already rotting they were vomiting up a little more of their own death.

Damien Hirst acknowledging the Turner Prize, perhaps?

No, that is Salvador Dalí in 1942, recounting his work for the Surrealist film *Le Chien Andalou.*

The fact is that performances like Mr. Yegge's "Art Piece No. 1" do not challenge established taste. To a great extent they *are* established taste. Such phenomena are a dime-a-dozen these days. They fill the special exhibition galleries of virtually every art museum the world over. Remember, to take just one example, "Sensation," the infamous exhibition of British art that appeared at the Brooklyn Museum in the fall of 1999? Remember the portrait of the Virgin Mary festooned with cut-outs from pornographic magazines and clumps of elephant dung? Remember the pubescent female mannequins studded with erect penises, vaginas, and anuses, fused together in various postures of sexual coupling? Or the portrait of a child molester and murderer made from what looks like a child's hand prints? Or Damien Hirst's bisected animals (pigs, cows) in plexiglass tanks full of formaldehyde?

To an extent frightening to contemplate, performances like "Art Piece No. 1" and exhibitions like "Sensation" represent the new Salon taste: the taken-for-granted taste of the art establishment. It used to be that the Salon looked to the past and resisted aesthetic innovation. The Salon of today insists on the *appearance* of innovation and forgets the past. Again, this situation is not new. On the contrary, we have been living with the consequences of the vertiginous fact that anything can be art for many years: since the 1960s, certainly, and perhaps, in essentials, since the 'teens, when the Dadaist crusader Marcel Duchamp unveiled his "ready-mades" and impishly offered them to the public as works of art.

But there are some important differences between then and now. Duchamp's outrageousness oscillated between the banal and the shocking. One day he would come up with an ordinary bottle rack or snow shovel, the next day with a urinal (which, in more innocent days, was thought shocking). Either way, the art public widely considered Duchamp's activities outrageous. Moreover, Duchamp *meant* them to be outrageous. We sometimes forget that the professed aim of Dada was not to extend but to explode, to destroy the category "art." But something unexpected happened. "I threw the bottle rack and the urinal into their faces as a challenge," Duchamp noted contemptuously some years later, "and now they admire them for their aesthetic beauty."

Duchamp's "They" was not the public—not yet—but taste-makers and suitably enfranchised members of that ever-growing congregation, "the art world." Duchamp's own motives were, to put it mildly, mixed. But his exasperation is understandable. Looking back at the unfolding drama of avant-garde culture in this century, we see that the remarkable thing was not really the phenomenon of Dada. At bottom, it was just one of many late-Romantic expressions of nihilistic *Weltschmerz*. What *was* remarkable was its quick certification as a legitimate form of artistic expression. Who would have thought it possible? A coat rack? A urinal? A moustache on the Mona Lisa? All right as jokes perhaps: but could anyone have predicted that such objects would be lovingly absorbed into some of the world's finest collections of art? And yet it happened. Dada is now an academic and museological topic of impressive pedigree, the subject of exhibitions and monographs and doctoral dissertations.

What happened to Dada set an ominous precedent. Among other things, it demonstrated the extent to which the outrageous can be trivialized by being institutionalized: assimilated into the predictable cycle of museum exhibitions, curatorial safekeeping, and critical commentary. To be sure, every now and then a Robert Mapplethorpe or Andres Serrano, a Damien Hirst or Jeff Koons, will come along to inspire a *frisson* of anxiety and unhappiness. Yet, really, what is most striking about such figures is not how "controversial" they are—or were—but how quickly they are docketed and filed away as certifiable examples of contemporary art—even "great" contemporary art, if we are to believe the encomia of some noteworthy critics. The politically correct commentary elicited by Robert Mapplethorpe's photographs depicting homosexual sadomasochistic practices provided one vivid example of this phenomenon. Discussing the infamous self-portrait that showed Mapplethorpe with a bullwhip protruding from his rectum, one highly respected critic dilated on its pleasing "classical" composition.

My favorite example of critical complicity in the trivialization of outrage is provided by the English so-called artists Gilbert & George. For those fortunate souls unacquainted with Gilbert & George, it is enough to say that they specialize in a kind of scatological Pop Art. They create large, brightly colored square or rectangular photomontages. Images of the two men, often naked, sometimes in various obscene postures, occupy the foreground of most of the pictures, some of which cover an entire wall. The background usually consists of photographic images of bodily fluids or waste products, magnified beyond recognition except when the waste product is excrement: then the image is merely grotesquely enlarged. Fond of using dirty words, Gilbert & George tend to title their works after the bodily effluvia they portray.

It is part of Gilbert & George's act to pose as moralists whose art is wrestling with deep existential and religious questions. "We believe our art can form morality, in our time," George tells us in one typical statement. The critics have been eager to believe it. In the mid-1980s, Simon Wilson wrote that Gilbert & George had "come to be seen as being among the leading artists of their generation" and that the young men who populate their pictures are "equivalents, performing the same function in art, of the classicizing male figures of Michelangelo and Raphael." In 1995, when Gilbert & George exhibited what they called their "Naked Shit Pictures" in London, Richard Dorment, writing in the London *Daily Telegraph*, invoked the Isenheim altarpiece as a precedent. John McEwen, in *The Sunday Telegraph*, spoke of Gilbert & George's "self-sacrifice for a higher cause, which is purposely moral and indeed Christian." Not to be outdone, David Sylvester, in *The Guardian*, wrote that "these pictures have a plenitude, as if they were Renaissance pictures of male nudes in action." About their last exhibition in New York, the distinguished critic Robert Rosenblum delivered himself of the following:

> Brilliantly transforming the visible world into emblems of the spirit, Gilbert & George create from these microscopic facts an unprecedented heraldry that, in a wild mutation of the Stations of the Cross, fuses body and soul, life and death. Once again, they have crossed a new threshold, opening unfamiliar gates of eternity.

To which I will only add, Amen.

This situation—a situation in which any object or activity can be baptized as art—makes it difficult to get one's bearings. Familiarity may not always breed contempt, exactly; but it does tend to inspire a certain complacency. We are tempted to overlook, to take for granted, what has become blatantly familiar, no matter how odd or repugnant it is in itself. Habit dulls us. We look and register the presence of things without really seeing or understanding them. It may be worth pausing, then, to remind ourselves just how much the meaning of the word "art" has mutated over the course of this century. Words like "freedom," "innovation," and "originality" have typically accompanied this process of mutation. It is clear that, for many, the expansion of art has been synonymous with some imperative promise of liberation: not only aesthetic liberation, but social, political, and even, it seems, what we might call metaphysical liberation.

Yet here as elsewhere in human affairs there has generally been a gap between promise and fulfillment. From our vantage point at the dawn of a new millennium, what might have looked like freedom a few decades ago may now seem like irresponsible license; what struck some as cleverly innovative may now appear merely idiosyncratic or indeed perverse. Consider: is it not odd that, in many quarters, the word "art" has degenerated into a kind of honorific that is bestowed or withheld for reasons that have nothing to do with aesthetic quality or achievement? What does it mean—to take a few contemporary examples—that someone can package his own feces and distribute the result as works of art? Or that someone can have herself videotaped undergoing a series of disfiguring cosmetic surgeries and on that basis be hailed as a bona fide "performance artist"? Or that someone who is ill can successfully designate his hospital room a work of art? Such examples can be multiplied indefinitely, as anyone who has visited a gallery or museum devoted to contemporary art well knows.

The truth is that the prevailing situation is one that is good for cultural hucksters but bad for art—and for artists. It is especially bad for young, unestablished artists, who find themselves scrambling for recognition in an atmosphere in which the last thing that matters is aesthetic quality. In one sense, what we have been witnessing is the application of the principle of affirmative action to culture. Art confers prestige, celebrity, wealth; it is a social and economic blessing; therefore, its perquisites must be available to all regardless of talent or accomplishment. The logic is impeccable: only the premise and the consequences are disastrous. If anything can be a work of art, then it follows that anyone can be an artist. Such ideas are not confined to the fringe. They are, in various degrees, a staple of establishment prejudice. One recalls Mr. John Hightower, a Rockefeller apparatchik who was briefly director of New York's Museum of Modern Art in the late 1960s. In one memorable effusion, Mr. Hightower publicly delivered himself of the opinion that "I happen to think that everybody is an artist."

Of course, Mr. Hightower represents something of a special case: it is not often given to us to encounter fatuousness so deliciously blank and unadorned. But what matters is the extent to which Mr. Hightower was a bellwether. Perhaps few people in his position would have been so incautious; it surely would have occurred to most museum directors that indiscriminately bestowing the title of "artist" might have undesirable consequences for the status of the collections over which they preside. Yet Mr. Hightower articulated an assumption that, to one degree or another, informs much contemporary thinking about art and culture. It is a quintessentially Sixties assumption— there was a lot of starry-eyed talk about "unleashing creativity" then—but it is not *only* a Sixties assumption. It continues to resonate. The irony is that it is an assumption that conspires to rob artists of the things that should matter most to them: their talent and their art.

There are other ironies, too. There are more artists per

square inch in Western society today than ever before. Museums and galleries of contemporary art have sprouted like so many mushrooms across America, Europe, Australia, and parts of Asia. Everywhere one turns there are appeals to "support the arts." And yet, and yet . . . is there not also a widespread sense of staleness, futility, disenchantment? And does this not have a lot to do with the character of today's celebrity art—what we might call "art-world art"?

When we look around at the contemporary art scene, we are struck not only by its promiscuous nature—by the fact that it is a living illustration of the proposition that anything can count as art today—but also by certain telltale symptoms. I believe that these symptoms tells us a great deal not only about the character of contemporary art but also about the character of contemporary culture: about what we value, what we aspire to, who we believe we are as human beings. It is not a flattering portrait.

In the first place there is the issue of novelty. Anyone looking at the art world today cannot fail to be struck by its obsession with novelty. For those in thrall to the imperatives of the art world, the first question to be asked of a given work is not whether it is any good but whether it represents something discernibly new or different. Of course, the search for novelty has long since condemned its devotees to the undignified position of naïvely re-circulating various clichés: how little, really, our "cutting edge" artists have added to the strategies of the Dadaists, the Futurists, the Surrealists. But the appetite for novelty—even if the result is only the illusion of novelty—is apparently stronger than the passion for historical self-awareness. Never mind that the search for novelty is itself one of modernity's hoariest maneuvers: for susceptible souls its siren call is irresistible.

A second, related, symptom is the art world's addiction to extremity. This follows as a natural corollary to the obsession with novelty. As the search for something new to say or do becomes ever more desperate, artists push themselves to make extreme gestures simply in order to be noticed. But here, too, an inexorably self-defeating logic has taken hold: at a time when so much art is routinely extreme and audiences have become inured to the most brutal spectacles, extremity itself becomes a commonplace. After one has had oneself nailed to a Volkswagen (as one artist did), what's left? Without the sustaining, authoritative backdrop of the normal, extreme gestures—stylistic, moral, political—degenerate into a grim species of mannerism. Lacking any guiding aesthetic imperative, such gestures, no matter how shocking or repulsive they may be, are so many exercises in futility.

It is in part to compensate for this encroaching futility that the third symptom, the desire to marry art and politics, has become such a prominent feature of the contemporary art scene. When the artistic significance of art is at a minimum, politics rushes in to fill the void. From the crude political allegories of a Leon Golub or Hans Haacke to the feminist sloganeering of Jenny Holzer, Karen Finley, or Cindy Sherman, much that goes under the name of art today is incomprehensible without reference to its political content. Indeed, in many cases what we see are nothing but political gestures that poach on the prestige of art in order to enhance their authority. Another word for this activity is propaganda, although at a moment when so much of art is given over to propagandizing the word seems inadequate. It goes without saying that the politics in question are as predictable as clockwork. Not only are they standard items on the prevailing tablet of left-wing pieties, they are also cartoon versions of the same. It's the political version of painting by number: AIDS, the homeless, "gender politics," the Third World, and the environment line up on one side with white hats, while capitalism, patriarchy, the United States, and traditional morality and religion assemble yonder in black hats.

The trinity of novelty, extremity, and politics—leavened by frantic commercialism and the cult of celebrity—goes a long way toward describing the complexion of the contemporary art world: its faddishness, its constant recourse to lurid images of sex and violence, its tendency to substitute a hectoring politics for artistic ambition. It also helps to put into perspective some of the changes that have taken place in the meaning and goals of art over the last hundred years or so. Closely allied to the search for novelty is a shift of attention away from beauty as the end of art. From the time of Cubism, at least, most "advanced" art (which is not necessarily synonymous with "good" art) has striven not for the beautiful but for more elliptical qualities: above all, perhaps, for the *interesting*, which in many respects has usurped beauty as the primary category of aesthetic delectation.[1]

At the same time, most self-consciously avant-garde artists have displayed considerably less interest in pleasing or delighting their viewers than in startling, shocking, even repelling them. Not for nothing are "challenging" and "transgressive" among the most popular terms of critical praise today. The idea, of course, is that by abjuring beauty and refusing to please, the artist is better able to confront deeper, more authentic, more painful realities. And perhaps

---

[1] Readers of Kierkegaard's book *Either/Or* will be familiar with the unhappy consequences of elevating the interesting from an aesthetic desideratum into a moral imperative.

he is. But one mustn't overlook the element of posturing that often accompanies such existential divagations. Nor should one forget the many counter-examples and counter-tendencies. In a famous statement from 1908, when he was almost forty, Henri Matisse wrote that he dreamt of "an art of balance, of purity and serenity, devoid of troubling or depressing subject matter, an art which could be for every mental worker, for the business man as well as the man of letters, . . . something like a good armchair which provides relaxation from physical fatigue." Matisse was one of the greatest and also most innovative painters of the twentieth century. Does this vision of balance and serenity diminish his achievement? To a large extent, the calamities of art today are due to the aftermath of the avant-garde: to all those "adversarial" gestures, poses, ambitions, and tactics that emerged and were legitimized in the 1880s and 1890s, flowered in the first half of this century, and that live a sort of posthumous existence now in the frantic twilight of postmodernism.

In part, our present situation, like the avant-garde itself, is a complication (not to say a perversion) of our Romantic inheritance. The elevation of art from a didactic pastime to a prime spiritual resource, the self-conscious probing of inherited forms and artistic strictures, the image of the artist as a tortured, oppositional figure: all achieved a first maturity in Romanticism. These themes were exacerbated as the avant-garde developed from an impulse to a movement and finally into a tradition of its own.

The French critic Albert Thibaudet summarized some of the chief features of this burgeoning tradition in his reflections on the Symbolist movement in literature. Writing in 1936, Thibaudet noted that Symbolism "accustomed literature to the idea of indefinite revolution" and inaugurated a "new climate" in French literature: a climate characterized by "the chronic avant-gardism of poetry, the 'What's new?' of the 'informed' public, . . . the proliferation of schools and manifestos," and the ambition "to occupy that extreme point, to attain for an hour that crest of the wave in a tossing sea. The Symbolist revolution," Thibaudet concluded, "might perhaps have been definitively the last, because it incorporated the theme of chronic revolution into the normal condition of literature." Commenting on this passage in his classic essay "The Age of the Avant-Garde" (1972), Hilton Kramer observed that

> the "new climate" of 1885 has indeed become the "normal condition" of a good deal more than literature. It has become the basis of our entire cultural life. Thibaudet's "What's new?" is no longer the exclusive possession of a tiny "informed" public. It is now the daily concern of vast bureaucratic enterprises whose prosperity depends on keeping the question supplied with a steady flow of compelling but perishable answers.

The problem is that the avant-garde has become a casualty of its own success. Having won battle after battle, it gradually transformed a recalcitrant bourgeois culture into a willing collaborator in its raids on established taste. But in this victory were the seeds of its own irrelevance, for without credible resistance, its oppositional gestures degenerated into a kind of aesthetic buffoonery. In this sense, the institutionalization of the avant-garde—what Clement Greenberg called "avant-gardism"—spells the death or at least the senility of the avant-garde.

The road to this senility really begins with the "anti-art" movement of Dadaism. For with Dada the "chronic revolution" of which Thibaudet spoke is itself revolutionized, turned on its head. In this sense, Dada did not seek to provide yet another fresh answer to the question "What's new?" On the contrary, Dada sought to subvert the entire context in which the question gained urgency. That the extreme strategies of Dada, too, were quickly incorporated as part of that "chronic revolution" suggests that Thibaudet may have been justified in identifying the Symbolist revolution as "definitively the last." From this perspective, Dada, and every subsequent innovation, by definition appears as a variation on an already defined theme: an anti-theme, really, whose very negativity provides a foil for the ceaseless play of novelty. But in fact the incorporation of Dada into the fabric of the avant-garde did have consequences. For one thing, Dada altered the tenor of the avant-garde: Dada's adamant nihilism helped to short-circuit the essential seriousness of art. Dada might seek to occupy extreme points, but it did so out of a systematic contrariness: it had no ambition "to attain for an hour that crest of the wave in a tossing sea" because it had given up on the whole idea of art as a spiritual quest. Indeed, Dada was an art form that had given up on art.

In this respect, anyway, Dada appears as a kind of forerunner of Pop Art, the next stop on the itinerary. The architect Philip Johnson once observed that Postmodernism insinuated "the giggle" into architecture. He was, alas, right about that, and the same can be said about Pop Art: it insinuated the giggle into art. If there was a certain grimness about Dada's insouciance, Pop Art specialized in remaking art in the image of Camp. Pop Art was Dada lite: just as cynical, but without the kind of intellectual scruples that, for example, led Duchamp to abandon art for chess. Pop Art was a smirking form of nihilism, an art whose features compose themselves into a rictus of narcissistic despair while its practitioners eagerly dip their hands into the till of artistic celebrity and commercial success.

Many of these elements came together in the protracted assault on civilization that we sum up in the epithet "the Sixties." It was then that the senility of the avant-garde went mainstream: when a generalized liberationist ethos and anti-establishment attitude infiltrated our major cultural institutions and began forming a large component of established taste.

But the problem is not, or not only, numbers. The real issue is not the existence but the widespread celebration of such images and behavior as art. As a society, we suffer today from a peculiar form of moral anesthesia: an anesthesia based on the delusion that by calling something "art" we thereby purchase for it a blanket exemption from moral criticism—as if being art automatically rendered all moral considerations beside the point. George Orwell gave classic expression to this point in "Benefit of Clergy: Some Notes on Salvador Dalí" (1944), a review of Dalí's autobiography, *The Secret Life of Salvador Dalí.* Acknowledging the deficiency of the philistine response to Dalí's work—categorical rejection along with denial that Dalí possessed any talent whatever—Orwell goes on to note that the response of the cultural elites was just as impoverished. Essentially, the elite response to Dalí was the response of *l'art pour l'art,* of extreme aestheticism. "The artist," Orwell writes,

is to be exempt from the moral laws that are binding on ordinary people. Just pronounce the magic word "Art," and everything is O.K. Rotting corpses with snails crawling over them are O.K.; kicking little girls in the head is O.K.; even a film like *L'Age d'Or* [which shows among other things detailed shots of a woman defecating] is O.K.

A juror in the Mapplethorpe trial in Cincinnati memorably

summed up the paralyzed attitude Orwell described. Acknowledging that he did not like Mapplethorpe's rebarbative photographs, he nonetheless concluded that "if people say it's art, then I have to go along with it."

"If people say it's art, then I have to go along with it." It is worth pausing to digest that terrifying comment. It is also worth confronting it with a question: Why do so many people feel that if something is regarded as art, they "have to go along with it," no matter how offensive it might be? Part of the answer has to do with the confusion of art with "free speech." [2] Another part of the answer has to do with the evolution and what we might call the institutionalization of the avant-garde and its posture of defiance.

You know the drill: black-tie dinners at major museums, *tout le monde* in attendance, celebrating the latest art-world freak: maybe it's Damien Hirst with his animal carcasses packed into glass tanks of formaldehyde; maybe it's the Chapman brothers with their pubescent female mannequins festooned with erect penises; maybe it's Mike Kelley with his mutilated dolls or Jeff Koons with his por-

---

2 More precisely, it has to do with the confusion of art with a debased idea of free speech that supposes any limits on expression are inimical to freedom. Moral and aesthetic objections cannot always be answered simply by appealing to the First Amendment. In the 1920s, John Fletcher Moulton, a British judge, observed that "there is a widespread tendency to regard the fact that [one] can do a thing as meaning [one] may do it. There can be no more fatal error than this. Between 'can do' and 'may do' ought to exist the whole realm which recognizes the sway of duty, fairness, sympathy, taste, and all the other things that make life beautiful and society possible." One of the most destructive aspects of our culture has been the evisceration of that middle ground of "duty, fairness, sympathy, taste," etc.— everything that Lord Moulton congregated under the memorable category of "obedience to the unenforceable."

nographic sculptures depicting him and his now-former wife having sex or Cindy Sherman with her narcissistic feminism or Jenny Holzer with her political slogans. The list, obviously, is endless. And so is the tedium. Today in the art world, anything goes but almost nothing happens. As with any collusion of snobbery and artistic nullity, such spectacles have their amusing aspects, as Tom Wolfe, for example, has brilliantly shown. In the end, though, the aftermath of the avant-garde has been the opposite of amusing. It has been a cultural disaster. For one thing, by universalizing the spirit of opposition, it has threatened to transform the practice of art into a purely negative enterprise. In large precincts of the art world today, art is oppositional or it is nothing.

What can be done? For one thing, it is time that we recognized that art need not be adversarial or "transgressive" in order to be good or important. In this context, it is worth noting that great damage has been done—above all to artists but also to public taste—by romanticizing the tribulations of the nineteenth-century avant-garde. Everyone is brought up on stories of how an obtuse public scorned Manet, censored Gauguin, and drove poor Van Gogh to madness and suicide. But the fact that these great talents went unappreciated has had the undesirable effect of encouraging the thought that because one is unappreciated one is therefore a genius. It has also made it extremely difficult to expose fraudulent work as such. For any frank dismissal of art—especially art that cloaks itself in the mantel of the avant-garde—is immediately met by the rejoinder: "Ah, but they made fun of Cézanne, too: they thought that Stravinsky was a charlatan."

This is the easiest and also the most shallow response to criticism. It is yet another version of what philosopher

David Stove called "The 'They All Laughed at Christopher Columbus' Argument."[3] The idea is that we ought to welcome all innovators (moral, social, artistic, whatever) because all improvements in human life have come about as the result of some such "new beginning." The rub, of course, is that it works the other way, too. As Stove observed, "someone first had to make a new departure for any change for the *worse* ever to have taken place." This is perfectly obvious, and is reason enough to regard innovators with caution, to say the least.

If the Columbus Argument is puerile when applied to politics and morals, it is equally puerile when applied to art. In the first place, most artists whom we now associate with the nineteenth-century avant-garde did not set out to shock or "transgress" moral boundaries: they set out to make art that was true to their experience of the world. Today, the primary—often, it seems, the only—goal of many so-called "cutting edge" artists is to shock and transgress. The art is secondary, a license for bad behavior.

There is also the uncomfortable and unegalitarian truth that in any age most art is bad or failed art. And in our time, most art is not only bad but also dishonest: a form of therapy or political grumbling masquerading as art. Like everything important in human life, art must be judged on the basis of first-hand experience: no formula can be devised prescribing its assessment, including the formula that what is despised today will be championed as great work tomorrow. The art world today retains little of the idealism that permeated Romanticism, but it remains Romantic in its moralism and hubris about the salvific properties of art.

In one of his many jejune moments, Shelley wrote that

---

3 See above, pages 163–164.

poets were "the unacknowledged legislators of the world." This is an ambition that many artists continue, in more mundane ways, to harbor. But as W. H. Auden rightly pointed out "'The unacknowledged legislators of the world' describes the secret police, not the poets." Poetry, Auden said elsewhere, makes nothing happen: its province—like the province of all art—is in the realm of making not doing. An artist, as the word's history reminds us, is first of all someone who makes something. And just as a table can be well or poorly made, so, too, a poem or a painting can be well or poorly made. This is not the only criterion that we employ to judge a work of art, but it is a fundamental starting point that no disinterested critic can afford to abandon. Similar considerations apply to the ambition to make art "relevant" to contemporary social and political concerns. Of course, art cannot help being of its time and place. But the interesting question to ask about art that deliberately comments on its time is what makes it more than a mere commentary? What makes it art? As Goethe put it, "only the mediocre talent is always the captive of its time and must get its nourishment from the elements that time contains." The insistence that art reflect the tangled realities of contemporary life is a temptation that most artists should resist, if for no other reason than that giving in to that temptation is a prescription for ephemeralness.

What resources does an artist possess to combat the temptations of relevance? Apart from his talent, perhaps his greatest resource is tradition, for it is through tradition that he has his most palpable link with something that transcends the contingencies of the moment. As T. S. Eliot explained in a famous passage from his essay "Tradition and the Individual Talent," tradition is not simply "following the ways of the immediate generation before us in a blind or timid adherence to its successes." "Tradition," Eliot continued,

> is a matter of much wider significance. It cannot be inherited, and if you want it you must obtain it by great labour. It involves, in the first place, the historical sense, . . . and the historical sense involves a perception, not only of the pastness of the past, but of its presence; the historical sense compels a man to write not merely with his own generation in his bones, but with a feeling that the whole of the literature of Europe from Homer and within it the whole of the literature of his own country has simultaneous existence and composes a simultaneous order. This historical sense, which is a sense of the timeless as well as of the temporal and of the timeless and of the temporal together, is what makes a writer traditional.

Eliot's aestheticizing conception of the historical sense may not be the bulwark against arbitrariness that he hoped it would be. But by underscoring the element of transcendence, he reminds us that an embrace of tradition is not the enemy but the condition of genuine innovation. It is in this sense that we should understand the observation made by the German art historian Hans Sedlmayr that "many things that are classified as 'backward' . . . might be the starting-point of real inner progress." At a moment when the art world has abandoned art for political attitudinizing, the path forward begins with a movement of recuperation. In an age when anything can be a work of art, the question of whether something is art has ceased to be compelling: what matters is whether something is a good work of art, and about this the art world has rendered itself *hors de combat*.

Should we be pleased with this state of affairs? Or, to put it another way, is the celebrity of people like Damien Hirst or Jenny Holzer a good thing *for art*? My answer is no: it is a very bad thing. As Rochelle Gurstein observes in her recent book *The Repeal of Reticence*, "By now it should be obvious that there is something fraudulent, if not perverse, in the endless rehearsal of arguments that were developed to destroy nineteenth-century Victorians in a world where Victorians have long been extinct." The question remains: Where did we go wrong? What are we missing in the contemporary art world? Doubtless the list is a long one. But if one had to sum up volumes in a single word, a good candidate would be "beauty": What the art world is lacking today is an allegiance to beauty.

I know that this is both vague and portentous. But surely we have a very curious situation. Traditionally, the goal or end of fine art was to make beautiful objects. Beauty itself came with a lot of Platonic and Christian metaphysical baggage, some of it indifferent or even positively hostile to art. But art without beauty was, if not exactly a contradiction in terms, at least a description of *failed art*. And I might remark as an aside here how often this pattern repeats itself in contemporary life: if beauty was the traditional *raison d'être* of fine art, we now must have art that spurns beauty; if truth was the traditional goal of philosophy, we must now, postmodernists like Richard Rorty and others tell us, have philosophy that dispenses with truth; if ascertaining and elucidating facts was the traditional goal of historiography, we must now have historians who announce that there are no such things as facts and who pursue history as a new species of fiction; if procreation was the purpose of sex, we must now, according to radicals from Herbert Marcuse on down, foster a sexuality that has emancipated itself from the "tyranny of procreative eros" in order to champion what Marcuse called "polymorphous perversity." It is indeed a curious development.

But to return to art. The eclipse of beauty is not, I think, often talked about. But its absence has not gone entirely unremarked. I disagree with Peter Schjeldahl, the art critic for *The New Yorker*, about almost everything. But in a piece in the *The New York Times Magazine*, even Mr. Schjeldahl noted that "Beauty . . . has been quarantined from educated talk," and that "commerce travesties it and intellectual fashion demonizes it." His own examples of "the best art of our time"—he mentions among other delicacies photography by Cindy Sherman, a dirt-encrusted landscape by Anselm Kiefer, and the "rapturously perverse" photography of Robert Mapplethorpe—are not encouraging. He is surely right that something has happened to beauty. But what?

At the beginning of his book on modern art, the German art critic Julius Meier-Graefe defines painting as "the art of charming the eye by colour and line" and sculpture as the art of charming "the eye by means of form in space." Now when was the last time you heard someone talk about art "charming" the eye? And yet until quite recently, that specifically aesthetic pleasure was seen as being central to art. Thomas Aquinas defined beauty as *id quod visum placet*: that which being seen pleases. Still laboring in the aftermath of the avant-garde, much art today has abandoned the ambition to please the viewer aesthetically. Instead, it seeks to shock, discommode, repulse, proselytize, or startle. Beauty is out of place in any art that systematically discounts the aesthetic.

Of course, "beauty" itself is by no means an unambiguous term. In degenerate form, it can mean the merely pretty, and in this sense beauty really is an enemy of authentic artistic expression. It is not hard to find examples of this sort of thing. Edmund Burke, for example, in his book on the origin of our ideas of the sublime and beautiful, offers a list of the qualities he thinks are necessary for something to be beautiful:

First, to be comparatively small. Secondly, to be smooth. Thirdly, to have a variety in the direction of the parts; but fourthly, to have those parts not angular, but melted as it were into each other. Fifthly, to be of a delicate frame, without any remarkable appearance of strength. Sixthly, to have its colours clear and bright; but not very strong and glaring.

And so on. Frankly, I hesitated to cite Burke to this jocular purpose, both because I greatly admire him as a writer and because even this early book on aesthetics contains many profound and important things that my quotation out of context fails to acknowledge. Still, most of us will want to open a window after a page or two of such raptures about beauty.

How different is something like Rilke's idea of beauty in the first *Duino Elegy*:

Denn das Schöne ist nichts
als des Schrecklichen Anfang, den wir noch grade extragen,
und wir bewundern es so, weil es gelassen verschmäht,
uns zu zerstören.[4]

Or think of Dostoyevsky's contention that "Beauty is the battlefield on which God and the devil war for man's

---

4 "Beauty is only the beginning of a terror we can just barely endure, and what we admire is its calm disdaining to destroy us."

soul." The point is that, in its highest sense, beauty speaks with such great immediacy because it touches something deep within us. Understood in this way, beauty is something that absorbs our attention and delivers us, if but momentarily, from the poverty and incompleteness of everyday life. At its most intense, beauty invites us to forget our subjection to time and imparts an intoxicating sense of self-sufficiency. It has, as one philosopher put it, "the savor of the terrestrial paradise." This is the source of beauty's power. It both *dislocates*, freeing us, for a time, from our usual cares and concerns, and *enraptures*, seizing us with delight.

Art that loses touch with the resources of beauty is bound to be sterile. But it is also true that striving self-consciously to embody beauty is a prescription for artistic failure. This may seem paradoxical. But, like many of the most important things in life, genuine beauty is achieved mainly by indirection. In this sense, beauty resembles happiness as it was described by Aristotle: it is not a possible goal of our actions, but rather the natural accompaniment of actions rightly performed. Striving for happiness in life all but guarantees unhappiness; striving for beauty in art is likely to result in kitsch or some other artistic counterfeit.

The trick for artists, then, is not to lose sight of beauty but to concentrate primarily on something seemingly more pedestrian—the making of good works of art. The best guides to this task are to be found not in the work of this season's art-world darlings but in the great models furnished by the past. Although this lesson is rejected and ridiculed by the art world today, it is something that the tradition affirms again and again.

We live at a time when art is enlisted in all manner of extra-artistic projects, from gender politics to the grim linguistic leftism of neo-Marxists, post-struturalists, gender theorists, and all the other exotic fauna who are congregating in and about the art world and the academy. The subjugation of art—and of cultural life generally—to political ends has been one of the great spiritual tragedies of our age. Among much else, it has made it increasingly difficult to appreciate art on its own terms, as affording its own kinds of insights and satisfactions. This situation has made it imperative for critics who care about art to champion its distinctively aesthetic qualities against attempts to reduce art to a species of propaganda.

At the same time, however, I believe that we lose something important when our conception of art does not have room for an ethical dimension. That is to say, if politicizing the aesthetic poses a serious threat to the integrity of art, the isolation of the aesthetic from other dimensions of life represents a different sort of threat. Hans Sedlmayr articulated this point eloquently in the 1950s. The fact is, Sedlmayr wrote,

> that art cannot be assessed by a measure that is purely artistic and nothing else. Indeed such a purely artistic measure, which ignored the human element, the element which alone gives art its justification, would actually not be an artistic measure at all. It would merely be an aesthetic one, and actually the application of purely aesthetic standards is one of the peculiarly inhuman feature of the age, for it proclaims by implication the autonomy of the work of art, an autonomy that has no regard to men—the principle of *l'art pour art*.

Sedlmayr was hardly alone in this sentiment. Indeed, even so "advanced" a figure as Baudelaire understood that the ultimate measure of art must be extra-aesthetic. In his book *L'Art romantique*, Baudelaire wrote that

the frenzied passion for art is a cancer that eats up everything else; and, as the out-and-out absence of what is
proper and true in art is tantamount to the absence of art,
man fades away completely; excessive specialization of a
faculty ends in nothing. . . . The folly of art is on a par with
the abuse of the mind. The creation of one or the other of
these two supremacies begets stupidity, hardness of heart,
and unbounded pride and egotism.

And Julius Meier-Graefe made a similar point when discussing the liberation of modern art from the strictures of
religion. The severing of art from religion marked an important "emancipation" for mankind, he thought; but it
"entailed retrogression" for art. "Art was to be free,"
Meier-Graefe wrote, "but free from what? The innovators
forgot, that freedom implies isolation. In her impulsive
vehemence, art cast away the elements that made her indispensible to man."

What is it that makes art "indispensible," as Meier-
Graefe put it? That makes it more than "the diversion of
an idle moment"? If the politicization of art is constricting,
so too in a different way is a purely aesthetic conception of
art. By the nineteenth century, art had long been free from
serving the ideological needs of religion; and yet the
spiritual crisis of the age tended to invest art with ever
greater existential burdens—burdens that continue, in
various ways, to be felt down to this day. As we saw
above, Wallace Stevens articulated one important strand of
this phenomenon when he observed that "after one has
abandoned a belief in God, poetry is that essence which
takes its place as life's redemption."

The idea that poetry—that art generally—should serve
as a source—perhaps the primary source—of spiritual sustenance in a secular age is a Romantic notion that con-

tinues to resonate powerfully. It helps to explain, for example, the special aura that attaches to art and artists, even now—even, that is, at a time when poseurs like Andres Serrano and Bruce Nauman and Gilbert & George are accounted artists by persons one might otherwise have had reason to think were serious people. This Romantic inheritance has also figured, with various permutations in much avant-garde culture. We have come a long way since Dostoyevsky could declare that, "Incredible as it may seem, the day will come when man will quarrel more fiercely about art than about God." Whether that trek has described a journey of progress is perhaps an open question. It is no secret that Dostoyevsky thought it a disaster all around, for mankind as well as for art.

This much, I think, is clear: without an allegiance to beauty, art degenerates into a caricature of itself; it is beauty that animates aesthetic experience, making it so seductive; but aesthetic experience itself degenerates into a kind of fetish or idol if it is held up as an end in itself, untested by the rest of life. To put it another way, the trivialization of outrage leads to a kind of moral and aesthetic anaesthesia not the least of whose symptoms is the outrage of trivialization.

"The Two Cultures" Today

It is not a question of annihilating science, but of controlling it. Science is totally dependent upon philosophical opinions for all of its goals and methods, though it easily forgets this.
—Friedrich Nietzsche

[T]he more that the results of science are frankly accepted, the more that poetry and eloquence come to be received and studied as what in truth they really are,—the criticism of life by gifted men, alive and active with extraordinary power.
—Matthew Arnold

"THE CORRIDORS OF POWER" and "The Two Cultures": these phrases are essentially what remain of the once towering reputation of Sir Charles Percy Snow, novelist, pundit, and—as his harshest critic, F. R. Leavis, put it—"public relations man" for science. C. P. Snow (1905–1980) was the son of a provincial church organist who rose to public acclaim and a life peerage through a mixture of geniality, application, and talent—more or less in that order. He was the embodiment of a certain type of educated philistine: bluff, well-meaning, clubbable, so well-rounded as to be practically spherical. In the Thirties, Snow abandoned an incipient scientific career in order to

305

devote himself to writing. He published his first novel, a whodunit called *Death Under Sail*, in 1932. During the war, Snow's technical background helped win him the important post of overseeing recruitment for Britain's scientific research (hence his acquaintance with "the corridors of power"). And the novels kept appearing. By the Fifties, Snow's novel sequence *Strangers and Brothers* was occasionally compared to *A la recherche du temps perdu*.

Today, the word that seems most often used to describe his novels—on the rare occasions that they *are* described—is "inert." In a generous moment, Edmund Wilson defended Snow but anticipated the judgment of history in finding his novels "almost completely unreadable." "The corridors of power" furnished the title for one of Snow's novels; it is all that is left of the work. Things are a little different with "the two cultures." The phrase has lived on as a vague popular shorthand for the rift—a matter of incomprehension tinged with hostility—that has grown up between scientists and literary intellectuals in the modern world. Lack of precision has been part of its appeal: to speak of "the two cultures" is to convey regret, censure, and—since one is bold enough to name and appreciate a presumably unfortunate circumstance—superiority all at once.

Snow first used the famous phrase in 1956 as the title for an article in *The New Statesman*. The article provided the germ for his 1959 Rede Lecture at Cambridge University, *The Two Cultures and the Scientific Revolution*, which was subsequently printed in *Encounter* magazine in two installments. It is a brief, avuncular work. In book form it fits comfortably into fewer than sixty printed pages and is full of men who "muck in as colleagues," behavior that's "just not on," etc. Yet as as soon as it appeared, *The Two Cultures* became a sensation on both sides of the Atlantic.

The edition I have was published in 1961; by then the book was already in its seventh printing.

Its fame got an additional boost a year later when the critic F. R. Leavis published his attack on *The Two Cultures* in *The Spectator*. Originally delivered as the Richmond Lecture at Downing College, Cambridge, "Two Cultures? The Significance of C. P. Snow" is a devastating rhetorical fusillade. It's not just that no two stones of Snow's argument are left standing: each and every pebble is pulverized; the fields are salted; and the entire population is sold into slavery. Leavis spoke of "the preposterous and menacing absurdity of C. P. Snow's consecrated public standing," heaped derision on his "embarrassing vulgarity of style," his "panoptic pseudo-cogencies," his "complete ignorance" of history, literature, the history of civilization, and the human significance of the Industrial Revolution. "[I]t is ridiculous," Leavis wrote, "to credit him with any capacity for serious thinking about the problems on which he offers to advise the world." So much for Snow the sage. What about Snow the artist, Snow the novelist? "Snow is, of course, a—no, I can't say that; he isn't: Snow thinks of himself as a novelist," Leavis thundered, but in fact "his incapacity as a novelist is . . . total": "as a novelist he doesn't exist; he doesn't begin to exist. He can't be said to know what a novel is." It gets worse. Snow is "utterly without a glimmer of what creative literature is, or why it matters." "[N]ot only is he not a genius," Leavis concluded; "he is intellectually as undistinguished as it is possible to be."

Literary London was stunned and outraged by Leavis's performance (which was something of an official swan song, since he retired from teaching that year). At that time, a certain degree of rhetorical *politesse* still marked British literary journalism; Leavis had been the opposite of polite.

In the weeks that followed, *The Spectator* printed more than thirty irate letters, many from eminent personages, most of them siding firmly with Snow. It was an extraordinary outpouring. One correspondent deplored Leavis's "insincerity, incapacity and envy." Lord Boothby, claiming that there was "not a single constructive thought in his lecture," spoke of Leavis's "reptilian venom." Stephen Toulmin wrote that the lecture was "an insult to the audience and to Snow himself." Other indignant commentators dismissed Leavis's lecture as "ludicrously overdone," "a demonstration of ill-mannered, self-centered and destructive behaviour," or, more simply, "bemused drivelling."

The extreme reaction was partly a response to Leavis's own extremity: Lionel Trilling, reflecting on the controversy in *Commentary*, summed it up when he spoke of the "unexampled ferocity" and "bad manners" of Leavis's attack. In fact, Trilling agreed with much that Leavis had to say; but he could not abide the scorched-earth rhetoric: "it is," he wrote, "a bad tone, an impermissible tone." Perhaps so. But in the English response there was also a large element of snobbery: by 1960 Sir Charles was, well, Sir Charles: a member of the Athenaeum, a reviewer for *The New Statesman*, someone whom one *knew*. Thus Dame Edith Sitwell: "Dr. Leavis only attacked Charles because he is famous and writes good English." *Charles*, indeed.

The ruffled feathers of London's intellectual elite make for an amusing footnote to the cultural history of the period. But the questions raised by *The Two Cultures*—and by Leavis's searching criticisms of Snow's position—are something more serious. It is not simply that the gulf between scientists and literary intellectuals (and the general public, too, of course) has grown wider as science has become ever more specialized and complex. Because of the extremely technical nature of contemporary scientific dis-course—think, for example, of its deep reliance on abstruse mathematical notation—that gulf is unbridgeable and will only widen as knowledge progresses. The more pressing issue concerns the fate of culture in a world increasingly determined by science and technology. Leavis described C. P. Snow as a "portent" of our civilization because, in his view, Snow's argument epitomized modern society's ten-dency to trivialize culture by reducing it to a form of diversion or entertainment. Not that diversion and enter-tainment are necessarily bad things: they have their place; but so do art and high culture. The problem, as Leavis saw, is that the confusion of art and entertainment always proceeds in one direction: toward the adulteration, the trivialization, of art. For him, it was not surprising that *The Two Cultures* captured the public imagination: it did so precisely because it pandered to the debased notion of culture championed by established taste.

The year 2000 marks the fortieth anniversary of Snow's essay. As we look around the cultural landscape today, we see the debris of a civilization seemingly bent on cultural suicide: the triumph of pop culture in nearly every sphere of artistic endeavor, the glorification of mindless sen-sationalism, the attack on the very idea of permanent cul-tural achievement—in the West, anyway, the final years of the twentieth century were years of unprecedented material wealth coupled with profound cultural and intellectual degradation. C. P. Snow is hardly to blame for all this. He was merely a canary in the mine. But as such—as a symptom, a "portent"—he still has much to tell us.

Perhaps the first thing that one notices about *The Two Cultures* is its tone, which vacillates wildly between the cozily anecdotal and the apocalyptic. On the one hand, we find Snow busy meeting the physicist "W. L. Bragg in the buffet on Kettering station on a very cold morning in 1939." Without the narrative prop of High Table dinner conversation at Cambridge, Snow would be lost. On the other hand, he insists that the problem he has outlined is a "problem of the entire West." "This is," Snow writes toward the end of his lecture, "one of the situations where the worst crime is innocence." In some "afterthoughts" about the two-cultures controversy that he published in *Encounter* in 1960, Snow refers solemnly to his lecture as a "call to action."

But what, exactly, is the problem? And what actions does Snow recommend we take? At one moment it's nothing much; the next it's everything and more. There is that "gulf of mutual incomprehension" between scientists and "literary intellectuals," of course. But it soon turns out that there are also the "three menaces" of nuclear war, overpopulation, and the "gap" between rich and poor nations. (There are many gulfs, gaps, chasms, caesurae in *The Two Cultures*; it sometimes seems that Snow's entire argument has fallen into one of them.) On one page the problem is reforming the schools so that "English and American children get a reasonable education." Well, OK. But a few pages later the problem is mobilizing Western resources to industrialize India. And Africa. And Southeast Asia. And Latin America. And the Middle East—all in order to forestall widespread starvation, revolution, and anarchy. Snow envisions tens of thousands of engineers from Europe and North America volunteering "at least ten years out of their lives" to bring the "scientific revolution" to the underdeveloped parts of the world. Reality check: in Snow's mind, the Soviet Union was way ahead of the West in dealing with these vast imponderables. This is, he says, partly because the Russians have a "passionate belief in education." But it is also because they have a "deeper insight into the scientific revolution than we have, or than the Americans have." That explains why the world is clamoring for Russian automobiles and airplanes, you see, and also why the Soviets happened to manage their own economy so much more brilliantly than did the West.

If all this seems like a terrible muddle, it is. In truth, there are three sorts of problems in *The Two Cultures*: trivial, non-existent, and misunderstood. Some, such as the famous gulf, gap, or chasm between scientists and literary intellectuals, are both trivial and misunderstood. Sure, it would be nice if "literary intellectuals" knew more science. But the gulf, gap, chasm that Snow deplores will never be bridged—from this side of the gulf, at any rate—by anyone lacking a good deal of highly specialized training. And, *pace* Snow, it's not at all clear that the gulf really matters.

As several critics have pointed out, Snow's terminology can be exceedingly slippery. He begins with a dichotomy between the world of literary intellectuals and the world of physical scientists. (And he eschews anything more elaborate: "I have thought a long time about going in for further refinements," Snow writes, "but in the end I have decided against it": No wonder the biochemist Michael Yudkin, in a perceptive article on *The Two Cultures*, noted that Snow often seems "more concerned with the number two than the term 'culture.'") But in order to further his gulf-gap-chasm thesis, Snow is soon using "literary intellectual" interchangeably with "traditional culture." This fusion yields the observation that there is "an unscientific," even an "anti-scientific" flavor to "the whole 'traditional' culture." What can this mean? Aristotle, Euclid, Galileo, Copernicus, Descartes, Boyle, Newton, Locke, Kant: are there any more "traditional" representatives of "the whole 'traditional' culture'"? There's not much anti-scientific aroma emanating from those quarters.[1] The real burden of Snow's thesis was accurately summed up by Leavis: "there are the two uncommunicating and mutually indifferent cultures, there is the need to bring them together, and there is C. P. Snow, whose place in history is that he has them both, so that we have in him the paradigm of the desired and necessary union."

At the beginning of his lecture, Snow affects a generous even-handedness in his attitude toward scientists and literary intellectuals. There's a bit of criticism for both. If literary types tend to be quite appallingly ignorant of even rudimentary scientific concepts (Snow seems astounded that his writer friends cannot define such basic concepts as mass, acceleration, etc.), then it turns out that many scientists are unacquainted with the novels of Charles Dickens. But this show of even-handedness soon evaporates. The

---

[1] Among other things, Snow's lecture illustrates the fact that a mountain of confusion can be built from a grain of truth. For there *is* an ingredient of irrationalism in Western culture that regularly manifests itself in anti-scientific biases of one sort or another. Certain varieties of romanticism belong here, as do many less agreeable phenomena. But Snow, while he dances around this issue—it is what gives his whole "two cultures" thesis a superficial plausibility—never really comes to terms with it. In contemporary academic culture, a widespread suspicion of the achievements of science—often extending to an outright rejection of the idea of factual truth—can be seen in many radical movements and "theories." "Cultural constructivism," deconstruction, radical feminism, and other fashionable *ist*s and *ism*s are aggressively anti-empirical. Paul R. Gross and Norman Levitt expertly anatomize these disparate phenomena in *Higher Superstition: The Academic Left and Its Quarrels with Science* (Johns Hopkins, 1994). They show that this new hostility to science is part of a more general hostility to Western values and institutions, an anti-Enlightenment hostility that "mocks the idea that . . . a civilization is capable of progressing from ignorance to insight."

"culture" of science, Snow tells us, "contains a great deal of argument, usually much more rigorous, and almost always at a higher conceptual level, than the literary persons' arguments." Literary intellectuals are "natural Luddites"; scientists "have the future in their bones." This is a formulation that Snow rather likes. "If the scientists have the future in their bones," he writes later, "then the traditional culture responds by wishing the future did not exist." To clinch his argument that literary intellectuals (a.k.a. "the traditional culture") "wish the future did not exist," Snow holds up . . . George Orwell's *Nineteen Eighty-four*—as if that harrowing admonitory tale could have been written by anyone who did not have a passionate concern for the future!

Snow is especially impatient with what he takes to be the politics of "the traditional culture." He quotes approvingly an unnamed "scientist of distinction" who opined that literary intellectual writers tended to be "not only politically silly, but politically wicked. Didn't the influence of all they represent bring Auschwitz that much closer?" In this context, Snow explicitly mentions Yeats, Wyndham Lewis, and Ezra Pound. But his indictment is actually much broader: "nine-tenths" of the great literary figures of the early twentieth century (he specifies the period 1914–1950) are on his reckoning politically suspect. The "culture" of science, on the contrary, is optimistically forward-looking. But not, Snow hastens to add, *shallowly* optimistic. Scientists, too, appreciate the tragic nature of human life—that each of us "dies alone." But they are wise enough to distinguish, with Snow, between the "individual condition and the social condition" of man. There is, Snow writes, "no reason why, just because the individual condition is tragic, so must the social condition be." The prospect of social improvement (what Snow, echoing a character from *Alice in Wonderland*, picturesquely calls the prospect of "jam tomorrow") is a galvanizing force that allows the individual to transcend, or at least to forget, his private destiny.

Snow's argument operates by erasing or ignoring certain fundamental distinctions. He goes to a literary party, discovers that no one (except himself) can explain the second law of thermodynamics, and then concludes triumphantly: "yet I was asking something which is about the equivalent of *Have you read a work of Shakespeare's?*" But, as Leavis notes, "there *is* no scientific equivalent of that question; equations between orders so disparate are meaningless." The second law of thermodynamics is a piece of specialized knowledge, useful or irrelevant depending on the job to be done; the works of Shakespeare provide a window into the soul of humanity: to read them is tantamount to acquiring self-knowledge. Snow seems blind to this distinction.[2] A similar confusion is at work in Snow's effort to neutralize individuality by assimilating it to the project of "social hope." That may sound nobly altruistic. But, as Leavis asks, "What *is* the 'social condition' that has nothing to do with the 'individual condition'?"

> What is the "social hope" that transcends, cancels or makes indifferent the inescapable tragic condition of each individual? Where, if not in individuals, is what is hoped for . . . to be located? Or are we to find the reality of life in hoping for other people a kind of felicity about which as

2 Curiously, he also seems oblivious of the extent to which the second law of thermodynamics has impressed itself—vividly if not always accurately—upon the imaginations of modern artists, philosophers, and theologians via the concept of entropy: the thought that the universe is ineluctably "winding down" has proven to be a deeply unsettling but also fertile metaphor.

proposed for ourselves ("jam," Snow calls it later—we die alone, but there's jam to be had first) we have no illusions?

Leavis here exposes the central philistinism, the deeply *anti*-cultural bias, of Snow's position: the idea that the individual is merely a fungible token, a representative type, whose ultimate value is purely a function of his place in the tapestry of society.

In the end, Snow is a naïve meliorist. For him, a society's material standard of living provides the ultimate, really the only, criterion of "the good life"; science is the means of raising the standard of living, ergo science is the arbiter of value. Culture—literary, artistic culture—is merely a patina or gloss added to the substance of material wealth to make it shine more brightly. It provides us with no moral challenge or insight, because the only serious questions are how to keep increasing and effectively distributing the world's wealth, and these are not questions culture is competent to address. "The upshot" of Snow's argument, Leavis writes, "is that if you insist on the need for any other kind of concern, entailing forethought, action and provision, about the human future—any other kind of misgiving—than that which talks in terms of productivity, material standards of living, hygienic and technological progress, then you are a Luddite."

It is worth pausing at this point to note that Leavis grants Snow's subsidiary argument that improvements in scientific education would be a good thing. Leavis is not "anti-scientific." *Of course* "standards of living, hygienic and technological progress" are important. None of that is at issue. Nor is Leavis in any way suggesting that one should "defy, or try to reverse, the accelerating movement of external civilisation . . . that is determined by advancing technology." Barring a world-extinguishing catastrophe, the progress of science is inexorable. Leavis accepts that. What he denies is that science is a *moral* resource—he denies, that is to say, that there is any such thing as a "culture" of science. Science tells us how best to do things we have already decided to do, not why we should do them. Its province is the province of *means* not *ends*. That is its glory—and its limitation.

This is something that the editors of *The Spectator* grasped much more clearly than the many correspondents who wrote in to complain about Leavis's essay. One word that is missing from Snow's essay, they note in an unsigned editorial, is "philosophy"—"that effort to impart moral direction that was found in the best nineteenth-century English writers." Chief among "the best nineteenth-century English writers" was Leavis's own model and inspiration, Matthew Arnold. It is one of history's small but delicious coincidences that in 1882, nearly eighty years before C. P. Snow's Rede Lecture, Arnold was chosen for that honor. His Rede Lecture—"Literature and Science"—was itself a kind of "two cultures" argument. But his point was essentially the opposite of Snow's. Written in response to T. H. Huxley's insistence that literature should and inevitably would be supplanted by science, Arnold argued that, "so long as human nature is what it is," culture would continue to provide mankind with its fulcrum of moral understanding.

The *tenor* of Arnold's lecture could not have been more different from Leavis's. "The tone of tentative inquiry, which befits a being of dim faculties and bounded knowledge, is the tone I would wish to take," Arnold noted with un-Leavisite modesty. But his argument anticipated Leavis in striking detail. Both are concerned with what Leavis called "the cultural consequences of the technological revolution." Both argued passionately against the trivialization of culture, against what Arnold dismissed as "a superficial humanism" that is "mainly decorative." And both looked to culture to provide a way of relating, in Arnold's words, the "results of modern science" to "our need for conduct, our need for beauty." This is the crux: that culture is in some deep sense inseparable from *conduct*—from that unscientific but ineluctable question, "How should I live my life?" Leavis's point was the same. The stunning upheavals precipitated by the march of science and technology had rendered culture—the arts and humanities—both more precarious and more precious. Leavis understood that the preservation of culture—not as entertainment or diversion but as a guide to "conduct"— was now more crucial than ever. If mankind was to confront the moral challenges of modern science "in full intelligent possession of its humanity" and maintain "a basic living deference towards that to which, opening as it does into the unknown and itself unmeasurable, we know we belong," then the realm of culture had to be protected from the reductive forces of a crude scientific rationalism.

The contemporary relevance of this argument can hardly be overestimated. We live at a moment when "the results of science" confront us daily with the most extreme moral challenges. Abortion on demand, nanotechnology, the prospect of genetic engineering—the list is long and sobering. But more challenging that any particular application of science is the widespread assumption that *every* problem facing mankind is susceptible to technological intervention and control. In this situation, the temptation to reduce culture to a reservoir of titillating pastimes is all but irresistible. Rock music, "performance art," television, video games (not to mention drugs, violence, and promiscuous sex): we are everywhere encouraged to think of ourselves as complicated machines for consuming sensations—the more, and more exotic, the better. Culture is no longer an invitation to confront our humanity but a series of opportunities to impoverish it through diversion. We are, as Eliot put it in *Four Quartets*, "distracted from distraction by distraction." C. P. Snow represents the smiling, jovial face of this predicament. Critics like Arnold and Leavis offer us the beginnings of an alternative. Many people objected to the virulence of Leavis's attack on Snow. But given the din of competing voices, it is a wonder that he was heard at all.

Francis Fukuyama
and the End of History

*[T]he whig historian can draw lines through certain events, . . .
and if he is not careful he begins to forget that this line is
merely a mental trick of his; he comes to imagine that it
represents something like a line of causation. The total result
of this method is to impose a certain form upon the whole
historical story, and to produce a scheme of general history
which is bound to converge beautifully upon the present—all
demonstrating throughout the ages the workings of an obvious
principle of progress.*
—Herbert Butterfield, *The Whig Interpretation of History*

*"If this is the best of all possible worlds," he said to himself,
"what can the rest be like?"*
—Voltaire, *Candide*

I T IS DIFFICULT to remember an article in an intellectual
political quarterly that made as big a splash as did Francis Fukuyama's "The End of History?" when it appeared in
the Summer 1989 issue of *The National Interest*. While the
response was far from unanimously favorable, it was extraordinarily large and passionate. Such prominent figures
as Allan Bloom, Irving Kristol, Gertrude Himmelfarb,
Samuel P. Huntington, and Daniel Patrick Moynihan wrote

in the pages of *The National Interest* to comment on the fifteen-page piece. The article became something of a cause célèbre, attracting heated commentary across the U.S. as well as in Europe, Asia, and South America. Its millenarian title, sans question mark, soon became a slogan to be bruited about in Washington think tanks, the press, and the academy. The young Fukuyama, then a deputy director of the U.S. State Department's Policy Planning Staff, quickly emerged as a minor celebrity, replete with a position at the RAND corporation and a generous book contract allowing him to expand on his ideas. Even those who took issue with the article—"I don't believe a word of it," was Irving Kristol's rejoinder to its main thesis—were careful to praise the author's intellectual sophistication. Rarely has the word "brilliant" been used with such cheery abandon: perhaps here, in the response to "The End of History?," were those "thousand points of light" we had been hearing so much about at the time.

Why the fuss? Writing at a moment when Communism was everywhere in retreat, it was hardly surprising that Fukuyama should have proclaimed the end of the Cold War and "unabashed victory of economic and political liberalism." Such proclamations were already legion. What commanded attention was something far more radical. Claiming to distinguish between "what is essential and what is contingent or accidental in world history," Fukuyama wrote that

> What we are witnessing is not just the end of the Cold War, or a passing of a particular period of postwar history, but the end of history as such: that is, the end point of mankind's ideological evolution and the universalization of Western liberal democracy as the final form of human government.

"The end of history as such," "the evolution and the universalization of Western liberal democracy as the final form of human government": these were the sorts of statements—along with Fukuyama's professed conviction that "the ideal will govern the material world *in the long run*" —that rang the alarm.

Some of the negative responses to Fukuyama's article, as he was quick to point out, were based on a simplistic misreading of his thesis. For in proclaiming that the end of history had arrived in the form of triumphant liberal democracy, Fukuyama did not mean that the world would henceforth be free from tumult, political contention, or intractable social problems. Moreover, he was careful to note that "the victory of liberalism has occurred primarily in the realm of ideas or consciousness and is as yet incomplete in the real or material world."

What he did maintain, however, was that liberal democracy was the best conceivable social-political system for fostering freedom; and therefore—because "the ideal will govern the material world *in the long run*"—he also claimed that liberal democracy would not be superseded by a better or "higher" form of government. According to Fukuyama, other forms of government, from monarchy to communism to fascism, had failed because they were imperfect vehicles for freedom; liberal democracy, allowing mankind the greatest freedom possible, had triumphed because it best instantiated the ideal. In this sense, what Fukuyama envisaged was not the end of history—understood as the lower-case realm of daily occasions and events—but the end of History: an evolutionary process that represented freedom's self-realization in the world. The "end" he had in mind was in the nature of a *telos*: more "fulfillment" than "completion" or "finish."

True, one might still ask whether the career of History

so understood is anything more than a speculative fancy—whether, indeed, the ambition to distinguish between "what is essential and what is contingent or accidental in world history" is not bootless, given man's limited vision and imperfect knowledge. In any event, the idea of the end of History is hardly novel. In one form or another, it is a component of many myths and religions—including Christianity, with its vision of the Second Coming. And anyone familiar with the interstices of nineteenth-century German philosophy will remember that the end of History also figures prominently in the philosophies of G. W. F. Hegel and his disgruntled follower Karl Marx. It is perhaps worth noting, too, that one important difference between most religious speculation about the end of History and versions propagated by philosophers is hubris: orthodox Christianity, for example, is gratifyingly indefinite about the date of this eventuality. Hegel harbored no such doubts or hesitations. What he called *"the last stage of History, our world, our own time"* was ushered in by Napoleon's armies at the Battle of Jena in October 1806. "As early as this," Fukuyama writes, "Hegel saw . . . the victory of the ideals of the French revolution, and the imminent universalization of the state incorporating the principles of liberal democracy." It is Fukuyama's view that "the present world seems to confirm that the fundamental principles of sociopolitical organization have not advanced terribly far since 1806."

As Fukuyama acknowledges, the philosophy of Hegel, especially as interpreted by the Russian-born Marxist philosopher and French bureaucrat Alexandre Kojève, was the chief theoretical inspiration for "The End of History?" Whatever else can be said of Hegel's philosophy, or its interpretation by Kojève, there can be no doubt that it demands an extraordinarily cerebral view of the world. In the famous lectures that he gave in the 1930s on Hegel's first book, *The Phenomenology of Spirit*, Kojève tells us that History "cannot be *truly* understood without the *Phenomenology*," and, moreover, that "there is History *because* there is philosophy and *in order that* there may be Philosophy."[1] For those less persuaded of philosophy's determinative importance in human affairs, such statements may help explain why Hegel, in the preface to the *Phenomenology*, should have defined "the true" as *der bacchantische Taumel, an dem kein Glied nicht trunken ist*: "the Bacchanalian whirl in which no member is not drunk." Inebriation of some sort, at any rate, would seem desirable when entering such heady waters.

Curiously, Fukuyama's attitude toward the end of History is deeply ambivalent. On the one hand, faithful Hegelian that he is, he regards it as the final triumph of freedom. He speaks of nations or parts of the world that are still "stuck in history" or "mired in history," as if residence in the realm of history were something it behooved us to change. On the other hand, he foresees that

---

1 Kojève (1902–1968) was immensely influential, not only as a philosopher but also as a member of the French Ministry of Economy and Finance. Implacably anti-American, he dreamed of a resurgent Latin Empire. He was instrumental in the formation of the European Economic Community and encouraged de Gaulle to block British membership in the EEC. Kojève impressed nearly everyone he came in contact with. Allan Bloom described him as "the most brilliant man I ever met." Raymond Aron thought him "more intelligent than Sartre." Kojève once described himself as a "strict Stalinist." He meant it. As was revealed in 1999, Kojève was a Soviet spy for nearly thirty years. As Daniel Johnson reported in the London *Daily Telegraph*, this "miraculous mandarin turns out to have been a malevolent mole. Nobody of his eminence has ever been exposed as a traitor on this scale before."

"the end of history will be a very sad time," partly because he believes that the things that once called forth "daring, courage, imagination, and idealism will be replaced by economic calculation," and partly because "in the post-historical period there will be neither art nor philosophy, just the perpetual caretaking of the museum of human history." Thus he acknowledges "a powerful nostalgia for the time when history existed" and even suggests that the prospect of perpetual ennui that awaits mankind "after" History may "serve to get history started once again."

When we turn to Fukuyama's elaboration of his thesis in *The End of History and the Last Man* (1992) we find that he has collected a number of careful hedges and qualifications to place around the ideas he put forward in "The End of History?" For example, he continues to insist that there has been "a common evolutionary pattern for *all* human societies—in short, something like a Universal History of mankind in the direction of liberal democracy." But instead of presenting this Universal History as the record of an ineluctable dialectic, he now admits that it is "simply an intellectual tool." Early on in *The End of History and the Last Man*, Fukuyama repeats his claim that

> We cannot picture to ourselves a world that is *essentially* different from the present one, and at the same time better. Other, less reflective ages also thought of themselves as the best, but we arrive at this conclusion exhausted, as it were, from the pursuit of alternatives we felt *had* to be better than liberal democracy.

But at the very end of his book he hesitates, suggesting that the evidence for necessary progress—evidence that the "wagon train" of history is moving in the right direction, that the lead wagons have in fact reached their destination—is "provisionally inconclusive." The generous response to such tensions is that they render Fukuyama's discussion richer and more nuanced; the skeptical response is that, in an effort to answer his critics, he has opened himself to the charge of inconsistency on fundamental issues.

Fukuyama claims at the outset that *The End of History* is not simply a restatement of his famous article. Perhaps, then, we should call it a re-presentation and expansion of the ideas he articulated in "The End of History?" Divided into four parts and some thirty chapters, the book painstakingly presents the case that history possesses a structure and direction, that the direction is up, and that we in the liberal West occupy the final summit of the historical edifice. What's new is a lot of detailed philosophical discussion. Fukuyama provides a summary of Plato's speculations about the origin of our sense of honor and shame as well as a long discussion of the famous master/slave dialectic in Hegel's *Phenomenology.* Following Hegel, he presents the "struggle for recognition" as the "longing" that drives history, and concludes that liberal democracy offers the most complete and "rational" satisfaction of that longing possible. The last part of the book is essentially a meditation on his claim that the end of history will be "a very sad time." Fukuyama is particularly worried that the satisfactions of living at the end of history will leave mankind so dull and complacent that his spiritual life will atrophy and he will find himself transformed into that flaccid creature, Nietzsche's "last man," described in *Thus Spoke Zarathustra* as "the most despicable man" who is "no longer able to despise himself."

Like the article that occasioned it, *The End of History* also provides two quite disparate views of the world. On

EXPERIMENTS AGAINST REALITY

one side we have Fukuyama the conservative political analyst, commenting in lithe, well-informed prose on the state of the world. This gentleman is hardheaded, wry, and full of quietly witty obiter dicta. "In America today," he writes, "we feel entitled to criticize another person's smoking habits, but not his or her religious beliefs or moral behavior." Moreover, this Fukuyama recognizes that, whether or not we are at the end of History, nothing has happened to cancel a nation's need for vigilance: "no state that values its independence," he insists, "can ignore the need for defense modernization." Indeed, one imagines that he would accede wholeheartedly to the wise observation of the Roman military commentator Flavius Vegetius: *si vis pacem, para bellum* ("If you want peace, prepare for war"). One is not surprised to find endorsements on the book jacket from such well-known figures as Charles Krauthammer, George F. Will, and Eduard Shevardnadze.

On the other side we have Fukuyama the philosopher, impressively erudite, deeply committed to a neo-Hegelian view of the historical process. This Fukuyama seems to put greater stock in ideas than facts (indeed, one suspects that he would scorn the distinction between ideas and facts as an artificial construct). He speaks often about "the motor" or "directionality" of history, "internal contradictions" that must be overcome, and "the complete absence of coherent *theoretical* alternatives to liberal democracy." He even suggests that "the present form of social and political organization is *completely satisfying* to human beings in their most essential characteristics." It is not quite clear what the Messrs. Fukuyama have to say to each other, though their co-habitation clearly makes for sensational copy.

We have nothing but good wishes for Fukuyama 1; about Fukuyama 2, however, we have grave reservations, not least because of the threat his ideas pose to his more commonsensical twin.

Like most world-explaining constructions invented by humanity, Hegel's dialectic acts as catnip on susceptible souls. Once one is seduced, everything seems marvelously clear and, above all, *necessary*: all important questions have been answered beforehand and the only real task is to apply the method to clean up the untoward messiness of reality. It is very exciting. "All of the really big questions," as Fukuyama puts it in his preface, "had been settled." But the problem with such constructs is that they insulate their adherents from empirical reality: since everything unfolds "necessarily" according to a preordained plan, nothing that merely *happens* in the world can alter the itinerary. As the philosopher Leszek Kolakowski observed in his book *Religion,*

> Monistic reductions in general anthropology or "histori-osophy" are always successful and convincing; a Hegelian, a Freudian, a Marxist, and an Adlerian are, each of them, safe from refutation as long as he is consistently immured in his dogma and does not try to soften it or make concessions to common sense; his explanatory device will work forever.

What one gains is an explanation; what one loses is the truth. There are good reasons—from the rise of multiculturalism to the state once known as Yugoslavia—to believe that what we are witnessing today is not the final consolidation of liberal democracy but the birth of a new tribalism. For those committed to the end of History, however, it's simply that "the victory of liberalism has occurred primarily in the realm of ideas or consciousness and is as yet incomplete in the real or material world."

Among the unpleasant side effects of adherence to such doctrines is the habit of intellectual arrogance. Hegel offers the supreme case in point. About his "firm and invincible faith that there is Reason in history," for example, the philosopher assures us that his faith "is not a presupposition of study; it is a *result* which happens to be known to myself because I already know the whole." It is cheering to possess knowledge of "the whole," of course, but a bit daunting for the rest of us. Not surprisingly, such arrogance also expresses itself about competing doctrines. Thus we find Fukuyama, supplementing Hegel with Nietzsche, explaining that "the problem with Christianity . . . is that it remains just another slave ideology, that is, it is untrue in certain crucial respects." How gratifying to be able to docket the whole of Christianity and file it away as an example of mankind's spiritual immaturity!

Perhaps the most obvious problem with Hegel's philosophy of history is that the "necessary" freedom which his system mandates can look a lot like unfreedom to anyone who happens to disagree with its dictates. As the German philosopher Hans Blumenberg observed, "If there were an immanent final goal of history, then those who believe they know it and claim to promote its attainment would be legitimized in using all the others who do not know it . . . as a mere means." The twentieth century has acquainted us in terrifyingly exquisite detail with what happens when people are treated as "moments" in an impersonal dialectic. We find ourselves in a situation where "real freedom," as Hegel puts it, demands the "subjugation of mere contingent will." It is hardly surprising that Leszek Kolakowski, writing about Hegel in *Main Currents of Marxism*, should conclude that "in the Hegelian system humanity becomes what it is, or achieves unity with itself, only by ceasing to be humanity." Once again, the contrast with

Christianity is illuminating. The good Christian, too, believes that freedom consists in the "subjugation of mere contingent will." But he endeavors to act not in accordance with "the Idea" as formulated by a nineteenth-century German philosopher but with God's will. Moreover, while Hegel insists that with the formulation of his philosophy "the antithesis between the universal and the individual will has been removed," Christianity has had the good manners to attribute a large dollop of inscrutability to God's will. By refusing to saddle mankind with "necessary freedom," Christianity preserves a large domain for the exercise of individual freedom in everyday life.

Fukuyama's commitment to the Hegelian dialectic leads him to some strange inversions. Early on in his book, he remarks that "it is possible to speak of historical progress only if one knows where mankind is going." But is this so? Is it not rather that what one needs in order to discern progress is knowledge of where mankind has *been*, not where it is going? And in any case, whom should we trust to furnish us with accurate reports about where mankind is going? Is G. W. F. Hegel, for all his genius, really a reliable guide? Is Fukuyama? No: history, a humble account of how man has lived and suffered, is what we require to declare progress, not prophecy.

It is important to stress that the issue is not whether mankind has made progress over the millennia. Surely it has. The exact nature and extent of the progress can be measured in any number of ways. The material progress of mankind has been staggering, especially in the last two hundred years. Ditto for mankind's political progress, despite the tyrannies and despotisms that remain. As Fukuyama points out, in 1790 there were only three liberal democracies in the world: the United States, France, and Switzerland. By 1990 there were sixty-one. That is remarkable progress. But it is also *contingent* progress, reversible by the same means that accomplished it in the first place: the efforts of individual men and women.

Indeed, one of the great casualties of Hegel's system is the whole realm of individual initiative. Fukuyama has told us that "in the post-historical period there will be neither art nor philosophy," precisely because at the end of History nothing remains for those disciplines to accomplish. But how often, even before Hegel, has that end been proclaimed. Gilbert Murray, in *The Classical Tradition in Poetry*, recalled being told that "one of the very earliest poems unearthed in Babylonia contains a lament that all reasonable subjects for literature are already exhausted." And just about the time Hegel was proclaiming the end of History, we find the French painter Eugène Delacroix observing that "Those very ones who believe that everything has been said and done, will greet you as new and yet will close the door behind you. And then they will say again that everything has been done and said."

It is also worth noting, as the philosopher David Stove pointed out in his response to Fukuyama's original article, that

> the mixture which Fukuyama expects to freeze history forever—a combination of Enlightenment values with the free market—is actually one of the most explosive mixtures known to man. Fukuyama thinks that nothing will ever happen again because a mixture like that of petrol, air, and lighted matches is widespread, and spreading wider. Well, Woodrow Wilson thought the same; but it is an odd world view, to say the least.

One of the most serious moral problems with the idea of the end of History is that it implacably transforms everything outside the purview of the theory into a historical "accident" or exception, draining it of moral significance. Hegel's system tells us what *must* happen; what actually does happen turns out not to matter much. Fukuyama admits that "we have no guarantees" that the future will not produce more Hitlers or Pol Pots. But in his view, evil, e.g., the evil which produced the Holocaust, "can slow down but not derail the locomotive of History." More: "At the end of the twentieth century," he writes, "Hitler and Stalin appear to be bypaths of history that led to dead ends, rather than real alternatives for human social organization." But what can this mean? The Lisbon earthquake of 1755 was the tragedy that sparked *Candide*, Voltaire's attack on Leibniz's dictum that ours was necessarily "the best of all possible worlds." What philosophical empyrean need one inhabit in order to regard the course of history since 1806 as the reprise of a completed symphony? How far shall we trust a "Universal History" that relegates the conflagrations of two world wars and the unspeakable tyranny of Hitler and Stalin to epiphenomenal "bypaths"? I submit that any theory which regards World War II as a momentary wrinkle on the path of freedom is in need of serious rethinking.

If Fukuyama's commitment to Hegel is itself problematic, so at times is his interpretation of Hegel's teaching. For it is not at all clear that Hegel himself was a champion of anything like what we call liberal democracy. Fukuyama complains that people have labeled Hegel "a reactionary apologist for the Prussian monarchy, a forerunner of twentieth-century totalitarianism, and . . . a difficult-to-read metaphysician." Let's grant that the bit about totalitarianism is moot. What about the rest? No one is going to give Hegel a prize for limpid prose. Perhaps, as Fukuyama says, Hegel was par excellence the "philosopher of free-

EXPERIMENTS AGAINST REALITY

dom." Perhaps. Certainly he talked about freedom a great deal. He was fond, for example, of claiming that "the History of the World is nothing other than the progress of the consciousness of Freedom." We must of course hope that that notion is a consolation to the multitudes whom the dialectic has consigned to the uncomfortable (but, alas, necessary) role of unfreedom in the lower-case day-to-day history we all merely live through.

But liberal democracy? No doubt it was just one of those lucky strokes of fortune, an example of life imitating art: still, it is remarkable that "*the Germanic world*" of the nineteenth century should emerge as the political zenith of Hegel's system, *primus inter impares* of "those nations on which the world spirit has conferred its true principle." *Mirabile visu*, convenience once again jibes seamlessly with necessity. But question: was Hegel's Prussia, the Prussia of Metternich, of Frederick William III, et al., a "liberal democracy"? Did Hegel believe that it was? Fukuyama is surely correct that to have a liberal democracy, the people must be sovereign. But in *The Philosophy of Right* Hegel seems to think that the sovereign should be sovereign. "The monarch," he tells us, is "the absolute apex of an organically developed state," "the ungrounded self-determination in which finality of decision is rooted," etc. He says, further, that constitutional monarchy such as we see in . . . oh, well, in nineteenth-century Prussia, for example, is "the achievement of the modern world, a world in which the substantial Idea has won the infinite form." In other words, Hegel likes it.

Or at least he *appears* to like it. In a footnote, Fukuyama acknowledges that Hegel overtly supported the Prussian monarchy. He nevertheless maintains that, "far from justifying the Prussian monarchy of his day," Hegel's discussion in *The Philosophy of Right* "can be read as an esoteric critique of actual practice." Presumably, it is by virtue of some such "esoteric critique" that Hegel, champion of the Prussian state, turns out—*truly, essentially*—to be an enthuasiast for Kojève's "universal homogenous state," a.k.a. liberal democracy. It is nice work if you can get it.

It may also be worth pointing out a curious inconsistency in Fukuyama's account of the end of History. If, as Hegel's famous slogan has it, "the real is the rational and the rational is the real," how are we to understand Fukuyama's "provisional inconclusiveness"? Indeed, how are we to understand his suggestion that nostalgia, or boredom, or evil might "re-start" history? What, is mere nostalgia a match for the imperatives of History? Can boredom contravene "God's walk through the world," as Hegel once described the process of history? If the end of History is a logical and metaphysical necessity, how are we to understand Fukuyama's hesitations? In fact, his ambivalence contributes greatly to his book's vividness, for it provides a little space for reality to enter. But considered on his own—i.e., Hegel's—terms, Fukuyama would seem to be a disappointing dialectician.

It should go without saying that none of these criticisms is meant to deny that the Hegelian system possesses tremendous *aesthetic* appeal. The panoramic drama of absolute being struggling to achieve perfect self-knowledge in history: it is an imposing tale of a thousand and one nights for the philosophically inclined. The inconvenient question is only whether the story it tells is true. Perhaps, as Kierkegaard suggested, Hegel was a man who had built a palace but lived in the guard house.

Fukuyama's own addiction to palace building shows itself in a response to critics that he published in the Winter 1989–1990 issue of *The National Interest*. "In order to refute my hypothesis," he writes "it is not sufficient to suggest that the future holds in store large and momentous events. One would have to show that these events were driven by a systematic idea of political and social justice that claimed to supersede liberalism." But this would be the case only if one grants Fukuyama's premise—that we are in possession of a "systematic idea of political and social justice." In fact, it may be that what we need is not a better theory but less theory.

In this respect, as possibly in others, a good antidote to the Hegelian juggernaut is the mild doctrine of the Spanish-born American philosopher George Santayana. In *Character and Opinion in the United States* (1920), Santayana distinguishes between "English liberty," which is "vague," "reticent," and involves "perpetual compromise," and "absolute liberty," which he describes as "a foolish challenge thrown by a new-born insect buzzing against the universe." "In the end," Santayana suggests, "adaptation to the world at large, where so much is hidden and unintelligible, is only possible piecemeal, by groping with a genuine indetermination in one's aims"—that is, by rejecting the inflated promises of absolute liberty for the more modest satisfactions of local freedom. To the partisan of the Hegelian dialectic or any other "fixed programme or, as he perhaps calls it, an ideal," this capitulation to uncertainty will doubtless seem strange. But the Danish Prince was right: "There are more things in heaven and earth, Horatio, than are dreamt of in your philosophy."

Josef Pieper:
Leisure and Its Discontents

The first principle of all action is leisure. Both are required, but leisure is better than occupation and is its end; and therefore the question must be asked, what ought we do when at leisure?
—Aristotle, Politics

The poore, the foule, the false, love can
Admit, but not the busied man.
—John Donne, "Breake of Day"

Neither plenitude nor vacancy. Only a flicker
Over the strained time-ridden faces
Distracted from distraction by distraction
Filled with fancies and empty of meaning
Tumid apathy with no concentration. . . .
—T. S. Eliot, Four Quartets

O NE CAN LEARN a lot about a culture from the words and ideas it pushes into early retirement. Our own age is rich in such conceptual emeriti, as anyone who has pondered the recent careers of terms like "disinterested," "manly," "respectable," or "virtuous" (to take just four) knows well. One of the greatest casualties resulting from this policy of premature superannuation concerns the word "leisure," an idea that for the Greeks and for the doctors of the Church was inextricably bound up with the highest aspirations of humanity. For Plato, for Aristotle, for Aquinas, we live most fully when we are most fully at leisure. Leisure—the Greek word is σχολή, whence our word "school"—meant the opposite of "downtime." Leisure in this sense is not idleness, but activity undertaken for its own sake: philosophy, aesthetic delectation, and religious worship are models. It is significant that in both Greek and Latin, the words for leisure—σχολή and *otium* —are positive while the corresponding terms for "busyness"—ἀσχολία and *negotium* (whence our "negotiate")— are privative: *not* at leisure, i.e., busy, occupied, engaged. And for us? Of course, we still have the *word* "leisure." But it lives on in a pale, desiccated form, a shadow of its former self. Think for example of the phrase—and the odious object it names—"leisure suit": it goes quite far in epitomizing the unhappy fate of leisure in our society.

At first blush, it might seem odd that leisure should survive predominantly in such degraded form today. After all, the United States and Western Europe have never been richer or more concerned with "quality of life" issues. By every objective measure, we can certainly *afford* leisure. (The real question is whether we can afford to lose sight of it.) We are daily confronted by an army of experts and a library of self-help books urging us to salvage "quality time" for ourselves, our family, our friends. What time could be of higher quality than leisure, understood as Aristotle understood it? (Cardinal Newman was right when he observed that, about many subjects, "to think correctly is to think like Aristotle.") But all such remedial gestures serve to underscore the extent to which our society has devoted itself to defeating genuine leisure, replacing it where possible with mere entertainment (what the Greeks called παιδιά, "child's play"), and disparaging efforts to preserve oases of leisure as the pernicious indulgence of an outmoded elite.

Probably the most profound meditation on the meaning of leisure is a little book by the German neo-Thomist philosopher Josef Pieper called in English *Leisure, the Basis of Culture*. It consists of two essays, the title piece (in German *Musse und Kult*, "Leisure and Worship") and "The Philosophical Act," both of which Pieper wrote in 1947. The two were published together in English in 1952 in a volume introduced by T. S. Eliot. In 1999, this volume was reissued by St. Augustine's Press in a new translation with an introduction by the English philosopher Roger Scruton. Pieper, who died in November 1997 at the age of ninety-three, is pretty much a forgotten figure today. But in the Fifties and Sixties he commanded wide respect and exerted considerable intellectual influence.

The introduction by Eliot to *Leisure, the Basis of Culture*—the first of many books by Pieper to appear in English—is one sign of the seriousness with which he was regarded. Another sign was the book's reception by reviewers. (The present edition includes excerpts from the original reviews.) *The Times Literary Supplement* devoted a long and admiring piece to the book, as did *The New Statesman*. *The Spectator* was briefer but no less admiring: "These two short essays . . . go a long way towards a lucid explanation of the present crisis in civilization." The book was also widely noticed in this country: reviews from *The Nation*, the *Chicago Tribune*, *Commonweal*, and *The San Francisco Chronicle* are included here. The review by Allen Tate in *The New York Times Book Review* probably did as much as Eliot's introduction to stimulate interest in Pieper.

It is doubtful that this new edition will generate anything like that level of response. One reason, of course, is that we are dealing with a new edition of material first published fifty years ago. But a deeper reason is that the loss Pieper describes was more keenly felt in the late Forties and early Fifties than it is now. We are farther than ever from inhabiting a culture that esteems genuine leisure. But that distance acts as an anesthetic, dulling the sense of loss and, hence, the pulse of interest.

Pieper not only wrote about leisure. He was also a writer whose work requires leisure (I do not mean simply "spare time") if it is to be properly read. Not that he is "difficult" or overly technical. On the contrary, Pieper wrote with a glittering simplicity—for once a genuinely "deceptive simplicity"—but the tintinnabulation of unleisured life deafens us to such quiet dignity. We must stop to listen if we are to hear these arguments, and stopping and listening are among the most difficult things to accomplish in a world that rejects leisure. Pieper's simplicity is the hard-won simplicity that comes at the end of an intellectual journey. It is the fruit of confident mastery, like *The Tempest* or Beethoven's Op. 135 quartet. Pieper had no use for jargon or technicalities. His favored form is the long essay made up of short sentences. His books—almost all are fewer than 150 pages—sport many quotations from philosophers—from Aristotle, Plato, Aquinas, Descartes, Kant. And yet they somehow escape seeming academic.

In a curious way, this is at least in part because of the subjects Pieper wrote about. Although he wrote important books about Plato, he was first of all a specialist in the philosophy of Thomas Aquinas. His *Guide to Thomas Aquinas*, for example, is a splendid introduction to the intellectual and social world inhabited by the philosopher. It is true that Aquinas does not always elicit clarity and simplicity from his commentators. But Pieper wrote about him not as an academic subject but as someone who had irreplaceable things to say about the moral and intellectual realities of life—our life. He manages to make Aquinas's vocabulary seem the most natural language possible for discussing the subject at hand. (He manages the same trick with Plato and Aristotle.) This is a testimony to Pieper's rhetorical skill, the highest rhetorical achievement being to make itself invisible.

It also says something about the naturalness of the categories that Aquinas (like Aristotle and Plato before him) used to discuss moral questions. Pieper first made his name with a series of essays on the so-called Cardinal Virtues—prudence, justice, fortitude, and temperance. These terms—especially when taken all together—can seem curiously dated to modern ears. Yet in his book *The Four Cardinal Virtues* (1965) Pieper shows with beguiling straightforwardness that, by whatever names we choose to call them, prudence, justice, fortitude, and temperance are indispensable to the common realities of human life.

As is often the case with things that are indispensable, the importance of these principles goes unnoticed until they collapse. Then their centrality snaps into focus. In *No One Could Have Known* (1979), an autobiography that takes Pieper from his birth in a small village outside Münster to 1945 and the end of World War II, he recounts a chilling story from 1942 when he worked as a psychologist in the German army. Hitler's surprise attack on the Soviet Union had put German troops deep into Russia. Pieper encountered a young man of eighteen "who still had the look of a child about him." He wore the uniform of a volunteer "driver auxiliary" and worked for the Nazis behind the front. Pieper asked the boy what he did.

> "Lately we did practically nothing but transport Jews."
> I pretended to be puzzled, not to understand. "Were the Jews being evacuated? Or where did you drive them?"

"No, they were driven into the forest. And there they were shot."

"And where did you collect them?"

"The Jews used to wait in the market square. They thought they were being resettled. They had suitcases and parcels with them. But they had to throw them onto a big pile. And straight away the Ukrainian militia went after the things."

"And then you drove them to the forest. But the shooting—you were told about it later; it's only hearsay."

Then the boy got very angry in the face of so much distrust and stupidity. "No! I saw it myself. I saw them being shot!"

"And what did you say about that?"

"Oh well, of course you feel a bit funny at first. . . ."

And then?

And then, presumably, moral anesthesia takes over and you stop thinking about it. In one sense, Pieper's work aims to provide an antidote to such moral insensibility. Philosophy, of course, is a futile weapon against tyranny. (A point underscored by Stalin when he contemptuously asked how many divisions the Pope commanded.) But philosophy is not at all futile in helping to create a moral climate intolerant of tyranny. (Which helps to explain why it can be said that in the end the Pope prevailed over the tyranny of Communism.)

Not that we can necessarily trust everything that goes under the name of philosophy. In his introduction to the original edition of *Leisure, the Basis of Culture*, T. S. Eliot remarked on the widespread feeling that philosophy had somehow lost its way—philosophy, he added, in "an older meaning of the word," as a source of "*insight* and *wisdom*." Philosophy in this "ampler sense" had been

overtaken by various technical specialities, of which logical
positivism was a conspicuous example. (In retrospect, Eliot
suggested, logical positivism will appear as "the counterpart of surrealism: for as surrealism seemed to provide a
method of producing works of art without imagination so
logical positivism seems to provide a method of philos-
ophizing without insight and wisdom.") Pieper's chief importance was to provide a compelling counterexample. "In
a more general way," Eliot wrote, Pieper's "influence
should be in the direction of restoring philosophy to a
place of importance for every educated person who thinks,
instead of confining it to esoteric activities which can affect
the public only indirectly, insidiously, and often in a distorted form."

Well, Pieper did provide the example. But it cannot be
said that he provided the influence or restoration Eliot
hoped for. With some notable exceptions, philosophy—or
the activity that goes under that alias in the university
today—is every bit as impoverished and lost in bootless
specialization as it was when Eliot wrote forty-five years
ago. More so perhaps, if for no other reason than that
there are so many more people calling themselves philosophers today than then. Logical positivism was sterile. But
at least it made sense. Examples prove little, of course,
since in the realm of human endeavor there is never a
drought of absurdity. Yet it tells us *something* about the
current state of philosophy that Gilles Deleuze and Félix
Guattari, two much-idolized French philosophers, should
have published a book called *What Is Philosophy?* (1991)
in which we learn that

> philosophical concepts are fragmentary wholes that are not
> aligned with one another so that they fit together, because
> their edges do not match up. They are not pieces of a jig-

saw puzzle but rather the outcome of throws of the dice. They resonate nonetheless, and the philosophy that creates them always introduces a powerful Whole that, while remaining open, is not fragmented: an unlimited One-All, and "Omnitudo" that includes all the concepts on one and the same plane.

Which means . . . what? Perhaps, as Messrs. Deleuze and Guattari tell us a bit later on, that "if philosophy is re-territorialized on the concept, it does not find the condition for this in the present form of the democratic State or in a cogito of communication that is even more dubious than that of reflection." Or perhaps it is just ominous-sounding nonsense.

If Pieper is right, the current disarray of philosophy should come as no surprise. For philosophy in that "ampler sense" that Eliot spoke of (and that Aristotle famously observed in the beginning of the *Metaphysics*) depends on leisure. Philosophy in this sense is not primarily a mode of analysis but an attitude of openness: it is "theoretical" in the original sense of θεωρητικός: i.e., a contemplative attitude of beholding. It is one of the many ironies of contemporary academic life that what is called "theory" today means more or less the opposite of what the word θεωρία meant for the Greeks. For any self-respecting practitioner of the more modish forms of Lit. Crit., "theory" involves the willful imposition of one's ideas upon reality. In its original sense, however, theory betokened a patient receptiveness *to* reality. In this sense, philosophy, the theoretical activity par excellence, not only depends upon leisure but is also the fulfillment or the end of leisure. Consequently, the obliteration of leisure natur-ally leads to the perversion of philosophy.

It also leads to a perversion of culture, at least in so far as culture is understood not as an anthropological datum but as the repository of humanity's spiritual self-understanding: "the best," in Matthew Arnold's phrase, "that has been thought and said in the world." Leisure guarantees the integrity of high culture, its freedom from the endless round of means and ends that determines everyday life. It was Pieper's great accomplishment to understand the deep connection between leisure and spiritual freedom. "With astonishing brevity," Roger Scruton observes in his introduction, "he extracts from the idea of leisure not only a theory of culture and its significance, not only a natural theology for our disenchanted times, but also a philosophy of philosophy—an account of what philosophy can do for us . . . in a world where science and technology have tried to usurp the divine command."

Of course, there are many obstacles. For one thing, as Scruton notes, "leisure has had a bad press. For the puritan it is the source of vice; for the egalitarian a sign of privilege." There is also the related problem of simple pragmatism. If "maximizing profits" is a kind of categorical imperative, how can leisure—genuine leisure, not simply periodic vacations from labor—be justified? What is the use of something that is self-confessedly useless?

Defending leisure is always an audacious undertaking. It was particularly audacious in 1947 when a war-torn Germany was desperately trying to mend its ravaged physical and moral fabric. Especially at such times, leisure is likely to seem a luxury, a dispensable indulgence that distracts from the necessary work at hand. Pieper acknowledges the force of this objection. "We are engaged in the re-building of a house, and our hands are full. Shouldn't all our efforts be directed to nothing other than the completion of that house?" The answer is that the task of building or rebuilding is never merely a problem of engineering. If it were, human life could likewise be reduced to a problem of animal husbandry. Something more is needed: a vision of society, of the vocation of humanity. And the preservation of that vision is intimately bound up with the preservation of leisure. Even at a time of emergency such as faced Europe in the aftermath of World War II—perhaps especially at such times—the task of rebuilding requires a hiatus in which we can confront and reaffirm our humanity. The name of that hiatus is leisure. "To build our house," Pieper writes, "implies not only securing survival, but also putting in order again our entire moral and intellectual heritage. And before any detailed plan along these lines can succeed, our new beginning, our re-foundation, calls out for a defense of leisure."

We are not now in the exigent state of Europe in the late 1940s. But more than ever we live in a world ruled by the demands of productivity, the demands of work. Every human enterprise is increasingly subject to the scrutiny of the balance-sheet. "Rest," vacations, "breaks" are acknowledged necessities, but only as unfortunate requirements for continued productivity. Consequently, "free time," no matter how ample, is not so much a leisured alternative to work as its diastolic continuation. The world is increasingly "rationalized," as the sociologist Max Weber put it, increasingly organized to maximize profits and minimize genuine leisure. Now even more than when Pieper wrote we face the prospect of a "leisure-less culture of 'total work,'" a world that excludes the traditional idea of leisure *in principle*. Pieper found the perfect motto for this attitude in a passage quoted by Weber in *The Protestant Ethic and the Spirit of Capitalism*: "One does not only work in order to live, but one lives for the sake of one's work, and if there is no more work to do one suffers or goes to sleep." It is part of Pieper's task to show us how the attitude implicit in this credo "turns the order of things upside-down."

It is a measure of how far the imperative of "total work" has taken hold that the opposing classical and medieval ideal—that, in Aristotle's phrase, we work in order to be at leisure—seems either unintelligible or even faintly immoral to us. Even purely intellectual activity is rebaptized as "work" in order to rescue it from the opprobrious charge of idleness. The image of "intellectual work" and the "intellectual worker" presents us with a vision of the world whose ideal is busyness. René Descartes promised that by using his scientific method, man could make himself the "master and possessor of nature." Three centuries of scientific and technological progress have done a lot to prove Descartes right. Pieper's question is what happens when that technological model of knowledge is taken to be definitive of human knowing *tout court*. Presented with a rose, we can observe and study it, or we can merely look and admire its beauty. For the intellectual worker, only the former is really legitimate. Wonder is "a waste of time." It produces nothing, nor does it further understanding. In this context, it is perhaps worth noting that Descartes hoped to explain extravagant natural phenomena such as meteors and lightning in such a way that "one will no longer have occasion to admire anything about what is seen." Far from being a prelude to insight, wonder for Descartes was an impediment to the technology of knowledge.

Of course, we should not wish to do without the extraordinary benisons of that technology. We live in a world deeply shaped by the Cartesian imperative, and the first response of any sane person must be "Thank God for that." But our first response needn't be our only response. Pieper's point is that the discursive knowledge—knowledge whose end is the analysis, manipulation, and reconstruction of reality—is not the only model of human knowing. The word "discursive," he points out, suggests a busyness, a "running to and fro" (Latin, *dis-currere*). Such knowledge—"investigating, articulating, joining, comparing, distinguishing, abstracting, deducing, proving"—gives us power over the world. But it says nothing about our vocation in the world. The *simplex intuitus*, the "simple looking" (*in-tueri*: to look upon) that leisure provides, alerts us not to our power over reality but to our ultimate dependence on initiatives beyond our control. Thus it is that leisure is both an openness to reality and an affirmation of mystery, of "not being able to grasp" that which one beholds. "Human knowing," Pieper writes, "has an element of the non-active, purely receptive seeing, which is not there in virtue of our humanity as such, but in virtue of a transcendence over what is human, but which is really the highest fulfillment of what it is to be human, and is thus 'truly human' after all." Both sides are necessary if we are to affirm our humanity fully. Knowledge is in this sense (as we saw above with E. R. Curtius) a "mutual interplay of *ratio* and *intellectus*," of discursive reason and receptive intuition.

It is one of the ironies of what Pieper calls the "world of total work" that although it underwrites our objective control *of* the world it also insinuates a corrosive subjectivism and relativism into our attitude *toward* the world. "The other, hidden, side of the same dictum . . . is the claim *made by* man: if knowing is work, exclusively work, then the one who knows, knows only the fruit of his own, subjective activity, and nothing else. There is nothing in his knowing that is not the fruit of his own efforts; there is nothing 'received' in it." The moral aspect of this refusal is a kind of spiritual imperviousness, "the hard quality of *not-being-able-to-receive*; a stoniness of heart that will not brook any resistance." In the end, it is like Humpty Dumpty in *Through the Looking-Glass*:

> "The question is," said Alice, "whether you *can* make words mean so many different things."
> "The question is," said Humpty Dumpty, "which is to be master—that's all."

As this story reminds us, imperviousness is no guarantee of invulnerability.

It is worth noting that Pieper's brief on behalf of leisure is not an attack on work as such. "What is normal," he acknowledges,

> is work, and the normal day is a working day. But the question is this: can the world of man be exhausted in being the "working world"? Can a human being be satisfied with being a functionary, a "worker"? Can human existence be fulfilled in being exclusively a work-a-day existence? Or, to put it another way, from the other direction, as it were: Are there such things as liberal arts?

In *The Idea of a University*, Pieper points out, Newman suggestively translates *artes liberales* as "knowledge possessed of a gentleman," that is to say, knowledge born of leisure. A good index of the spiritual plight that Pieper describes is the widespread collapse of liberal arts in our society. More and more, so-called liberal arts institutions are really vocational schools at best (at worst they are circuses of narcissism); the σχολή, the leisure, has effectively been drained out of school as "job training" is taken to be the sole justification for education.

Again, Pieper does not dispute the importance of training. We cannot do without "the useful arts"—medicine, law, economics, biology, physics: all those disciplines that relate to "purposes that exist apart from themselves." The question is only whether they exhaust the meaning of education. Is "education" synonymous with training? Or is there a dimension of learning that is undertaken not to negotiate advantage in the world but purely for its own sake? "To translate the question into contemporary language," Pieper writes, "it would sound something like this: Is there still an area of human action, or human existence as such, that does not have its justification by being part of the machinery of a 'five year plan'? Is there or is there not something of that kind?"

To answer yes is to affirm the province of leisure. It is to affirm the value of uselessness, the preciousness of a dimension free from the realm of work.

Historically, the origin of this realm is in the world of the religious cultic festival, the "Kult" of Pieper's German title. Leisure in the end is human action on holiday, on holy-day. A temple is a *templum*, a bit of space marked off and exempt from everyday uses: so too with leisure. Just as "there can be no unused space in the total world of work," so there can be no unused time. Leisure snatches a measure of time from precincts of purpose. What validates that exemption is the openness to reality that leisure presumes. The festival origin of leisure is ultimately a religious origin. In the formula of the Shakespeare scholar C. L. Barber, it traces a movement from "release to clarification" and yields "a heightened awareness of the relation between man and 'nature'—the nature celebrated on holiday." This is what underlies the link between leisure and worship. In this sense, the justification for leisure lies not in the refreshment it offers but in the reality it affirms.

It is only to be expected that a pragmatic age, an age

dominated by the imperatives of work, would seek to counterfeit leisure in order to appropriate the appearance of receptivity without actually receiving anything. But the natural human appetite for leisure is not satisfied by simulacra. "A festival," Pieper writes,

> that does not get its life from worship, even though the connection in human consciousness be ever so small, is not to be found. To be sure, since the French Revolution, people have tried over and over to create artificial festivals without any connection with religious worship, or even against such worship, such as the "Brutus Festival" or "Labor Day," but they all demonstrate, through the forced and narrow character of their festivity, what religious worship provides to a festival.

We may indeed be at the "dawn of an age of artificial festivals." But if so we are at the dawn of an age without leisure.

It is fitting that in this encomium to leisure, Pieper does not seek "to give advice or provide guidelines for action but only to encourage reflection." To the question "What is to be done?" the first answer must be: nothing. "There are certain things which one cannot do 'in order to . . .' do something else. One either does not do them at all or one does them because they are meaningful in themselves." In *Ash Wednesday*, Eliot asked: "Teach us to sit still." It is a difficult lesson. At the beginning of his introduction to *Leisure, the Basis of Culture*, Roger Scruton cites "an American president" (I wish I knew which one) who answered a fussy official with the command "Don't just do something: stand there!" It is a bit of advice that all of us—even the presidents among us—should learn to take seriously.

Index

Index

Index

Davenport-Hines, Richard, 99, 107
Davie, Donald, 69
Day-Lewis, Cecil, 65
de Gaulle, Charles, 323
de la Mare, Walter, 122
de Man, Paul, 12–13
Deconstruction, 3, 7, 9, 12–17, 23
Defert, Daniel, 244, 251, 254
Delacroix, Eugène, 330
Deleuze, Gilles, *What Is Philosophy?*,
    341–342
Derrida, Jacques, 7, 9–13, 17–18,
    21–23, 238; *Dissemination*, 9;
    "Plato's Pharmacy," 10
Descartes, René, 311, 345; influence
    of, 223, 338
Dial, The, 68
Dickens, Charles, 113, 312; *Our
    Mutual Friend*, 68
Dickinson, Emily, 28
Donne, John, 335
Donoghue, Denis, *The Arts Without
    Mystery*, 41; *Walter Pater: Lover
    of Strange Souls*, 28–34, 40–44
Dorment, Richard, 283
Dostoyevsky, Fyodor, 119, 300–301,
    304
Duchamp, Marcel, 280–281

Eliot, Andrew, 75
Eliot, George, 39–40; *Middlemarch*,
    33
Eliot, T[homas] S[tearns], 29, 46,
    48–49, 61–83, 96, 108, 118, 337,
    340–342; *After Strange Gods*, 73,
    81; anti-Semitism in, 72–74;
    "Arnold and Pater," 29, 43–44, 88;
    Ash Wednesday, 69, 80, 349;
    "Burnt Norton," 83; "A Dialogue
    on Dramatic Poetry," 82; *Four
    Quartets*, 63, 69, 79, 83, 109, 318,
    335; "The Function of Criticism,"
    49; "Gerontion," 63, 80, 109;
    "The Hollow Men," 62–63, 69,
    71, 80; *The Idea of a Christian
    Society*, 73; *Inventions of the
    March Hare*, 72; "Little Gidding,"
    61; "The Love Song of J. Alfred
    Prufrock," 29, 63, 67, 109;
    "Morning at the Window," 67;
    Murder in the Cathedral, 80; *Notes
    Towards the Definition of Culture*,

79; *Old Possum's Book of
    Practical Cats*, 80; "Portrait of a
    Lady," 29, 67, 80; "Preludes," 29,
    67; *Prufrock*, 68, 74, 79; "Second
    Thoughts About Humanism," 79;
    "Tradition and the Individual
    Talent," 77, 296–297; *The Use of
    Poetry and the Use of Criticism*,
    82–83; *The Waste Land*, 63, 68,
    70, 76–80, 109
Elizabeth II, 116
Emerson, Ralph Waldo, 87, 138
Empson, William, 62
Encounter, 306, 310
Enlightenment, 5, 23–24
Epicureanism, 39
Epstein, Jacob, 52–54
Eribon, Didier, 240, 254
Euclid, 311
European Economic Community
    (EEC), 323
Existentialism, 193, 197, 236

Faber and Faber, 65
Fanon, Frantz, *The Wretched of the
    Earth*, 225
Feminism, in J. S. Mill, 161
Finkielkraut, Alain, 277
Finley, Karen, 287
Fish, Stanley, 11–12
Fisher, M[ary] F[rances] K[ennedy],
    The Art of Eating, 111
Fitzgerald, F[rancis] Scott, 29
Flaubert, Gustave, *L'Education
    sentimentale*, 223
Fleming, Ian, 126
Ford, Ford Madox, 29
Förster, Bernhard, 209
Forster, E[dward] M[organ], 29, 107
Förster-Nietzsche, Elisabeth, 208–209
Forum, 128
Foucault, Michel, 7, 12, 237–257; *The
    Archaeology of Knowledge*, 237;
    The History of Sexuality, 247, 252,
    256–257; *Madness and
    Civilization*, 251–252, 256; *Les
    Mots et les choses (The Order of
    Things)*, 254, 256; *Surveiller et
    punir (Discipline and Punish)*, 238
Franco-Prussian War, 206
Franz Josef, 146
Frederick William III, 332

Index

Index

Index

Index

Palestine Liberation Organization
(PLO), 226
Pall Mall Gazette, 170
Pater, Walter, 27–44, 81; education,
32–33; family background, 32–33;
influence of, 28–30, 84; *Marius the
Epicurean*, 39–40; *The
Renaissance*, 28, 30, 35–43;
"Sandro Botticelli," 27; "The
School of Giorgione," 28
Pattison, Emilia (Mrs. Mark), 33,
35–36
Pattison, Mark, 33
Pavlova, Anna, 122
Phillips, Adam, 42
Pico della Mirandola, 36
Pieper, Josef, 335–349; *Guide to
Thomas Aquinas*, 338–339;
Leisure, the Basis of Culture,
337–338, 340–349; *No One Could
Have Known*, 339–340
Pike, Burton, 136–137
Plath, Sylvia, 65
Plato, 5, 325, 336, 338; *Phaedrus*, 10;
Philebus, 233; *The Republic*, 5–6;
Symposium, 140, 148
Plutarch, 237, 239
Poetry Review, 127
Pol Pot, 165, 331
Pop Art, 282, 291
Pope, Alexander, 167–168
Posner, Richard A., 171; *The
Economics of Justice*, 168;
Overcoming Law, 20
Pound, Ezra, 29, 46, 49, 65, 68–69,
86, 313; "In a Station of the
Metro," 47; *Ripostes*, 47
Praz, Mario, *The Romantic Agony*, 30
Pritchett, V[ictor] S[awdon], 148, 151
Proust, Marcel, *A la recherche du
temps perdu*, 118, 129, 133, 306
Purcell, Victor, *The Sweeniad*, 70

Quinn, John, 69

Ransom, John Crowe, 94
Raphael, 283
Rede Lecture, 306, 316
Reiter, Heinrich, 139
Richardson, Joan, 90
Ricks, Christopher, 34, 72, 104–105,
115–116

Rilke, Rainer Maria, 106, 132, 141,
155, 193, 207; *Duino Elegies*, 300
Rimbaud, Arthur, 30, 230, 261
Ritschl, Friedrich, 204–206
Roberts, Michael, 48–49
Romanticism, 31, 41, 57, 59–60, 81,
137, 152–153, 230, 255, 258, 261,
264, 270, 281, 289, 295, 302–304
Rorty, Richard, 1, 7, 11, 16–23, 239,
298; *Consequences of Pragmatism*,
16–17; *Contingency, Irony,
Solidarity*, 17; *Philosophy and the
Mirror of Nature*, 17
Rosenblum, Robert, 283
Rousseau, Jean-Jacques, 9, 161, 165,
177; *Emile*, 45
Ruskin, John, 31–32
Russell, Bertrand, 54–55, 76

Sade, Marquis de, 165, 240, 250
Sadomasochism, 240, 242, 247–252,
282
Saint-Exupéry, Antoine de, 223
Saint-Just, Louis de, 165
Saintsbury, George, *History of English
Prosody*, 95
Salomé, Lou, 207
San Francisco Chronicle, The, 337
San Francisco Examiner, 278–279
Sanger, Margaret, 128
Santayana, George, 66, 87, 93;
*Character and Opinion in the
United States*, 334
Sartre, Jean-Paul, 193, 214–236, 238;
The Age of Reason, 220; *Being and
Nothingness*, 217, 221–223, 229,
231–236, 239; *La Cause du
Peuple*, 225; *Critique of Dialectical
Reason*, 216; family background
of, 214–216; *Nausea*, 218–219,
227, 232; *No Exit*, 233; *The Wall*,
218; *The War Diaries*, 220–224,
227; *The Words*, 214, 224, 227
Saturday Review, 35, 172
Scaevola, Gaius Mucius, 204
Scheler, Max, 46
Schiller, Friedrich von, 209; *On the
Aesthetic Education of Man*, 236
Schjeldahl, Peter, 299
Schopenhauer, Arthur, 200–202, 212,
258; *The World as Will and
Representation*, 204–205

357

Index

Roger Kimball is Managing Editor
of *The New Criterion* and an art critic
for the London *Spectator*. His previous
books include *Tenured Radicals: How Politics
Has Corrupted Our Higher Education* and
*The Long March: How the Cultural Revolution
of the 1960s Changed America*.